Library of Philosophy.

EDITED BY J. H. MUIRHEAD, LL.D.

GOD AND PERSONALITY

Library of Philosophy

General Editor : PROFESSOR J. H. MUIRHEAD, LL.D.

ANALYTIC PSYCHOLOGY. By G. F. STOUT. Two Vols. 21s. net.

APPEARANCE AND REALITY. By F. H. BRADLEY. 12s. net.

ATTENTION. By Prof. W. B. PILLSBURY. 10s. 6d. net

CONTEMPORARY PSYCHOLOGY. By Prof. G. VILLA. 10s. 6d. net.

HISTORY OF ÆSTHETIC. By Dr. B. BOSANQUET. 10s. 6d. net.

HISTORY OF ENGLISH UTILITARIANISM. By Prof. E. ALBEE. 10s. 6d. net.

HISTORY OF PHILOSOPHY. By Dr. J. E. ERDMANN.
    Vol. I. ANCIENT AND MEDIÆVAL. Third Edition. 15s. net.
    Vol. II. MODERN. Fifth Edition. 15s. net.
    Vol. III. SINCE HEGEL. Third Edition. 12s. net.

HISTORY OF PSYCHOLOGY: ANCIENT AND PATRISTIC. By G. S. BRETT, M.A. 10s. 6d. net.

MATTER AND MEMORY. By HENRI BERGSON. Translated by N. M. PAUL and W. S. PALMER. 10s. 6d. net

NATURAL RIGHTS. By Prof. D. G. RITCHIE. 10s. 6d. net

PHILOSOPHY AND POLITICAL ECONOMY. By Dr. J. BONAR. 10s. 6d. net.

RATIONAL THEOLOGY SINCE KANT. By Prof. O. PFLEIDERER. 10s. 6d. net

THE PHENOMENOLOGY OF MIND. By G. W. F. HEGEL. Translated by J. B. BAILLIE. Two Vols. 21s. net.

THOUGHT AND THINGS; OR, GENETIC LOGIC. By Prof. M. BALDWIN.

    Vol. I. FUNCTIONAL LOGIC.
    Vol. II. EXPERIMENTAL LOGIC. 10s. 6d. net per vol.
    Vol. III. REAL LOGIC (I., GENETIC EPISTEMOLOGY).

TIME AND FREE WILL. By HENRI BERGSON. Translated by F. L. POGSON. 10s. 6d. net.

VALUATION: THE THEORY OF VALUE. By Prof. W. M. URBAN. 10s. 6d. net.

THE PSYCHOLOGY OF THE RELIGIOUS LIFE. By G. M. STRATTON. 10s. 6d. net.

THE GREAT PROBLEMS. By Prof. BERNARDINO VARISCO. Translated by Prof. R. C. LODGE. 10s. 6d. net.

KNOW THYSELF. By Prof. BERNARDINO VARISCO. Translated by Dr. GUGLIELMO SALVADORI. 10s. 6d. net.

GOD AND PERSONALITY

BEING THE GIFFORD LECTURES
DELIVERED IN THE UNIVERSITY OF
ABERDEEN IN THE YEARS 1918 & 1919

FIRST COURSE

BY

CLEMENT C. J. WEBB

Fellow of St. Mary Magdalen College, Oxford

LONDON : GEORGE ALLEN & UNWIN LTD.
RUSKIN HOUSE   40 MUSEUM STREET, W.C. 1
NEW YORK : THE MACMILLAN COMPANY

First published in 1918

ERRATA.

P. 27, l. 18—For 'representat.on' read 'representative.'
p. 47, n. 21—For '*Eutzychen*' read '*Eutychen*.'
p. 68, n. 7, l. 6—For 'αὖ τοῦ' read 'αὀτοῦ.'
p. 101, n. 9, l. 6—For 'possessed by' read 'possessed or.'
p. 162, l. 3—Omit 'a.'
p. 220, l. 21—For 'easily' read 'early.'
p. 239, l. 5—For 'fuller' read 'fullest.'

DEDICATED

IN AFFECTIONATE GRATITUDE

TO THE MEMORY OF

A GREAT THINKER AND A GREAT TEACHER,

JOHN COOK WILSON,

SOMETIME WYKEHAM PROFESSOR OF LOGIC

IN THE UNIVERSITY OF OXFORD

PREFACE

In giving these Lectures to the public, I desire in the first place to express my sincere thanks to the Senatus Academicus of the University of Aberdeen, who, by honouring me with their invitation to fill a place which has been filled in the past by men of my unworthiness to succeed whom I am acutely sensible, have given me a welcome opportunity of drawing together my thoughts, such as they are—and I am very well aware of their inadequacy —upon a subject of central importance in the Philosophy of Religion, and of deep concern to many persons who, while laying no claim to philosophical culture, are anxious to form a reasonable judgment of the value to be attached to the religious language and imagery with which they are familiar.

In the second place, I have to thank my own College in Oxford for generously granting me leave of absence in term time to enable me to avail myself of the invitation I had received from Aberdeen.

Lastly, I wish to acknowledge the manifold help which I have received from my wife in the work of preparing the Lectures alike for delivery and for publication.

A correspondent of an Aberdeen journal which did me the honour of printing very full reports of my Lectures quoted as a comment upon them and upon Gifford

Lectures generally the famous lines beginning 'Myself,
when young, did eagerly frequent.' I may perhaps take
occasion here to say that it never occurred to me that
such discussions as these could be other than 'about it
and about' or could, under the most favourable circumstances, be of service in the way of religion to any one
except by assisting towards the expression or defence of
a religious experience of which the hearer or reader was
already in possession.

I am greatly indebted to my friend and former pupil,
Professor Loveday, for his kindness in reading the proofs
of this book and for making a number of valuable
suggestions for its improvement.

SYLLABUS

LECTURE I

Our subject to be Personality and especially the place
to be assigned to it in our conception of God. Individuality, but not Personality, has already been treated by
Gifford Lecturers. The distinction illustrated by the
difference of view between Lotze and Mr. Bosanquet, the
former attributing Personality, the latter denying Personality but attributing Individuality to the Absolute. Personality in God to be discussed before Personality in
man. This order of treatment defended on grounds
historical and philosophical. The problem of Personality indicated by Dr. Merz as that to which we are invited
by the course taken by the history of thought during the
last half-century. Embarrassment alike of the scientific
and the philosophical movements of this period in the
presence of this problem ; which has also been raised for
many in an acute manner by the present war. The fact
that the history of the notion of Personality will compel
us to deal with the theological doctrines of Christianity
suggests a digression on the attitude to be adopted in
these Lectures towards those doctrines. Programme
of the following Lectures.

LECTURE II

Persona in classical Latin. The modern meaning of the
word Person is conditioned by its theological use as equivalent to ὑπόστασις. Original meaning of ὑπόστασις.
Substantia, though probably at first intended as a trans-

9

lation of it, comes to be used render οὐσία. History of
the philosophical use of ὑπόστασις and its relation to
οὐσία and ὑποκειμένον. Difference in meaning between
οὐσία and ὑπόστασις utilized in the formulation of the
Christian doctrine of the Trinity. *Substantia* being
already appropriated to represent οὐσία in Latin, another
word was required to correspond with ὑπόστασις and was
found, probably by Tertullian, in *persona* ; of which
πρόσωπον, in its theological use, seems to be a translation.
The words *persona* and ὑπόστασις, as applied to the distinctions recognized by Christian theology within the
Godhead, supplement one another, each suggesting something which the other fails to suggest. The philosophical
use of Person begins in its theological use and is expressed
in the definition of Boethius, *Persona est naturae rationabilis individua substantia*. The attribution to the
Absolute of Personality by Lotze, and of Individuality,
but not of Personality, by Mr. Bosanquet, is partly explained by the adherence of the latter to the juridical
associations of the word Person, which for Lotze do not
determine its meaning. The history of the notion of
Personality after the time of Boethius marked by the stress
laid successively on *incommunicability* (among the Schoolmen), on *self-consciousness* (since Descartes), and on *will*
(since Kant), as characteristics of Personality.

LECTURE III

HISTORY OF THE NOTION OF PERSONALITY AS APPLIED TO
    GOD . . . .

The expression ' Personality of God ' of modern origin.
In Christianity, the only religion which has expressly
affirmed Personality to be *in* God, this affirmation was
until recent times made only in connexion with the doctrine
of the Trinity ; for even the Socinian assertion that God
is *one* person was originally brought forward merely as a
correction of the Trinitarian formula, not as the enunci-
ation of an important fundamental truth. Influences
tending during the seventeenth and eighteenth centuries
to detach the thought of Personality in God from Trinitarian associations, and so preparing the way for the now
familiar expression ' Personality *of* God.' An examination of various accounts of the divine nature, undertaken
with the view of satisfying ourselves whether they could
be described as accounts of a ' personal God,' leads to the

result that only so far as *personal relations* are allowed to exist between the worshipper and his God can that God be properly described as ' personal ' ; and that such personal relations are excluded alike by extreme stress on the ' immanence ' and by extreme stress on the ' transcendence' of the object of worship. This conclusion is illustrated by a review of certain great religious systems.

LECTURE IV

The Boethian definition being taken as a provisional starting-point, the question is raised of the relation of Personality to Individuality, which is there described as a factor in it. All persons are individual but only *rational* individuals are persons. The antithesis of *individual* and *universal* is considered, and while certain ways of thinking which appear to rest on a confusion of the two are criticized, it is maintained that reality is throughout and at every point both the one and the other. *Persons* are *individuals conscious of universality*, such consciousness occurring only when Individuality has attained a certain level of *development* or *evolution*. The thought of a perfect Individuality, in comparison with which our Personality is imperfect, raises again the question at issue between Lotze and Mr. Bosanquet, whether such an Individuality should be called ' personal.' It is found that the answer will depend upon the rank assigned to ethical predicates in the scale of values.

LECTURE V

Rationality the other factor in Personality beside Individuality recognized in the Boethian definition. Yet what is *rational* seems to be that in which *personal* differences disappear, and we are apt to explain as especially *personal* what is not *rationally* explicable in human conduct. This ' irrationality of the personal ' the chief inspiration alike of the demand for a personal God and of the reluctance of many to admit that demand to be legitimate. This reluctance natural from the point of view of Natural

Science, which treats the 'personal equation' as something to be discounted, of a philosophy which looks on Natural Science as the type of true knowledge, and also of such a philosophy as Fichte's, which represents the supreme system of Reality as a 'moral order.' But a philosophy like Mr. Bosanquet's, which does not so represent it, will refuse to ascribe personality to the Ultimate Reality, because it must transcend moral distinctions, whereas Personality and Morality go (as we saw) together. It is admitted on all hands that finite personality cannot be ascribed to the Absolute; but what is really meant by the attribution of personality to God is the affirmation that reciprocal personal relations may exist between the worshipper and him; and it is sometimes sought to evade the difficulty of affirming this in the case of the Absolute by distinguishing God from the Absolute and allowing God to be a finite person. The next Lecture to be devoted to the consideration of this suggestion.

LECTURE VI

It is sometimes thought that the doctrine of a Finite God would satisfy the claims at once of Religion and of Metaphysics. This conception appears in several forms. Three of these we may conveniently associate with the names of Mr. Bradley, Dr. Rashdall, and Mr. H. G. Wells respectively. The second and third of these, it is contended, fail because they abandon the attempt to identify God with the Absolute, and in so doing, abandon what is essential to Religion when once the stage of intellectual development is reached at which the question of this identification can be raised. By Mr. Bradley, on the other hand, this failure is admitted and the consequence proclaimed that Religion, like other forms of experience, is bound to break down under metaphysical criticism and stand convicted of involving a contradiction. After a full examination of this view, which leads incidentally to a discussion of the antithesis of 'immanence' and 'transcendence,' the conclusion is reached that Religion implies a paradox but not a contradiction, and that there is no necessary inconsistency between the recognition that the object of religious experience is the supreme Reality and the recognition that this experience is an experience of personal relations with its object ; nor yet between a personal intercourse of the worshipper with his God and the immanence of that God in his worshipper. The difficulties encountered in the course of this examination nevertheless press upon us the problem of the best language for expressing the dependence upon the Divine Spirit of the finite spirits which are conscious of standing in personal relations with him.

LECTURE VII

Of metaphors which may be used to express the relation of the Divine Spirit to our spirits, that of *creation* emphasizes the *difference*, and those of *procreation* and *emanation* the *identity* between the two terms of the relation. Thus the first will be appropriate to a doctrine which lays stress on divine transcendence. Such Scholasticism is said to have been, and we see an extreme recoil from its position in this respect in the philosophy of Signor Croce, which does not allow Religion to be anything but an immature form of Philosophy. An attempt to unite the advantages of the metaphors of creation and procreation by the conception of a Mediator, who is the *Son* of God and so distinguished from *created* spirits. Such a conception may be objected to as (1) mythological, (2) logically leading to an infinite regress.

1. It may be regarded as a myth, but in the sense which Plato gives to the word, a sense in which myth has a legitimate place in philosophy. As is shown by the examination of Plato's usage, it is proposed to employ it just where Plato would employ a myth, in dealing with the nature of the Soul, which is the meeting-place of Universal and Individual, of Philosophy and History. The conception will be found apt to help us in expressing our relation to God in terms which avoid encouraging either an irreligious pride or an abject servility.

2. It need not lead to an infinite regress. Such a regress only becomes inevitable when there is no ground for introducing a middle term between two others which is not equally a ground for introducing a further middle term between the first middle term and either of the extremes. But in the present instance this is not the case. The Mediator represented as the archetype and ideal completion of the nature found to exist imperfectly

in finite souls. But a new complication is introduced when the latter are regarded as not only *imperfect* but *sinful ;* and we are constrained to pass on to the problem of *Sin.*

LECTURE VIII

A general discussion of the Problem of Evil not to be attempted here, but only of the bearing of our consciousness of moral Evil or Sin upon our conception of Divine Personality. It is true that what would be a criminal act, if brought about by a person, is not blamed when due to a natural force or the activity of an irrational animal. But to extend this to an assertion that there is no question of Evil in the world, if the cause of the world be not regarded as personal, is a piece of illegitimate reasoning The question of the significance to be assigned to our moral consciousness in the formation of a general view of the world cannot be put aside altogether. To a view which assigns it no significance beyond the sphere of human action the world must appear fundamentally irrational and incoherent. Hence the denial of Divine Personality does not enable us to rid ourselves of the problem of the existence of Evil. On the other hand a religious experience which implies a personal relation of our souls to God, if it gives to the sense of Sin a peculiar poignancy, yet provides it with a more intelligible setting than it has in any other connexion. Those who, while attributing personality to God, would relieve him of responsibility for the evil in the world by refusing to identify him with the Absolute, do so at the cost of denying him Godhead in the true sense of the word. After a consideration of the extent to which our consciousness of Sin must modify the conception adopted in the last Lecture of the relation between our spirits and the Divine Spirit, we pass to an examination of Signor Croce's teaching with its extreme doctrine of immanence and reach the conclusion that a religious experience implying a personal relation of our souls to God affords a clue to the solution of the antinomy between a realized perfection and an eternal activity in God, and that in the light of this experience the mystery involved in that antinomy will be found not so much to baffle reason as to enlarge its scope and opportunity.

LECTURE IX

PAGE

The problem of Personality in God is at bottom the same as that of the distinction of God from the Absolute, and also as that of the relation of Religion to Philosophy. Though Religion may exist apart from the affirmation of Personality in God, yet the presence of an emotion of reverence akin to that experienced towards persons is a mark distinguishing Religion from Philosophy, which are both of them concerned with the Supreme Reality ; for although what is known to be less than this may receive religious honour, only to that which is taken to *be* this can the greatest religious reverence be paid in the end ; nor acn the religious consciousness forbear the demand that the Supreme God should be the Supreme Reality. On the other hand, apart from the religious consciousness the Absolute cannot be known as God. Hence Religion and Philosophy are intimately connected, yet always distinct. The Absolute being the ultimate principle of unity reached in the search characteristic of Philosophy for the One in the Many, we may inquire what light can be thrown upon its nature by the study of subordinate principles of unity, and how far it can be described in terms borrowed from our acquaintance with any of these. It cannot be adequately described as the Universal or as Substance, or even, despite the eloquent advocacy of M. Bergson, as Life ; although this last description may serve a useful purpose in purging from undesirable accretions what is yet in the end the more satisfactory account of it as Reason and Goodness in that close mutual union assigned to them in the Platonic philosophy. Yet even this account, as given by Plato, calls for a further development, which is in principle supplied in the identification, established with the help of religious experience on a Platonic foundation by Christian theology, of the living God, who in Plato's system is to the end less than the Good, with the Good which is in that system the Supreme Reality. Here we reach a definite contribution made by religious experience to our conception of the supreme principle of unity.

LECTURE X

PAGE

Religious Experience, on which it is rightly claimed that theology should be based, is not to be sought only in records of conversion or of mystical raptures, but in the public theologies and ecclesiastical polities wherein may be read " writ large " the normal religious experience of the peoples among whom they have arisen. The student of Natural Theology should seek to discover the universal significance of the tradition which he himself inherits ; and need not suppose that to classify religious experiences as ' higher ' or ' lower ' is to abandon the ideal of Natural Theology as expressing the outcome of reflection on the whole religious experience of mankind. He must, however, use for his classification a suitable criterion ; which is to be found in the capacity of a religion to encourage and be encouraged by moral and intellectual progress in its votaries, yet only so far as this is done by exhibiting the specific nature of Religion in a particular manner. No historic religion has maintained and developed itself in an atmosphere of higher intellectual and moral culture than Christianity, which more than any other has laid stress upon personality in God ; and this stress is no extrinsic or accidental feature of this religion, but the fuller development of a factor to some degree present in all Religion, viz. the doctrine of divine transcendence. The recognition of personality in God adds to the intelligibility and moral efficacy of such religious ideas as those of Sin, Forgiveness, Justice, Sacrifice, Union; and although the language of Religion is always metaphorical, we must distinguish the metaphor with which it can dispense without danger to its claim to be real experience and that which is its only means of describing it. The difficulty of ascribing Personality to God, arising from what we called in a former lecture ' the irrationality of the personal,' met by the consideration that Reason as manifested in the artist affords a better analogy for use in that connexion than Reason as manifested by the mathematician or the moralist ; especially if the notion of Evolution is to be taken seriously. The Lecture concludes with some remarks on the relation of this account of Divine Personality to that contained in the Christian doctrine of the Trinity.

GOD AND PERSONALITY

LECTURE I

THE SUBJECT PROPOSED

IN these two courses of Lectures on the foundation of
Lord Gifford, I propose to consider the subject of Personality and especially the place to be assigned to Personality in our conception of the nature of God, the knowledge of whose nature and attributes is, according to the
will of the Founder, to be the theme of the Gifford
Lecturers.

In looking over the titles of previous courses of Gifford
Lectures I do not find the words Person or Personality
occurring, but I find more than once the words Individual
and Individuality. The remarkable series delivered at
Aberdeen by the eminent American philosopher, whose
loss we have since had to lament, Josiah Royce, dealt
with *The World and the Individual* [1] ; the distinguished
German biologist Professor Driesch discoursed in the
same University on *The Science and Philosophy of the
Organism*,[2] a topic which he subsequently resumed in a
work called *The Problem of Individuality* ; [3] while at
Edinburgh Dr. Bernard Bosanquet took for the subject

[1] 1900 and 1901.   [2] 1907 and 1908.   [3] London, 1914.

of one course *The Principle of Individuality and Value*,[4] and of another *The Value and Destiny of the Individual*.[5] It is obvious that the topic of Individuality is near akin to that of Personality, and in the lectures to which I have referred the lecturers had certainly chiefly though not solely in view those Individuals which we call Persons. But I think that there is still room for a discussion of Personality on its own account. For it would be readily allowed that not all Individuals are Persons ; and, on the other hand, we may speak of Personality as belonging to beings which we should not naturally or unhesitatingly call Individuals. Thus, on the one hand, some psychologists speak of alternating *personalities* in one and the same *individual* ; and, on the other hand, it is often maintained that a community such as a State, though consisting of many *individuals*, may be said to possess *personality*.

Again, it may be observed that, while it would not be disputed that only to *individuals* occupying a high grade in the scale of existence would the title of *persons* be usually given, yet some thinkers, such as Mr. Bosanquet, would strenuously deny the applicability of that title to the Ultimate Reality or the Absolute, while they would, on the contrary, maintain that it is only of the Absolute that *Individuality* in its full sense is predicable.[6]

Nor have we to do with a mere preference of one form of words to another when we find a philosopher with whose works Mr. Bosanquet is so familiar and in many ways so sympathetic as Lotze saying, not of Individuality but of Personality, just what Mr. Bosanquet says of

---

[4] 1911.   [5] 1912.

[6] See *Principle of Individuality and Value*, p. 72 : " In the ultimate sense there can be only one Individual."

Individuality, that it is properly attributable to the Supreme Reality only.7 In the difference between the two ways of speaking there finds expression a profound divergence of view between the two philosophers. While, then, a discussion of Individuality and a discussion of Personality must obviously to a considerable extent occupy common ground, we shall find that, in consequence of choosing Personality rather than Individuality as our main topic, we shall be, as it were, moving over that ground in a somewhat different direction from that taken by those who have preferred to concern themselves primarily with Individuality. In particular I shall endeavour to keep in close touch with the problem suggested by the expression, now so familiar, 'a personal God,' and shall make it my principal business to examine what is involved alike in the demand for 'a personal God' and in the rejection of that demand, and to arrive at some conclusion as to the rights and wrongs of the controversy between those who ascribe and those who refuse to ascribe Personality to God. I say to God, not to the Absolute or the Ultimate Reality ; for we shall find that there are not a few who would allow or even insist upon the ascription of Personality to God, but only if by 'God' they may be understood to mean something other than the Ultimate Reality ; while they agree with those who would altogether repudiate faith in a 'personal God,' in denying Personality to the Absolute.

It might seem that I should be following the most natural and convenient course for such a discussion as I am proposing to undertake if I were to begin with an examination of what we mean by Personality in ourselves

7 See *Microcosmus*, ix. 4, Eng. tr. ii. p. 688 : " Perfect Personality is in God only."

and to pass thence to an inquiry as to the legitimacy of extending the conception to that in which we " live and move and have our being." We should thus, it may be thought, be starting from the firm ground of that which lies nearest to ourselves, and beginning with the primary object of the conception we have set ourselves to consider. To begin with God, however accordant with the custom of antiquity or with the piety of Dogberry,[8] might seem an unpromising method of procedure for any one who hopes to reach an assured and scientific conclusion. Nevertheless I propose to devote my first course to the topic of Personality in God and the second to that of Personality in man, and must therefore endeavour to justify as best I can the order which I have adopted.

My grounds for adopting it are of two kinds : historical and philosophical. As a matter of fact it will be found on inquiry that not only has the development of the conception of personality been profoundly affected by the discussions which were carried on in the Christian Church concerning the mutual relations of the persons of the Trinity and the union of the divine and human natures in the person of Christ, but that philosophical discussion of the nature of human Personality is posterior in time to these theological discussions. Nay, it may even be said that it was the religious and theological interest in the Personality of Christ, conceived as being at once God and man, which actually afforded the motive and occasion of undertaking the investigation of the nature of Personality in men generally. In placing therefore the consideration of Personality in God before the consideration of the Personality in man, I shall be, at any rate, following the clue given by the history of thought. But there are

---

[8] *Much Ado about Nothing*, Act IV, Sc. 2.

reasons of a more philosophical order which may be alleged in support of my procedure. Personality is not merely something which we observe in men ; rather it is something which, though suggested to us by what we find in men, we perceive to be only imperfectly realized in them ; and this can only be because we are somehow aware of a perfection or ideal with which we contrast what we find in men as falling short of it. In such cases we rightly begin with thinking out the ideal and then considering the experienced facts in the light of it. We deal thus even with such a notion as that of Straightness in geometry, into our conception of which there does not enter that element of value which is involved, for example, in our notion of Justice or of Courage. It is, however, to this latter class of objects of thought, the class of what we may call ideals, that Personality belongs ; although I should readily admit that it is not to be conceived with the same definiteness and precision and consequently with so large a measure of general agreement as Justice or Courage.

Such a consideration of Personality as what it is in itself, apart from what appear as obstacles and hindrances to its full realization extraneous to its proper nature, when thus undertaken prior to any consideration of it under limiting and qualifying circumstances, quite naturally assumes the form of a discussion of Personality in God : and this is not to be distinguished from a discussion of the place and value of Personality in the universe. For the view that God, the Supreme Reality, has personality, not only in the sense in which the Absolute must possess all excellences which belong to any form of reality embraced within its systematic unity, but properly and pre-eminently ; and the view that it is possessed by a Being or Beings of far higher rank and more enduring significance in the scale of existence than men, but cannot be affirmed of the all-embracing Reality, within the unity of which men and such a higher Being or Beings would be distinguishable elements, factors or moments ; lastly, the view that only of beings like men, the unstable product of certain rare and transient conditions which are found to have presented themselves in a certain region within the infinity of Space, at a certain period within the infinity of Time, can Personality be intelligibly affirmed : all these views are at once replies to the question Is there a personal God, and if so, in what sense ? and also to the question, What is the rank or significance of Personality in the universe ? I would also here take occasion to point out that the order of treatment which I have chosen does not necessarily commit him who chooses it to the belief that Religion, as an attitude towards something other than ourselves, has objective value. For one might hold, with Feuerbach,[9] that Religion is an illusion in which we project as it were a shadowy image of ourselves upon the background of a world in which there exists as a matter of fact no higher being than ourselves ; but that this is the natural and only way in which we can discover the structure of our own souls ; since a direct vision of our own spiritual nature is to our minds as impossible as is a direct vision of our outward form to our bodily eyes ; so that only by means of a shadow or a reflected image can we become acquainted with either the one or the other.

The learned author of the *History of European Thought in the Nineteenth Century*,[10] Dr. Merz, has lately, in his very

---

[9] In his book *Das Wesen der Christenthums*, which George Eliot translated into English.   [10] Edinburgh, etc., 1896–1914.

interesting essay on *Religion and Science*,[11] indicated the problem of Personality as the problem to the consideration of which the course taken by the discoveries and speculations of the last age particularly invites at the present time the attention of philosophers ; and this because, whether we are exploring the nature of the world of objects in the presence of which we stand or tracing to its origin our consciousness of that world, we shall meet at last confronting us in our path this mystery of Personality. For, on the one hand, it is only through Personality —through our intercourse with persons quickening in us a personal response—that (to quote the words of Dr. Merz [12]) we gain in the earliest period of our earthly existence that entry into a world of Reality which enables us to distinguish our self from a not-self ; and, on the other hand (to cite the same writer again), " Personality always impresses us as the most powerful instance of individual existence." I welcome this confirmation by so high an authority of conclusions which I had independently reached, and which the observations that follow are intended to reinforce.

Mr. Rudyard Kipling in the *Jungle Book* has made us all familiar with the picture of a human child stolen by wolves in earliest infancy, brought up by and among animals without any intercourse with other human beings, yet arriving in due course at intellectual maturity and the exercise of reason. What little evidence there is concerning the fate of children thus stolen does not, I believe, suggest that such would have been the history of a real Mowgli ; and though one would not desire unduly to discourage an adventurous imagination bent on reconstructing the past history of our species and the genesis

[11] Edinburgh, etc., 1915.   [12] *Religion and Science*, p. 174.

of Reason upon earth, certainly intercourse with other persons seems to be within our experience an indispensable condition of the development of Rationality and Personality in human beings.[13]

I think that Dr. Merz is calling attention to a fact well worthy of our consideration when he points out that knowledge of objects always begins within our experience in a personal environment, and that it is probably through personal intercourse that we come to that discrimination of our selves from what is not ourselves which is involved in knowledge. Nevertheless, even if we content ourselves with saying that we have no conception of knowledge except as a personal activity, we shall still be admitting that in attempting to explore the nature of knowledge we are confronted by the fact of personality as the presupposition of that which we are exploring. So, too, we must agree with Dr. Merz that the progress of knowledge itself must sooner or later bring us face to face with this same fact of Personality as the highest form of life, and that, as students of living nature are more and more coming to recognize the impossibility of a merely mechanical or chemical account of life, we shall be no less compelled at last to admit that the study of life at a level below that of Personality will not suffice to solve the problem of Personality itself.

But while the progress of thought is thus forcing upon our attention this problem of Personality, it is not too much to say that both the scientific and the philosophical speculation of the last age showed a marked tendency to start aside (like Balaam's ass) when it found this mysterious apparition standing in the way. In the case

[13] Cp. Reid *On the Active Powers*, Essay V c. 2 (ed. Hamilton, ii. p. 641).

of scientific speculation this is obvious, and is readily
to be accounted for. It is characteristic of Science
(as we now commonly use the word) to concern itself with
generalities ; and it is precisely preoccupation with the
individual that marks off the sphere of History from that
of Science. No doubt the data of Science are found in
the observation of individuals ; but the moment that the
observation has been made, if it is to be turned to scientific
account at all, the result is, so to say, stripped of its historical circumstances, and presented as true not of that
thing, but of anything of that kind. Who made the
observation, and upon what individual object it was
made, these are questions the answers to which are only
interesting to Science so far as they guarantee the correctness of the observation ; and that once assured, they may
be forgotten. History is primarily concerned with persons ;
Science, on the other hand, can treat them only as speci-
mens, and the ' personal equation ' is important only as a
source of error to be discounted.

The embarrassment of Science in the presence of
Personality is thus not only easily explicable, but in view
of its special task legitimate. More remarkable is the
embarrassment of the very philosophy which during the
past century has made it its business to repress the over-
vaulting ambitions of Natural Science and to insist that
a method which necessarily abstracts from the spiritual
factor must be inadequate to the complete interpretation
of the experience of a spiritual being. Yet it is hard to
deny that the history of recent thought suggests embarrassment in the presence of Personality on the part
of this philosophy as well as on the part of Science. The
reasons for this embarrassment will become more evident
at a later stage of this inquiry. I will at present confine

myself to pointing out that, like the embarrassment of Science, it was largely due to the task which this philosophy had set itself, especially as represented by its illustrious progenitor, Kant, and by those British thinkers who towards the end of the last century devoted themselves to spreading the knowledge of Kant's work and of developing his principles among the inheritors of the tradition of the great British empiricists, Locke and Hume.

This task may be said to have been that of combating the scepticism of Hume by insistence on the principles of construction or synthesis which, though neglected or misrepresented by the empiricists, are really involved in the process of the scientific understanding. The traditional alliance between Natural Science and the empirical philosophy had caused the real inconsistency between them to be overlooked. Yet Natural Science implied the existence of objects which, though they could be felt, could not really be reduced to a combination of feelings. Hence, it was contended, the mind which was capable of Natural Science must be more than the mere aggregate of sensations to which Hume had shown it must be reduced if one were to be faithful to the implication of Locke's theory of knowledge ; a theory which still, a century later, was in essentials that in vogue among British men of science.[14] The mind must possess in itself—independently of any experience by way of separate sensations—those principles of synthesis and construction, to which Kant had given the name of *categories*. But Natural Science, as we have already seen, takes no account of Personality

[14] Professor Gibson has well pointed out in his recent book on *Locke's Theory of Knowledge* that Locke was himself much less of an empiricist than he appears in Green's criticism of him, which I was following in the text.

except as a possible source of errors in observation ; the principles of synthesis and construction which it employs are those which abstract from the difference of individual minds from one another. Hence a philosophy mainly concerned with the criticism of the procedure of Natural Science will concentrate its attention upon the principles of construction and synthesis of which Natural Science makes use rather than upon one which it can only recognize as a disturbing factor whose influence must be discounted before any trustworthy results can be attained.

But if, in tracing the recent history of thought, one is thus struck by a certain failure on the part of at least two representative groups of thinkers to come to grips with the problem of Personality, we shall not be surprised to find also that this very failure has provoked a marked tendency in other quarters to place this problem in the forefront of philosophical debate. No representation of this tendency, however, appears to me to have so dealt with the problem as to render superfluous or belated a further attempt to contribute to its discussion ; though I cannot hope that that which I have to offer will do more than, at the utmost, indicate some difficulties or suggest some considerations which have not always been borne in mind by others who have turned their thoughts in the same direction.

It is a profound saying of Tertullian's : *Habet Deus testimonia totum hoc quod sumus et in quo sumus.*[15] Nothing in ourselves, nothing in our environment can be utterly irrelevant to the subject presented to these Lectures by their Founder, the subject of Natural Theology. And so I need, I think, make no apology if I advert to the special circumstances in which these Lectures were

[15] *Adv. Marc.* i. 10.

delivered and suggest that they also invite our attention to the particular topic which I had chosen for my theme. The great and terrible war in which at the time of the delivery of these Lectures our country had been engaged for nearly four years has, I think, modified very greatly the attitude of thoughtful men, not especially occupied with the study of philosophy, but inquisitive concerning the great questions which life propounds to us all, towards the problem of Personality in God and in men. The time that preceded the war was a time in which even intelligent people could seriously doubt whether there would ever be another armed conflict on a great scale between civilized Powers ; a time in which the whole story of war which has filled so much of human history, with all its suffering and all its heroism, all its brutality and all its sacrifice, had become to many educated men among ourselves something legendary, a tale of

> . . . old, unhappy, far-off things
> And battles long ago. [16]

In such a time a certain way of regarding Personality had become familiar, which it is not too much to say the war has for a great number of persons completely reversed, making it seem important where it had seemed insignificant, and insignificant where it had seemed important. On the one hand the progress of scientific discovery, opening up to the imagination new and overwhelmingly vast vistas of Time and Space ; the rapid fading of beliefs which appeared to be bound up with the discarded cosmology of the Middle Ages, and seemed to appeal to the trustworthiness of traditions the authority of which had been irremediably shattered by the advance

[16] Wordsworth, *The Solitary Reaper.*

of historical knowledge and criticism ; and lastly the gradual loosening of ties which had largely depended for their sanctity and binding force upon the validity of these same beliefs : all these things had for multitudes of our contemporaries dwarfed into insignificance the ephemeral life of the human individual upon this planet and obliterated his once ' sure and certain hope ' of another life when that was over. On the other hand, the same changes of outlook had made that very ephemeral life seem to him who had to live it his one chance of happiness, of which he would do wisely to make the very fullest use in the few years allotted him. The realization of individual personality had come to seem at once supremely important as an object of human endeavour, and supremely unimportant from the point of view of the universe, wherein humanity itself was no more than the " child of a thousand chances 'neath the indifferent sky." [17]

Now for many the war has reversed all this. Men who were believed by others—who may even have believed themselves—to have asked from life no more than the largest possible measure of happiness for their individual selves, by whom the assertion that country and State were sacred realities which could claim from them a real devotion or self-sacrifice was felt to have about it something romantic or theatrical—an echo of picturesque but absurd times ' when knights were bold '—such men have not hesitated, nay, more, have after hesitation deliberately resolved to risk everything they could call their own—comfort, prospects, happiness, life—as of no account when set in the balance against their country's call. Death has become a familiar acquaintance to us all ; if we are to hold up our heads at all, we cannot afford

[17] Sir W. Watson, *The Hope of the World*, § 7.

to rate so high as we did the earthly life which death cuts short, and the opportunity of happiness which it holds for the individual. But this very depreciation of the value to the individual of that separate personality, to give which what seemed its solitary chance of full development had been reckoned the one thing worth caring about, has revived in the hearts of mourners who have lost those in whom their own hopes were bound up the old reluctance to believe that this life is all, the old faith that Personality has a greater significance in the universal scheme than accords with the suggestions of physical science ; it has revived also both in those who are fighting and those whom they have left at home the old instinct of prayer and therewith the demand, even in unexpected quarters, for one who can " hear the prayer " [18], for what we are apt to call a personal God.

No doubt it is possible to say that all this ought to make no difference to a philosophic ' spectator of all time and all existence.' Even this great war, what is it in the immensity of the stellar universe but a very little thing, " a trouble of ants in the gleam of a million million of suns " ? [19] If before it began there was no proof of the existence of a personal God who can hear our prayers, no reasonable probability that consciousness survives bodily death, the intensity of our private sorrows and the recrudescence of ancient habits cannot alter the laws of evidence. But I am not now concerned to defend the change of attitude towards the problem of Personality of which the war has been the occasion ; only to note it as an additional reason for attempting at this time to make up our minds what we ought to think about that problem itself.

[18] Psa. lxv. 2.   [19] Tennyson, *Vastness.*

In tracing this history we shall, as I have already intimated, find ourselves compelled to take note of the discussions of Christian theologians respecting two points of central importance in Christian theology, the union of the divine and human natures in the person of Christ, and the coexistence of three persons in the nature of God. It was the desire of Lord Gifford that the subject of Natural Theology should be treated by the Lectures on his Foundation without reference to or reliance upon any supposed special exceptional or so-called miraculous revelation. That I shall not be in any way contravening the spirit of this provision in the will of the Founder by giving a historical survey of views in support of which their propounders would certainly have invoked the authority of a special revelation, with the intention of showing the influence exerted by these views on the usage of the terms Person and Personality—this would be, I imagine, readily admitted. But I do not think that I shall be unfaithful to Lord Gifford's wishes, wishes to which moreover he was with great wisdom careful not to bind his beneficiaries too strictly, only intending, as he says, " to indicate leading principles," if I take seriously, as possible materials for the view of Personality that I desire to recommend to you, conceptions suggested by theological doctrines which will come before us in the course of our historical survey. So long as they are not treated as authoritative or as sacrosanct and immune from criticism, there can be no more inconsistency with a free scientific treatment of our subject in such a use of them, despite the belief of those who first put them forward in their peculiar claim to be considered as revealed, than there is in a like use of the doctrines of any philosopher, which we may find useful in guiding us to a conclusion of our own ; and we may be very sure that Lord Gifford had no thought of requiring of his Lecturers an impossible independence of all previous speculation. I shall, therefore, not hesitate to seek in the conceptions suggested by the dogmas of the Christian Church the same kind of help as I should seek in those implied in the systems of the masters of philosophy : and shall feel my conscience in doing so quite free from any scruple arising from Lord Gifford's desire that his Lecturers should treat their subject " without reference to or reliance on any supposed special, exceptional, or so-called miraculous revelation." At the same time I must confess that my view of the relation of Natural Theology to the historical religions is probably not quite the same as that which was taken by the Founder of these Lectures. I have elsewhere [20] given my reasons for holding that Natural Theology is to be regarded not after the manner suggested by certain expressions in Lord Gifford's will, as a science consisting of truths reached altogether independently of a historical religion, but rather as the result of reflection on a religious experience mediated in every case through a historical religion. Hence I do not think it possible for our subject to be (in Lord Gifford's words) " considered just as astronomy or chemistry is," and that because it cannot, in my judgment, be rightly described, as Lord Gifford seems to have thought that it could be described, " as a strictly natural science." But I should not regard the difference between Natural Theology and the ' strictly natural ' sciences, such as astronomy or chemistry, as consisting in the fact that in the former our thought is not to be allowed free play as in the latter, but must be exercised within the limits imposed by authority, or by

[20] *Studies in the History of Natural Theology*, p. 271.

assumptions which are not open at any time to reconsideration and criticism. I should rather regard it as depending on a characteristic shared by Natural Theology with such other subjects as Moral Philosophy, Political Philosophy, and the Philosophy of Art. Wherever there is found any one of the kinds of reflection which we describe by these names, it cannot but originate in the special moral, political, or æsthetic experience of a particular people ; although, at the same time, the claim made for such reflection to be a branch of Philosophy implies the faith that every experience of the sort can ultimately be placed in an intelligible relation with every other and be shown to have its function as a member of the resultant system.

So too I should hold that a definite type of religious experience, expressed in a historical religion, is presupposed in every system of Natural Theology ; while the ultimate goal of all human speculation which can be so named must be a system which presupposes all the religious experience of mankind ; an experience to which indeed those who regard Religion as genuine experience, and not as mere illusion throughout, cannot surely deny the name of Revelation.

From the history of the notion of Personality and of the application of it to God I shall pass to a consideration of the motives which have led to an attempt to find Personality in God, and of the difficulties which such an attempt encounters. We shall find ourselves in the course of this investigation examining the conceptions implied in such phrases as ' divine immanence,' ' divine transcendence,' and ' a finite God.' Lastly I shall venture to put before you certain conclusions to which I have been led by my reflections on these motives for seeking Personality in God and on the difficulties involved in such a search.

This programme will bring us to the end of the present course. The following course I propose to devote to an inquiry into the bearing of my conclusions, reached in the former course, as to Personality in God upon the view which we should take of Personality in men, as exhibited in the various spheres of human activity—in conduct, in politics, in art, in science, in religion ; and also upon what, borrowing an expression from the title of Mr. Bosanquet's Gifford Lectures, to which I have already referred,' I will call the question of the ' value and destiny of the individual ' person.

My next Lecture will deal with the history of the word Person and with the notion of Personality in general.

LECTURE II

HISTORY OF THE NOTION OF PERSONALITY IN GENERAL

IT is a well-known fact that in its original use the word *persona* was the designation of the *mask* worn by the actor on the ancient Roman stage and came to be used of the *actor* himself and his *part* in the play ; and hence of the *part* that a man plays in social intercourse generally, and especially those forms of social intercourse in which, as in legal transactions or in the official relations of public magistrates, a definite task is assigned, just as in a play, to a particular man, to which all that he is or does when not engaged in the performance of that task is irrelevant. In classical Latin *persona* did not acquire that vague use as equivalent to 'human being' generally in which 'person' is among ourselves so often employed. It is possible no doubt to quote one or two passages even in classical Latin which may seem to contradict this statement.[1] But even in these I think we should be more nearly correct in translating *persona* by 'party' than in translating it by 'person.' The word 'party,' even when it was, as in old English (to use the expression of the *New English Dictionary*), "common and in serious use" for an individual person, had not wholly lost the

[1] E.g. Suet. *Ner.* § 1 ; Juv. *Sat.* iv. 15.

meaning belonging to it in the legal or mercantile phraseology from which it was borrowed. It meant the man
or woman concerned in the transaction of which mention
was being made. When a reference of this sort to a *part*
played by the person in question in a definite affair involving
other *parties* is wholly absent, as when one speaks of ' an
old party ' or ' a stout party,' the expression is, except
as jocular, not recognized in educated English ; and it
is probably due to its undignified associations, as vulgarly
employed in such colloquialisms, that the use of the
word for an individual person in solemn and sacred
contexts, such as those in which the English divines of
the seventeenth century were not afraid to avail themselves of it, has now become impossible.

If in classical Latin *persona* did not, on the one hand,
acquire the vague colourless sense which *person* has among
ourselves when we use it to mean no more than ' individual human being,' neither did it, on the other, come
to be expressive of what may be supposed to distinguish
the inner life of a human being from that of an animal—
self-consciousness, moral purpose, æsthetic emotion,
intellectual point of view. The possibility of such a
use of it—the philosophical use of it, as we may call
it—which we assume in such a discussion of *Personality*
as I am undertaking in these Lectures, lay no doubt in this,
that *persona* always implied that the being so designated
had a part to play in some kind of social intercourse, such
as is represented in a drama ; and that of such social
intercourse no mere animal but only a human being is
capable. But the appropriation of the word to express
the dignity of the rational human being in his consciousness
of a special function and worth in relation to his fellow-
men would, though assisted by the juristic associations

of the term, probably not have taken root in the modern languages of Europe had *persona* not come to be used by the Latin-speaking theologians of the Christian Church as the equivalent of the Greek ὑπόστασις.

This word ὑπόστασις, which literally means ' a standing under or below,' was in classical Greek used only of that which has settled down at the bottom—dregs, that is, or sediment ; or else of the position of one who lies in ambush, standing concealed under some kind of cover. But it came at a later period to signify what we may call real concrete existence as opposed to a mere appearance with nothing solid or permanent underlying it. There can be little doubt that it was among the Stoics that this usage arose ; but actual examples of its use by writers of this School are lacking. The corresponding verb, however, occurs in the great Stoic moralist Chrysippus in a related sense [2] ; and the word itself is employed in the pseudo-Aristotelian treatise *de Mundo*, which was most likely written in the first century of our era, and in a passage of it which probably repeats the views of the Stoic Posidonius, the master of Cicero, to express the corporeal reality which comets, for example, have, and mere effects of light, such as rainbows, have not.[3] About the same time the appearance in the letters of Seneca of the Latin *substantia*, which must have originated as a translation of ὑπόστασις, to express real concrete existence, testifies to the acquisition by the Greek word of this signification in the preceding generation at latest ; and it is interesting to note that the ecclesiastical

[2] Plutarch, *Moralia*, 1081 F : Χρύσιππος . . . τὸ μὲν παρῳχημένον τοῦ χρόνου καὶ τὸ μέλλον οὐχ ὑπάρχειν ἀλλ' ὑφεστηκέναι φησί. It is noticeable, in view of the later history of the word ὑπόστασις, that it is *not* the actual present for which ὑφεστηκέναι is here reserved.

[3] 4.395, a 30. See Zeller, *Phil. der Griechen*, 3rd ed. III. i p. 644 f.

historian Socrates has preserved for us the record of a protest made against its use in this sense as a barbarous novelty by an Alexandrian scholar who may have lived as early as the time of Augustus.[4] Neither Seneca nor Quintilian, who in the next generation often uses *substantia* in the way to which I have referred, regards it as corresponding to the Greek οὐσία, which signifies *being* in the widest sense.[5] But the latter employs it in connexions where οὐσία might have been used in Greek [6]; and it came afterwards to be the usual rendering of that word, for which both the two Roman writers just mentioned lamented the absence of a proper Latin equivalent in common use.

It is remarkable that the word *essentia*, which might have seemed to be the natural representative for οὐσία in Latin, although it could claim the great authority of Cicero, and although other distinguished writers, Seneca among them, attempted to introduce it in this capacity, failed to establish itself until some centuries later, and left the place in philosophical terminology which its patrons intended for it, to be filled by *substantia*.[7] That sub-

4 See Socr. *Hist. Ecc.* iii. 7. The scholar in question was the grammarian Irenæus, otherwise called Minucius Pacatus. His date, however, is not certain, and he has by some been placed as late as the reign of Hadrian.

5 See Seneca, *Ep.* 58 § 6. Quintilian, *Inst. Or.* iii. 6 § 23.

6 See *Inst. Or.* ii. 15 § 34, iii. 6 § 39, ix. 1 § 8. We know from Pseudo-Augustine *Princ. Rhet.* c. 5 that de *substantia* in the last of these passages, as the description of a subject of legal investigation, corresponds to περὶ τῆς οὐσίας in the terminology of the rhetorician Theodorus of Gadara, who flourished in the reign of Augustus.

7 See Seneca, *Ep.* 58 § 6; Quintilian, *Inst. Or.* iii. 6 § 23, viii. 3 § 33; Sidonius Apollinaris *præf. ad. carm* 14; Quintilian (ii. 14 § 2, iii. 6 § 23) says that Plautus used *essentia*, but, if he did so, it is not likely to have been in a philosophical context. Augustine (*de Moribus Manichæis* ii. 2 § 2, *de Trin.* v. § 9) still speaks, in the fifth

stantia could fill this place implies a close approximation in meaning between ὑπόστασις and οὐσία, making a discrimination between them a task of some difficulty.

The first unquestionable extant example of the use of ὑπόστασις itself in a sense hardly distinguishable from that of οὐσία is in the anonymous work of an author who was probably younger than Seneca and older than Quintilian, and who belonged, not to the cultivated society of the capital, but to a people which more than any other within the Empire resolutely held itself aloof in religious isolation from the main stream of contemporary life. This work is that which we call the Epistle to the Hebrews.

At the very outset of this Epistle the Son of God is described as the χαρακτὴρ τῆς ὑποστάσεως, the " express image of the substance" of his Father.[8] Our Authorized Version of the Bible, influenced by the technicalities of the later theology, has *person* in this passage ; but the Revised Version has replaced this word by *substance*. We also find the word in another work of the same age, also by a Jewish writer, the so-called *Wisdom of Solomon* [9] ; the interpretation of it in this place is doubtful, but, in the judgment of the Revisers of 1894, it refers, as in the Epistle to the Hebrews, to the *nature* or *being* of God. Another Hellenistic Jew, the Alexandrian philosopher, Philo, certainly employs the cognate verb with this reference.[10] We may also note that the word in the sense of *subsistence* or *continuance*—a sense which would easily pass into the sense of *nature* or *essence*—is

century, of *essentia* as an unfamiliar word, and describes *substantia* as the recognized Latin rendering of οὐσία.

[8] Heb. i. 3. [9] xvi. 21.
[10] *Quod deterius potiori insidiari soleat*, § 160 (ed. Cohn i. p. 294).

already found in the LXX version of the Psalms,[11] as well
as in less closely related senses in that of the Prophets.[12]
There is nothing but what is natural in a term which
would thus be familiar to readers of the Greek Old Testament domesticating itself in the language of the Christian
Church ; and it was, as has already been observed, due
to its employment in Christian theology that it came to
be rendered by, and so to affect the usage of, the Latin
persona.

To make this episode in the career of the word ὑπόστασις
fully intelligible it will be necessary to look back for a
few minutes to an earlier period in the history of Greek
philosophical terminology and consider those difficulties
in determining the proper use of the word οὐσία, *being*
or *reality*, with which Aristotle's discussion of its ambiguities makes us acquainted.[13] It is easy to see that this
word might naturally enough be applied to the characteristic nature of a thing, by a description of which we
should answer the question ' What *is* it ? ' But as, if
this question were raised about several things of the
same kind, we might give exactly the same answer in
the case of each, the *being* or *essence*, as we may say,
of a thing might seem to be something common to it
with others, or, in the language of the logicians, a ' universal.' On the other hand, it was argued by Aristotle
that nothing could be properly considered as an οὐσία,
or real being, which was not something existing, so to say,
upon its own account, something to which attributes
might belong, but which could not belong in this way to
anything else ; which was, in the phrase which had come

[11] Psa. xxxviii. (xxxix.) 6 ; lxxxviii. (lxxxix.) 48.
[12] Jer. x. 17 (τὴν ὑ. σοῦ=thy substance, i.e. thy property) ;
Ezek. xxvi. 11 (τὴν ὑ. τῆς ἰσχυος σου=the support of thy strength).
[13] *Metaph.* Z. 1–3, cp. Δ 8.

to be appropriated to such a thing, a ὑποκείμενον, a *subject* or *substratum*. Hence a mere 'universal' such as 'man,' which is no more what I am than it is what you are or what you are than what I am, could not be rightly called οὐσία, but only an individual being, this or that individual man, for example Socrates or Callias, in whom are met together the two mutually complementary conditions of full reality, namely a *distinguishable nature* of its own and that *concrete independence* which cannot be ascribed to what is only an accident or attribute of something else. But the term ὑποκείμενον, which is used to indicate this latter note of a real being, could be and was employed also as a designation of that abstraction of indeterminate, unqualified potentiality which Aristotle called ὕλη or Matter. Greek philosophy was haunted, as it were, by the thought of this Matter, lying at the root of whatever is susceptible of any kind of development ; in itself without form or character of any kind, but capable of receiving any and so becoming some particular thing, qualified in some definite way. Matter, thus understood, might be called the ultimate ὑποκείμενον or substratum of everything in this lower world. Now it was, I take it, because this word ὑποκείμενον might be thus used, and so could not be restricted to the concrete individual thing, in which some form or nature, describable in general terms which are applicable to more things than one, is realized in this or that instance, this or that man, this or that horse, that there was felt in the post-Aristotelian period of Greek philosophy to be room for a word appropriated to this last signification only. Such a word was found in ὑπόστασις, a word involving practically the same metaphor as ὑποκείμενον, but without the associations of ὑποκείμενον with mere indeterminate Matter. Thus it is that ὑπόστασις comes into use as a philosophical term, often equivalent to οὐσία, which for Aristotle is most properly used of the concrete individual of a certain kind; but of Aristotle's two notes of real being, its *intelligible character* and its *concrete independence*, emphasizing the latter, as οὐσία emphasized the former.

This difference of emphasis between the two words οὐσία and ὑπόστασις sufficiently accounts for the use made of them respectively by the Christian Church in the eventual formulation of her theology. When constrained to give systematic expression to the implications of the divine Name of Father, Son, and Holy Ghost, the use of which had been characteristic of Christianity at least from the time of its first appearance on the stage of the Græco-Roman world as a claimant to universal allegiance, she worked out a terminology in which οὐσία was appropriated to the one Divine Nature, ὑπόστασις to the distinctions within it designated by the three titles, Father, Son, and Spirit.

As is well known to students of theology, the settlement of this terminology was a long and controversial process. The discrimination of οὐσία from ὑπόστασις was not readily accepted; for, whatever difference of emphasis there may have been between the two words, they were at first, both inside and outside of the Christian Church, generally considered on the whole as synonymous. They were so both in the language of Origen, in whose writings the description of the members of the Trinity as three ὑποστάσεις first occurs, and also in that of his fellow-student at Alexandria, Plotinus. We should, indeed, expect the associations of the word to be the same for them both. The use of ὑπόστασις by Plotinus and by the Neo-Platonic philosophers generally is a subject which needs a fuller investigation than it seems yet to have received. For Plotinus, so far as I understand him—but he is a very difficult author and I make no claim to more than a superficial acquaintance with his writings—ὑπόστασις and the corresponding verb seem to signify the *concrete actuality* of that to which they are applied. Such a concrete actuality does Origen attribute to each member of the Christian Trinity where he speaks of them as three ὑποστάσεις [14]; and Plotinus to each member of his corresponding triad—the Supreme Good, Intelligence, and the World Soul; which, in the title of one of the essays by him which his disciple Porphyry collected into the fifth Ennead,[15] are described as the three ἀρχικαὶ ὑποστάσεις, primary or original realities.

The word οὐσία, on the other hand, though, as we have seen, generally regarded as synonymous with ὑπόστασις—and so treated not only by Plotinus but by Origen—was obviously more readily applicable to something which was shared by several concrete actualities, but was itself not actual apart from or outside of them. Hence, as we have seen, in the final settlement of the terminology of the Christian doctrine of the Trinity the divine οὐσία was said to be one, the divine ὑποστάσεις three. This terminology was so far, however, not distinguishable from that which might be used in discriminating the one identical human nature of Peter, James, and John from the individuality in which the three men differ each from each. But, since the Christian Church had no intention of surrendering the confession that " the Lord our God is one," [16] which had been the characteristic note of the faith of the parent community of Israel, out of

---

[14] *In Joan.* ii. 6.　　　[15] *Enn.* v. I.
[16] Deut. vi. 4 ; cp. Mark xii. 29.

which she had arisen and whose Scriptures she retained as her own, it was in itself a defect in this part of her theological phraseology that it did not, as it stood, more decisively exclude the interpretation which would assimilate the unity of the Godhead to the merely specific unity in which three several men partake. Now it so happened that a deficiency in the philosophical vocabulary of the Latin-speaking as compared with that of the Greek-speaking churches proved of service in helping to remedy this defect.

We have already seen that *substantia* came to be regarded in philosophical Latin as the representative of the Greek οὐσία, and that, despite the high authority of no less a master of the language than Cicero, *essentia*, which was afterwards to be found useful in this capacity, long failed to obtain a sure footing in the language. Hence arose a difficulty in rendering into Latin the discrimination between οὐσία and ὑπόστασις necessary to the orthodox expression of the doctrine of the Trinity. For *substantia*, which would naturally have been used for ὑπόστασις, of which it was the direct translation, was wanted to represent οὐσία ; what, then, was to stand for ὑπόστασις?

It would seem to have been to Tertullian that the currency—if not the discovery—was due of a word to serve this purpose which was ultimately to take the place of ὑπόστασις in the theological phraseology of the Western Church and to suggest a useful variant for it in that of the Eastern. This word was no other than *persona*,[17] which, as we have seen, meant primarily a part played in some form of social intercourse, and secondarily the player of such a part. Though used in the connexion of which we are now speaking to stand for ὑπόστασις,

[17] See Tert. *adv. Praxean*, cc. 11, 12 (Migne, *Patr. Lat.* II, 167, c,d).

it had already a more nearly literal representative in Greek, namely πρόσωπον; and this is not unknown to Greek theology as a synonym of ὑπόστασις when employed in formulating the doctrine of the Trinity. But there seems reason to conjecture that the introduction of this latter word into Greek theological terminology was due to the reaction of the Western usage upon the language of the East. It first appears in its theological reference in the writings of Hippolytus, who though he wrote in Greek, was himself a Western, a presbyter of the Roman Church, and to a considerable extent in theological and ecclesiastical sympathy with his African contemporary Tertullian.[18] This is not the place to discuss the question of the literary relation of Tertullian to Hippolytus. If we could be certain that Hippolytus' use of πρόσωπον was independent of Tertullian, or should even suppose—what is not likely—that it suggested Tertullian's use of persona, the evidence would still point to the Eastern Church having borrowed the use of πρόσωπον from the Western, in which Latin (already, no doubt, though Hippolytus still wrote in Greek, by his time the medium of ordinary intercourse), became with Tertullian the language of theological literature as well.

In any case persona became the principal Latin representative of the Greek ὑπόστασις in its theological sense, and we shall see that the use of its more literal rendering πρόσωπον as an alternative expression for ὑπόστασις in Greek balanced the suggestion contained in the use of ὑπόστασις of a too complete distinction of Father, Son, and Spirit within the Godhead, as complete

---

[18] Hippolytus contra Noetum § 14 (ed. Lagarde, p. 52); Ref. Haer. ix. 12 (ed. Duncker, p. 458).

as that of three men within the human species, by a
suggestion of an exactly opposite kind. For πρόσωπον
had (principally, as one may suppose, because it had not
acquired the legal associations of *persona*) made still
less progress than *persona* towards the modern philosophical use of *person*. Primarily, indeed, it meant the *face*,
not, like *persona*, the actor's mask (which was properly
in Greek προσωπεῖον). So far as it had come to be used
at all for an individual human being it was probably
rather through taking the 'face' to stand for the man,
as we speak of counting *heads*, than through being used
for a *dramatis persona*, although it is found also in this
sense. This being the history of the term πρόσωπον, we
are not surprised to find that even more than *persona*
did it suggest a mere *aspect* or *rôle*. Several such aspects
might be presented, several such rôles discharged by the
same individual at different times. Thus πρόσωπον,
used of Father, Son, and Spirit, might suggest, did one
but forget that one might also say ὑπόστασις, that
the distinction between them was one of as superficial,
perhaps of as temporary a character as that between the
different aspects the same man may wear on different
occasions, or the different parts he may take in different
conversations.

Thus what we may call the philosophical use of *person*
in the modern European languages has been determined
by the use in the formulation of the Christian doctrine
of the Trinity of ὑπόστασις and *persona* as equivalent
expressions ; and we shall find that ambiguities derived
from the very different origins of the two words thus
associated together have left undeniable traces in the
treatment of the word *person* by different thinkers in our
own time. For the history of philosophical terms is very

far from encouraging the writer of philosophical books in the belief that he can say with Humpty Dumpty in *Alice Through the Looking Glass* that " when I use a word, it means what I choose it to mean—-neither more nor less." [19] To Boethius at the beginning of the sixth century of our era we owe the definition of *persona* which became the standard definition for the writers of the Middle Ages and which is still perhaps, take it all in all, the best that we have. It occurs in his treatise—we will speak of it as his, for, though his authorship has been doubted by good scholars, the weight of the evidence is, I think, on the whole in favour of it [20]—against Nestorius and Eutyches, whose names were associated respectively with two opposite views of Christ's personality, reckoned by the main body of the Christian Church as alike heretical.

This celebrated definition runs as follows : *Persona est naturæ rationabilis individua substantia* [21] : the indi-

[19] c. 6.

[20] In my *Studies in the History of Natural Theology*, p. 143, I expressed a different opinion ; but I now doubt whether the Council of Chalcedon is the assembly referred to in the preface ; and, if it is not, the chief argument against the authenticity of the treatise disappears. On the other hand, I cannot but think it possible that in the *Anecdoton Holderi*, to which Usener appeals as deciding the question by the unexceptionable authority of Cassiodorus, the copyist of the extract from the latter's letter may, as Nitzsch supposes, have interpolated the names of works already ascribed in his time to Boethius. Still, as it stands, the external evidence is in favour of Boethius's authorship, while I do not feel so strongly as Nitzsch the difficulty of supposing the writer of the *Consolatio Philosophiæ* to have composed a Christological treatise which, while abounding in learning and in the appreciation of intellectual subtleties, gives no sign of a deep personal religious interest in the doctrines expounded.

[21] *Contra Eutychen et Nestorium*, c. 3. I take this opportunity of correcting the statement of the definition in my *Studies*, p. 143, where, through an oversight, the origin of which I cannot now explain, the false reading *subsistentia* was printed instead of the certainly correct *substantia*.

vidual subsistence of a rational nature. Here what I
may call the double-facedness of the term is brought out.
For when we use the word *person* we describe that which
we so designate as an individual, not as a universal which
may attach to many individuals. *Rational nature* taken
by itself as a universal is not a person. On the other
hand, neither is any individual a person whose nature is
not rational : and this, if we consider, means an individual
which is not aware of itself as an instance of a universal.
Thus an individual stone is not a person, because, though
we recognize that there is a common nature which it
shares with other stones, the stone itself is not aware of
this ; nor is an animal, such as a dog or a horse, a person ;
for although it may possess (for example in the form of
the attraction of sex) an instinctive awareness of the
presence in others of a nature common to them with
itself, yet we do not suppose that it reflects upon this so
as to form a general notion of this common nature. Nor
do we naturally apply the term *person* even to a human
infant which has not yet arrived at the stage of such
reflection. It is only to mature human beings that
within the sphere of our everyday experience we commonly apply it ; for only in them do we find a full recognition of his or her self as at once distinct from other selves
and as sharing along with other selves in a common
nature. It is true that a corporation may be a person
in law and may be treated like an individual man or
woman as a subject of rights and duties. This conception
of corporate personality I hope in my second course of
Lectures to examine more closely. But I think we must
admit that only with an apology or explanation should
we in ordinary discourse speak of a corporation or a community of any kind as a person ; to call it so without

qualification would be felt to be unnatural and pedantic.[22]
It may seem strange that this should be so if, as appears
to be the case, we find in the earlier stages of civilization
not the individual but the community to which he belongs
regarded as the primary subject of rights and duties ;
the crime of the individual involving the guilt of his clan
or tribe, and the wrong done to the individual calling for
the infliction of vengeance by any member of his tribe
upon any member of the offenders. But the development
of civilization has on the whole been marked by a tendency
to transfer, at any rate in respect of a large part of the
field of human conduct, this position as the subject of
rights and duties from the community to the individual
member of the community. When the remark is made,
which we often hear nowadays, that Personality is a
comparatively late discovery, it is due to a perception
of this historical fact. For (to quote some words which
I have written elsewhere) [23] so long as Personality is found,
not mainly in the individual, but rather in the community, so long Personality in our sense—the *individual
subsistence* of a rational nature—is not adequately recognized. On the other hand, so long as it is only
acknowledged in certain selected individuals, such as
a prince who, as in Hobbes's theory, absorbs the
personality of all his subjects, or a priest who is the
' parson ' or ' *persona* ' of the parish over which he
presides, so long there is an inadequate recognition of
the individual subsistence of a *rational nature* in
the multitude of which these are the selected representatives ; for the ordinary members of the multitude
are so far regarded as *mere individuals*, not properly

[22] Cf. my *Studies in the History of Natural Theology*, p. 143.
[23] *Studies in the History of Natural Theology*, p. 144.

persons in their own right, but only as such in and through their representatives.

I would further call attention to the fact that the two notes in the conception of *Personality* which are expressed in the definition of *persona* given by Boethius may be said to be emphasized the one rather by that word itself, the other by what is its Greek equivalent in this sense ; the rational nature rather by *persona*, the individual subsistence by ὑπόστασις. The word ὑπόστασις does not by itself convey any suggestion of a rational nature. There was nothing in its etymology to forbid its application even to a merely material thing. We have already seen that in one of the earliest instances of its scientific use, in the passage quoted above from the pseudo-Aristotelian *de Mundo*, it is even used to distinguish the solid corporeity of a comet from a mere effect of reflected light like a rainbow.[24] But the later usage of the word had tended to give to it dignified associations which made it suggest a higher kind of reality than could be ascribed to a mere inanimate thing. Boethius himself—if the treatise be really his—asserts, in the context of the definition of *persona* which I have been quoting, that the Greeks do not use ὑπόστασις even of irrational animals but only of rational beings. This is probably not true in the unqualified form in which it is here asserted. But it must have had some ground in fact ; and, if we take it to proceed from Boethius, it must be allowed very considerable weight. A man so well read in Greek literature, philosophical, scientific, and theological, as Boethius certainly was—he had translated into Latin Plato, Aristotle, Archimedes, and Euclid, as well as written on the chief theological controversies of the day—would scarcely

[24] *De Mundo* 4, 395, a. 30. See above, p. 37.

have made such a statement had it not held good in a notable majority of instances. We have already observed that not only was it the word used by the Christian theologians of the Father, Son, and Spirit whom they worshipped as one God, but it was also employed by Plotinus to designate the three members of his Trinity—the Supreme Good, the Intelligence, and the World-Soul—a Trinity suggested by the *Timæus* of Plato, and despite important differences, presenting a certain correspondence with the Trinity of the Christians. The use, then, of ὑπόστασις to denote the members alike of the Neo-Platonic and of the Christian Trinity suggests that Boethius was justified in calling attention to this association of special dignity with the word as characteristic of Greek thought as a whole during the period in which it had been used as a technical term of philosophy.

But if ὑπόστασις, despite the absence of any suggestion of the kind in the etymology of the word, had come to imply the individual subsistence not of any nature, but only of a *rational* nature, *persona* was from the first obviously inappropriate to any but a rational nature. Only a rational being could be an actor in a play or a party to a suit or contract. On the other hand, as has already been pointed out, there was lacking in *persona* (and perhaps still more in its Greek representative πρόσωπον) any decided suggestion of a permanent, inalienable, fundamental individuality. Rather did it carry with it the associations of an occasional, temporary, voluntary activity, although no doubt also of one which distinguished him who exercised it from the mass of his fellows and made him in some particular respect an outstanding figure. An individual man is not born a player, a litigant, or an official; when he ceases to act in any

of these capacities, he does not thereupon cease to be,
nor while he is acting in them do they absorb the whole
of his existence. ✓

I said in my first Lecture that when Lotze ascribes to
the Absolute Personality and Mr. Bosanquet Individuality
but not Personality, we have to do with something more
than a merely verbal difference. But though this is true,
the difference between them in this respect is a difference
upon which the history of the word *Person* will be found
to throw some light. We shall have at a later stage of
our inquiry to consider the deeper significance of it;
at present I desire to call attention to its verbal aspect.

Mr. Bosanquet is true to what may be said to be the Hegelian tradition, for which the legal associations of *persona* are
what on the whole determine the use of the words *Person*
and *Persönlichkeit*.[25] A *person*, to be a *person*, must stand
in relation to other *persons*, and it is where this relation
is of a merely judicial or legal character that the expression is especially in place; for in the higher kinds of such
relationship—in marriage or in the State—the parties
to the relation tend to lose their separate personality and
become.factors in the inclusive personality of the family
or of the State, which can then be treated as persons,
just because they stand over against other families or
other States with claims and counterclaims upon them,
such as the several men and women who constitute them
have upon one another when they are not conscious of
a higher unity superseding their mutual independence.
When Personality is viewed from this angle, it is intel-

[25] Hegel's use of 'person' is perhaps not quite consistent. Thus
he sometimes says that all living beings are *subjects* but that only
some are *persons* (*Phil. d. Rechts* § 35, *Werke*, viii. p. 71), sometimes that the *person* becomes a *subject* when passing from legality
to morality (ibid. § 105, p. 144).

ligible that it should seem an attribute wholly inapplicable
to the Absolute, which cannot stand in an external relation
to anything else. On the other hand, just because all
relations must fall within it, the Absolute alone can from
this point of view be called in the strictest sense an *individual* ; beings like ourselves who *are* persons are for
that very reason possessed only of a quasi-individuality ;
we are aware of ourselves as, in the phrase of Descartes,[26]
res incompletæ, beings whose nature cannot be fully
described without bringing in the mention of beings
other than ourselves, our relations to which constitute
what we ourselves are. To the all-inclusive reality of the
Absolute *personality* is inapplicable, but *individuality* is
its prerogative ; we, on the other hand, just because we
are *persons*, can only be called *individuals* in a qualified
sense and, as it were, by courtesy.

The way in which Lotze looks at Personality is quite
different. For him,[27] though each of us may only be able
to think of his self as contrasted with what is not self,
yet one may experience one's self " previous to and out
of every such relation " and " to this is due the possibility of its subsequently becoming thinkable in that
relation." That to which Personality can properly be
ascribed is an " inner core, which cannot be resolved
into thoughts " [28]; of this " inner core " we know the
meaning and significance " in the immediate experience
of our mental life " and " we always misunderstand it
when we seek to construe it."

We will not at present pursue further Lotze's account
of Personality, to which we must hereafter return. But

[26] *Medit*. iii. sub fin.
[27] See *Microcosmus*, ix. 4 § 4, Eng. tr. ii. p. 680,
[28] Ibid. p. 682.

what I have quoted from it is sufficient to explain why he, unlike Mr. Bosanquet, can ascribe Personality to the Absolute, and indeed in the strictest sense to nothing else. For only an Infinite Being can be supposed consciously to possess its whole nature in the manner in which we consciously possess that part of our experience which we feel to be most intimately our own. The considerations which determine Lotze in appropriating Personality to the Infinite are closely akin to those which determine Mr. Bosanquet to a like appropriation of Individuality to the Absolute. But that it is Personality which he can thus appropriate is due to the fact that with Lotze the legal associations of the word do not, as with Mr. Bosanquet, dominate his conception of its meaning, and that for him it corresponds more closely than with Mr. Bosanquet, faithful as he is to the Hegelian tradition of insistence on those legal associations, to ὑπόστασις as employed by the Greeks whose usage Boethius reports to us.

The general history of the word Person with its derivatives in philosophical terminology may be said to have moved on the whole throughout on lines determined for it by the process whose result is summed up in the Boethian definition of *persona*. Within these lines there has been a continual oscillation, according as the thought, emphasized by the Greek word ὑπόστασις, of independent and fundamentally unchangeable individuality, or the thought of social relationship and voluntary activity, suggested by the Latin word *persona*, has been uppermost. But it will be convenient, before leaving this general history of the word and the notions corresponding to it for a more particular consideration of the history of its application to God, to advert to certain aspects of Personality which, although they may be brought within the scope of the Boethian formula, were not so much emphasized in the earlier discussions which have chiefly occupied our attention hitherto as they have been in later times. I shall not attempt to discuss them exhaustively, but shall only conclude this Lecture by indicating them in a brief and summary manner.

Three such aspects of Personality may be noted. We may label them as *incommunicability*, *self-consciousness*, and *will* respectively. Stress was already laid upon the first of these, *incommunicability*, in a passage of the twelfth-century mystic Richard of St. Victor, which was often quoted by later Schoolmen ; and to dwell upon this feature of Personality was congenial to the tendency which from the middle of the thirteenth century manifested itself in mediæval philosophy towards preoccupation with the problem of Individuality. It is obvious that, in emphasizing the incommunicable nature of Personality, the writers whom I have in mind were attending to that side of the conception of Personality, as defined by Boethius, which is expressed by the words *individua substantia* and suggests the Greek word ὑπόστασις, rather than to that expressed by the words *naturæ rationabilis* which remind one more of the original associations of the Latin *persona*. It became the custom to use in defining *persona* phrases which, like *suppositum*, or *ens completum*, called attention chiefly to its concrete individuality, though of course with some such epithet as *intellectuale* to distinguish persons from *supposita* (concrete individuals) of a lower rank ; and this practice still persisted among the philosophical theologians of the sixteenth and early seventeenth centuries.[29]

[29] See Richard of St. Victor, *de Trin.* iv. 6, 8, 21, 22, 23, 24 (Migne

As we should expect, the new direction given to speculation by Descartes was not without its effect upon the
way in which the subject of Personality was approached.
It is well known that Descartes, after attempting to
carry doubt as far as it would go, had found one thing
which he could not doubt, namely the existence of his
own thinking self; since even to doubt he must think,
and to think he must exist; and that, starting from this
sole ultimate bedrock of certainty, he worked back to
assurance of the existence, first of God and then of the
world of objects. Now in following this procedure and
treating the mind of man as the one indubitable reality,
he broke away from the conviction, which the philosophy
of the Middle Ages had inherited from antiquity, that
the existence of something real other than the mind of
man was beyond question, and introduced into European
thought that pyschological bias, if I may so describe
it, the presence of which in so much of the speculation
of the last three centuries perhaps more than anything
else differentiates it from that of the preceding ages.
The change of point of view due to the introduction of
this bias is marked by the changes in philosophical terminology to which it has led. Thus *subjective* formerly
meant what belonged to the existence of things as they
were in themselves, independent of our perception or

Patr. Lat. cxcvi. 934 *seqq.*); Durandus a Sancto Porçiano *in Sent*
iii. 11, 2 § 10, ii. 3. 2 § 5; Duns Scotus *in Sent* (Op. Oxon.) I dist.
23, qu. 1. 4; Ockham *in Sent*. i. dist. 23, qu. 1.   Richard of
St. Victor held that the Boethian definition as it stood was in-
sufficient to distinguish the divine persons from the 'undivided
substance' of the Trinity.
  See also Melanchthon, *Loc. Theol. de tribus Personis Divinitatis*;
Turretinus, *Inst. Theol.* (1679) loc. III. qu. 23 §§ 4, 8; Bellarmine,
de Christo, ii. 4; Sherlock, *Vindication of the Doctrine of the Trinity*,
p. 69.

knowledge of them, *objective* what belonged to them as presented to or apprehended by consciousness. But now, since for Descartes the only thing whose existence was directly and indubitably certain was the conscious mind, this conscious mind has arrogated to itself the designation of Subject *par excellence* and *subjective* has come to mean what belongs to it, *objective* what is in any particular connexion contrasted with it.

There was another famous term, very similar in origin and history to *Subject* : I mean *Substance*. *Subject* of course originated as a rendering of ὑποκείμενον and *Substantia* as we have seen of ὑπόστασις, and I have already touched upon the early relationship of these two Greek terms.

Now the term Substance was for the philosophers of the age inaugurated by Descartes a fruitful source of embarrassment, just because the thought which it was apt to call up of an unperceived foundation, concealed underneath those immediate objects of our consciousness of which we are actually aware, was not easily harmonized with a philosophy which found in awareness or consciousness itself what is surest and deepest and most abiding. No wonder, then, that the notion of Personality was profoundly affected by this new set of the currents of thought, and that *self-consciousness*, that is *consciousness of self*, came to be considered the essence of Personality.

The expression ' self-consciousness ' probably originated in England, where we find it used by Locke [30] and other writers of his time and playing a considerable part in the Trinitarian controversy which agitated the learned of

[30] *Essay* ii. 27 § 16 (cp. ibid. §§ 23, 26) ; Sherlock, *Vindication*, p. 49; South, *Animadversions upon Dr Sherlock*, London, 1693, pp. 70 foll.

that country at the end of the seventeenth and the beginning of the eighteenth century. But it afterwards seems almost to have disappeared from the English language. As a philosophical term it was brought back into it in the nineteenth century by British thinkers who wrote under the influence of German idealism, as a translation of the German *Selbst-bewusstsein*, which itself may not improbably have been at first a rendering of the old English term.

Although Self-consciousness had no doubt been always implied in the definitions which spoke of a "naturæ *rationabilis* individua substantia" or of a "suppositum *intellectuale*," yet the changed attitude towards the old problems led to emphasis on what in those definitions was adjectival, almost or quite to the exclusion of what in them was substantive. When Christian Wolff, the Schoolman of the Enlightenment, defines *Person* as *Ein Ding das Sich bewusst ist*,[31] a thing that is conscious of itself, the words might stand as a translation of Ockham's *suppositum intellectuale*; yet the balance of the phrases is characteristically different. In Wolff's definition as compared with Ockham's the substantive is the vaguest, most colourless word which could be found, instead of one implying a whole metaphysical theory; while the adjectival clause describes in terms which at any rate seem unambiguous the activity which in the older formula is merely designated by a conventional epithet that might well be thought to stand itself in need of explanation.

Since the philosophical revolution which we associate with the name of Descartes, one other remains to be

---

[31] *Vernünftige Gedancken von Gott, der Welt, und der Seele* (Halle, 1751) § 924, p. 570, God (ibid. § 979, p. 603) *sich seiner bewusst ist*; but the word *Person* is not applied to him.

mentioned as having affected in an important degree
our way of regarding Personality. The name which we
connect with this revolution is that of Kant. Although
Descartes had broken away from the tradition of ancient
and mediæval thought in treating our own mental activity
as the one unquestionable fact of experience, he had
remained faithful to what had been the main (though
not the sole) tradition of the earlier schools in recognizing
the primacy of *cognition* among the forms of that activity.
It was Kant [32] whose proclamation of the primacy of the
practical over the theoretical reason gave the chief impulse
to the tendency, apparent in much recent speculation,
to find in *will* rather than in *cognition* the most fundamental characteristic of the experienced mental activity,
wherein rather than in anything underlying experience,
called 'substantial soul' or the like, the modern world
had come to seek the essence of Personality. It will not,
however, escape the notice of the practised student of the
history of thought that an emphasis on *will* rather than
on *cognition* may easily lead to the search for the true
sources of mental activity below (to use a now familiar
metaphor) 'the threshold of consciousness,' and thereby
to a reinstatement of something strangely like the
mysterious underlying substance or *suppositum* of the
older Schools, which the philosophy of experience believed
itself to have exorcised.

I have in the last few paragraphs of this Lecture very
briefly and summarily indicated movements of thought

[32] But Leibnitz already defines *persona* thus : " Persona est cuius
aliqua voluntas est, seu cuius datur cogitatio, affectus, voluptas,
dolor." This definition (which I have not been able to find) is
quoted by Wallace, *Essays on Moral Philosophy* VI (*Lectures and
Essays*, p. 273), without a reference to the work from which it is
taken.

the accurate description of which would require a much more extended treatment. But perhaps what I have said will be sufficient to form a background to our later investigations. And for the present I pass from the general history of the notion of Personality to the history of its application to God. This history will form the topic of my third Lecture.

LECTURE III

HISTORY OF THE NOTION OF PERSONALITY AS APPLIED TO GOD

As in the last Lecture, so in this, it is a historical investigation which will engage our attention. Having outlined the history of *persona* as a philosophical term, a history in tracing which we have often had to advert to its use in the formulation of theological dogma, I have now to invite you to a more particular consideration of its use and that of its recognized equivalents as applied to God.

It is so often taken for granted nowadays that the Personality of God is a principal tenet of Christianity that it is not without surprise that we find this expression not only entirely absent from the historical creeds and confessions of the Christian Church, but even, until quite modern times, in the estimation of all but the minority of Christians who reject the doctrine of the Trinity, regarded as unorthodox. Nevertheless it is beyond question that historically it was in connexion with the doctrine of the Trinity that the words ' person ' and ' personality ' came to be used of the Divine Being ; and that God was first [1] described as ' a person ' by certain theologians of

---

[1] But see p. 68 *n*. below for an anticipation of this language by Paul of Samosata in the third century

the sixteenth century not so much by way of positively asserting an important truth of theology as by way of denying that he was rightly said to be *three persons*. The most influential of the anti-Trinitarian divines of the Reformation period, Faustus Socinus, was followed by the compilers of the Racovian Catechism (the official standard of the first organized Church since the Reformation to profess Unitarianism) in expressly stating that, though God may rightly be said to be one Person, since in the case of an intellectual being numerical (as opposed to merely specific) unity is not to be distinguished from personality, yet belief in the unity of his Person is not necessary to salvation ; for those who hold that he exists in three Persons, however absurd their view, may obey his will as revealed by Christ, and so may be saved.[2]

It would be interesting to ascertain the first occurrence of the expression ' Personality of God ' as we are accustomed to find it used now, apart from any reference to the Christian doctrine of a Trinity of persons in one Divine Nature. There can in any case, I think, be little doubt that it should be sought among the writers of the eighteenth century, and in the period which historians of philosophy sometimes describe as that of the enlightenment.[3] I

---

[2] See Socinus, *Christianæ Religionis Institutio* (Opp.; p. 652) : *Catech. Racov., de Cognitione Dei* c. 1 (ed. Lat. 1609, p. 29). Servetus, on the other hand, called *Christ*, who in his view existed from the beginning of the world as the archetype of humanity, the ' person of God.' *Nec est alia Dei persona nisi Christus, non est alia, Dei hypostasis (de Trin. erronibus* ed. 1531, p. 112). His disciple, Valentinus Gentilis expressly denied the propriety of applying the term *persona* to God the Father (*Brevis Explicatio*, 1567, p. 3).

[3] On Wolff see above, Lecture II, p. 58. Kant, who defines *Person* (*Rechtslehre : Werke*, ed. Hart. vii. p. 20) as a being *dessen Handlung einer Zurechnung fähig sind*, could not have held the term applicable to one who was sovereign and not subject in the ' kingdom of ends.' I do not actually know of any instance of the use

may be allowed to indicate certain characteristics of the thought of this period, which would have assisted an expression with Unitarian associations, though not, so far as I know, employed by Unitarian writers (Priestley, for example, appears to avoid it) to escape, even in quarters where the Trinitarian theology was not abandoned, the suspicion which would have attached to it on that account in the preceding age. On the one hand several of the influences then most potent in the world of thought tended to draw away attention from Trinitarian speculations and to fasten it upon the unity of the Divine Nature. Such was the great progress made by mathematical and mechanical science in the period illustrated by the names of Galileo and Newton, revealing as it did with ever increasing clearness the unity of the material system, and thereby impressing with ever increasing force upon the mind the unity of its Cause, but at the same time encouraging an abstract and unhistorical mode of thinking, to which a doctrine like that of the Trinity, which seeks to construe the Highest in terms of a life of love, could make but little appeal. Such, again, was the movement in philosophy inaugurated by Descartes with its preference for ' clear and distinct ideas ' such as are especially afforded by the sciences to which I have just referred. To those in whom this preference was strong the mysterious and enigmatic character of the doctrine of the Trinity rendered it naturally uncongenial ; while there are perhaps at any time but few who, following the celebrated

of ' the Personality of God ' in our sense before Schleiermacher's *Reden über die Religion* II (*Über das Wesen der Religion*), but he speaks as though the expression were already known and by some insisted upon. Its currency in England is, however, most probably to be attributed to its appearance in Paley's *Natural Theology*, the 23rd chapter of which is devoted to ' The Personality of the Deity.' This work appeared in 1802.

counsel given to Priestley [4] by Bishop Horsley, to read the *Parmenides*, have learned from Plato that the conception of unity is also not without grave difficulties of its own.

Such, once more, was the philosophy of Locke, with its cautious resolve to plant its feet upon the firm ground of experience and to abjure excursions into regions with the knowledge of which our happiness or misery has nothing to do; and to the temperament characteristic of that age the regions of speculative theology which had exercised the subtle wits of Platonists and Schoolmen in earlier times were apt to appear regions deserving so to be described.

On the other hand, the view of St. Thomas Aquinas (which is now authoritative in the Roman Catholic Church) that, while Reason could demonstrate the unity of God, Revelation alone could make known to us the trinity of persons therein, had come to prevail among the adherents of tradition ; a view which relieves a theology claiming to be Natural or Rational from any obligation to trouble itself with a doctrine which is declared by its defenders to be of necessity altogether beyond its sphere.

When we consider the direction taken by these various currents of thought, we shall not be surprised to note in the philosophical theology of the eighteenth century, even among those who had no intention of abandoning the traditional doctrines, a marked tendency towards the Unitarian conception of deity, nor to find coming into use among theologians of all schools a phrase like ' the Personality of God,' which, in days when sensitiveness to the points of Trinitarian controversy was greater,

[4] In his fifteenth letter to Priestley. See Horsley's *Tracts in Controversy with Dr. Priestley* (Dundee, 1812), p. 287.

would have committed him who used it to a downright denial of the dogma of the Catholic Church. Accordingly we find Schleiermacher in the last year of the eighteenth century referring to it as an expression familiar to his hearers and Paley in the third year of the nineteenth devoting a chapter of his *Natural Theology* to the ' Personality of the Deity.' But even after this, it is surprising to find how little in use the phrase seems to have been at any rate among English divines until the nineteenth century had run more than half its course.

We have, then, as historians, to note this fact : that, while the affirmation of Personality *in* God has been a characteristic of Christian theological terminology since the third century of our era, the great majority of Christian theologians down to quite modern times have not affirmed in so many words the Personality *of* God. I am not, of course, asserting that the majority of Christian theologians, and indeed of Jewish and Mohammedan theologians as well, to mention no others, have not ascribed to God attributes which it may plausibly be argued can belong only to persons. At present I am concerned only with the actual ascription of Personality itself to God.

We have seen that the word *persona* was first used in theology to describe the respective bearers of the three names, Father, Son, and Spirit, the use of which, not alternatively but in combination, the Christian Church had early come to regard as necessary to express the fullness of the Godhead as apprehended in her worship ; and that only long afterwards did it begin to be employed of the Godhead as a whole. We have seen also that the application of the word to the members of the

Christian Trinity owed its currency to, if it was not originated by, Tertullian, the first of the great Christian theologians to write in the Latin tongue. Professor Harnack, to whose labours all students of the history of Christian dogma owe so great a debt, now admits that in his earlier discussion of the circumstances which may have recommended this word to Tertullian for use in this connexion, he laid an exaggerated stress upon its legal associations.[5] These must certainly not be left out of account ; but I think we should be nearer the truth in seeking our principal clue to the theological meaning of the term in the sense which it had come to bear and still bears in grammar, when we speak of the first, second, and third persons in the conjugation of a verb. A study of Tertullian's language will, I think, tend to show that what he had most often in his mind was the fact that the Scriptures contained passages of colloquy wherein both addressing and addressed, and sometimes also the subject of their discourse, were alike treated as divine.[6]

Now no doubt this uncritical use of Scripture texts as authoritative and unquestionable sources of information with respect to the Divine Nature, though not so many years since it seemed to most of our own forefathers quite fit and reasonable and is by no means even now extinct among our countrymen, may perhaps appear nowadays to a cultivated and academic audience to take away from the speculation which finds its starting-point therein any but a purely archæological interest. But to neglect that speculation altogether on this account would be unwise. For the thoughts of sincere and active minds are never fairly to be judged by a mere inspection of the

5 See *Dogmengeschichte*, 4th ed., i. p. 576*n*.
6 See Tertullian *adv. Praxean*, c.c. 11, 12.

form in which their reasonings are expressed. This form may often betray the presence of prejudice, illusion, or error, and we do well to be on the watch to detect any infection thereby of the substance of the conclusion; and yet that substance may itself prove to be in part, even in great part, sound and unaffected by the false opinions of the thinker.

And so in the present instance, when, in respect of Tertullian's reliance on his proof-texts from the Bible, one has made all allowances for his ignorance of Hebrew and of the history of the old Testament, for his bondage to the letter of the old Latin translation, and for his readiness to treat, in Matthew Arnold's famous phrase, 'literature' as 'dogma,' there still remains in the discussions to which I am referring a solid foundation with which we have to reckon. This solid foundation is the profound impression made by the attitude towards God attributed in the Gospels to the Founder of the Christian religion and the inference to which it had led that the personal relation—I use the term advisedly—of loving sonship in which Jesus Christ was there represented as standing towards his Father in heaven was the revelation of a permanent and essential feature of the divine life, further testimony to which it was then only natural that Christians should seek, and not surprising, considering their intellectual environment, that they should have been over-easily satisfied to find, in writings which they had always been taught to regard as verbally inspired.

It was only to express that which distinguished one from another of the members of the Trinity acknowledged by the Christian Church to exist within the unity of the Godhead that the word 'Person' was regularly employed in theology down to the period of the Reformation.7 During that period, even when the doctrine of the Trinity was disputed, the use of this word ' Person ' as applied to God was so closely associated with that doctrine that those who altogether rejected the doctrine, or at least desired to let it fall into the background, either avoided the word altogether or employed it merely in defining their attitude towards the traditional system. But in the course of the last two centuries, under the influences which I have indicated, the expression ' Personality of God,' apart from reference to the doctrine of the Trinity, has come into general use, and in what remains of the present Lecture I will endeavour to ascertain what is really intended by those who attach importance to maintaining the truth of that which they describe by this phrase.

This can perhaps most conveniently be done by considering certain representative accounts of the Divine Nature and making up our minds how far God as described therein can be considered as a ' personal God.'

It would be readily admitted, I suppose, on all hands that the God of Spinoza is not a ' personal ' God. But it will be worth while to spend a few minutes in asking ourselves what it is in the Spinozistic theology that

7 Where the unipersonality of God is suggested at all, it is merely as a negative to the doctrine of his tripersonality. Thus, to take examples from two authors belonging to two very different epochs, we find the heresiarch Paul of Samosata in the third century quoted as saying that God is one Person and his Logos, πρόσωπον ἕν τὸν θεόν ἅμα τῷ λόγῳ ὡς ἄνθρωπον ἕνα καὶ τὸν αὖ τοῦ λόγον (Frag. x. I. See *Journal of Theological Studies*, Oct. 1917, pp. 37 ff). And in the fourteenth century Durandus a Sancto Porciano, who opposed the view common in his day, and which of course had etymology upon its side, that *persona* must always imply a *relation*, observes that if, *sicut Gentiles imaginantur*, there be not a Trinity in the Godhead, then God would be a person, *illi naturæ vere competeret ratio personæ* (*in Sent.* i. dist. 23, qu. I, § 15).

satisfies us of this.   For the doctrine of the great Jewish
thinker may stand as the most highly developed and
therefore most adequately representative form assumed
by one widely diffused type of thought concerning the
nature of the Ultimate Reality—that type of thought
which may be conveniently designated by the popular
if ambiguous name of Pantheism.

No doubt, if by a Divine Person one were compelled
to mean, in accordance with strict historical propriety,
one of a plurality of beings within the Divine Nature,
the God of Spinoza could not be called ' a Person,' for
by God Spinoza undoubtedly means the absolute and all-
inclusive Reality.   This, however, is not by itself enough
to show that Spinoza's God ought not to be called personal.
For the God of Catholic Christianity is also, as we have
seen, not ' a Divine Person ' and it would seem strange
to deny that the God of Catholic Christianity is personal,
although he is not thought of as one Person but as three.
It is easy, however, to discriminate the Spinozistic conception of God in this respect from that of Catholic
Christianity.   Spinoza cannot, indeed, be said to admit
no distinctions in God.   On the contrary he admits, as
is well known, what he calls ' Attributes ' of God, in each
of which, just as, according to Catholic Christianity, in
each Person of the Trinity, the whole Divine Nature is
expressed.[8]   Of these only two, Thought and Extension,
are within the sphere of our knowledge ; but we have
no reason to suppose but that there is an infinite number
of others besides.[9]   But the relations of these Attributes
to one another are in no sense *personal* relations.

[8] See esp. the decrees of the Fourth Lateran Council, c. 2 (Mansi
xxii. 983).   Cp. Turretinus *Inst. Theol.* III. 27 § 1.   *Unaquæque
persona habet totam diuinitatem ;* John of Damascus, *de Fide*, iii. 6.
[9] *Eth.* i. def. 6, prop. 10; cp. *Ep.* 66 and see Joachim, *Study of the
Ethics of Spinoza*, pp. 39 ff.

However, as we have seen, the expression 'a personal God' is now often used without any thought of admitting a plurality of beings within the Divine Nature standing to one another in personal relations, whether after the manner of polytheism, wherein they are thought of merely as sharing in the Divine Nature just as all of us here share in the human, or after the manner of Catholic Christianity, in which the mutual unity of the three Divine Persons is of course regarded as of an infinitely closer and more intimate kind. When, however, the expression a 'personal God' is thus used, without reference to any plurality within the unity of the Divine Nature, what is really in the minds of those who so use it is, I think, always the possibility of personal relations—of worship, trust, love —between *oneself* and God. Now here again, so far from Spinoza denying the possibility of anything of this kind, it is well known that for him the supreme happiness of man is *amor intellectualis Dei*,[10] the love of God which comes of knowledge. But—and here is the crucial point at which any theology which is concerned to ascribe personality to God must take leave of Spinoza—it is abundantly clear that there is in this *amor intellectualis Dei* no question of *reciprocation*. According to Spinoza God neither "first loves us" nor does he return our love.[11] And it is just this impossibility of a *reciprocation* of love which makes it—despite the religious joy and peace which we cannot for an instant doubt that Spinoza experienced in his contemplation of the eternal and unchangeable nature of the Universe—impossible to speak of him as teaching the *personality* of God.[12]

---

[10] *Eth.* v. prop. 33.   [11] *Eth.* v. prop. 19.
[12] There is an ironical reference to the theological use of the word in *Cojitata Metaphysica*, ii. 8 § 1.

In modern times it has become usual to contrast divine *immanence* with divine *transcendence*. We shall have occasion at a later stage to examine this antithesis more closely ; but at present I am content to refer to it as one familiar to all who are acquainted with contemporary theological literature.

Now it might seem, from what has just been said, that it is because Spinoza regards God as *immanent* or rather as *immanent only*, that he cannot allow him to be *personal*. As to this suggestion, since we are still in this Lecture dealing with the history rather than with the validity of the conceptions under discussion, I will at this point only make the following observation. There are views of God as immanent and as immanent only, for which, although they would probably not in popular discussion be treated as affirmations of a *personal* God, it might be easier to make out a case that they are really such. I am thinking of such a view as finds expression in a striking sentence of the elder Pliny, *Deus est mortali adjuvare mortalem* [13] : ' This *is* God when one mortal helps another ' ; or again such as is offered to us by the Religion of Humanity inaugurated by Auguste Comte. Here it is in personal relations—relations of persons to persons—and in such relations only, that the Divine Nature is regarded as consisting. A God of this kind it is hard to say is not personal. Yet most people would be inclined to hesitate. Pliny indeed, as the context of the words I have quoted shows, meant little more than that, since there was nothing more divine than a man who helps his fellows, a ' saviour of society ' might be properly regarded as a God. And such a deified man might seem to be beyond question a personal

[13] *Hist. Nat.* ii. § 18.   See Prof. Gilbert Murray, *Four Stages of Greek Religion*, p. 139.

God. But the phrase used taken by itself may suggest a thought for which one might find a still better expression in more familiar words : " God is love, and he that abideth in love abideth in God and God in him." [14] So we read in the New Testament. Here it is plain from what goes before that the writer is thinking of the mutual love which should exist between the members of the Christian brotherhood, and which he does not hesitate to identify with the Divine Nature. Did we possess this passage as a fragment only, and were ignorant of other aspects of the author's religion, we might suppose that we had to do with a theology for which God was merely *immanent*. But should we not in that case hesitate to describe such a theology as the doctrine of a ' personal God ' ? And, when we turn to the Great Being of the Comtist faith, we should certainly be disposed to say that Humanity, though consisting wholly of persons standing to one another in personal relations, is not itself a Person with whom oneself or any other human being can be in personal relations. One is only in personal relations with some other human being whom, in relation to oneself, one would not call God. According to the language of Catholic Christianity on the other hand, every Person in God is himself God ; and we finite persons, who are not ourselves God, may stand in personal relations with these Divine Persons. Our later discussions may perhaps lead us to doubt whether full justice has been done to the views to which I have just been referring in the account here given of them. But I have been intentionally describing them according to their most obvious purport, in order to show that, while of some doctrines which make God immanent only one would hesitate—as one

[14] 1 John iv. 16.

would not in the case of Spinozism—to say that they did not make God personal, yet, on the whole, a God consisting of persons, each of whom is not entitled to be called God, and with whom as a whole we finite persons cannot stand in personal relations, is not what is generally called a personal God.

Thus, on the whole, we should not speak of a personal God, unless we supposed that we could stand in personal relations with him. And for those who conceive God as *merely* immanent, this would be impossible. But so it would be also for some who do not conceive God as immanent at all. This we may illustrate from the theology of Aristotle. If one meant by calling God personal no more than to ascribe to God a self-conscious individuality, we should certainly have to call the God of Aristotle a personal God. And yet I think that no one who is familiar with Aristotle's theology will deny that to do so would be to give a very misleading description of his teaching. Between the religion of Aristotle and that of Spinoza there is a close kinship. In both it is the splendid flower of a pure passion for knowledge, and in both it has nothing to do with relations between persons, such as the mutual love in which the New Testament writer whom I lately quoted finds the very essence of God. And so, though in a certain sense their theologies are diametrically opposed, that of the ancient thinker being an extreme doctrine of *transcendence*, and that of the modern an extreme doctrine of *immanence*, they are alike in this, that both may be said utterly to exclude such a possibility of personal communion between God and his worshippers as the expression ' a personal God ' at once suggests. Both philosophers, indeed, speak of a ' love of God.' By this expression Aristotle means not so much a conscious emotion (though man may doubtless be conscious of it in himself) as an instinctive movement by which everything in the universe which is not the supreme good is drawn towards it, as a lover towards his beloved ; for Spinoza it is indeed a personal activity of thought, *amor intellectualis Dei* ; but by both philosophers alike the possibility of reciprocation on the part of God is entirely excluded. That this is expressly explained by Spinoza I have already observed ; and, so far as regards Aristotle, the only activity which he held to be attributable to a being perfect and in need of nothing beyond himself, such as he conceived God to be, was the activity of knowledge ; and the only object which, according to him, was not unworthy of God's knowledge was his own eternally perfect nature. The God of Aristotle is not, indeed, like Spinoza's, an *immanent* God. For Spinoza our understanding or knowledge of God is a part of God's infinite understanding or knowledge of himself, and our intellectual love of him a part of the infinite love wherewith God loves himself.[15] Thus he can even speak of a love of God for us, although this does not mean something other than our love for God. It is a part of God's love for himself. This includes what can be called in a sense a love for us, since our minds and the thoughts which constitute them, so far as we think clearly and thoroughly, are parts of that one eternal system of thought which is, in Spinoza's language, God viewed under the attribute of Thought ; just as our bodies are parts of that eternal system of matter in motion which is God viewed under the attribute of Extension. The love of God for us, thus understood, is no reciprocation of our love for him, and so does not warrant us in describing the relation between us and God as a personal relation.

[15] *Eth.* ii. prop. 11, v. prop. 36.

But Aristotle does not and could not speak of a love of God for us in any sense. God, according to the principles of Aristotle's theology, can know and love nothing less than himself, and his being does not, like that of Spinoza's God, include our being within itself. He is utterly transcendent, and beyond the reach of personal communion. It is very instructive to study the modifications which Aristotle's faithful follower, St. Thomas Aquinas, has to introduce into his master's notion of God, in order to make room for the providence of God for man and the communion of man with God which his religious faith and religious experience demanded.[16]

Thus, though Aristotle's theology is an extreme doctrine of transcendence, while Spinoza's is an extreme doctrine of immanence, neither is a doctrine of a personal God ; and this agreement between them is closely connected with that likeness between the religious temperaments, if I may so speak, of the two philosophers which strikes at once those who are acquainted with the writings of both.

No doubt it would be possible to stand in genuine personal relations with such a 'saviour of society' as those whom Pliny, in the passage to which I referred earlier in this Lecture, and other Romans of his age were ready to salute with the title of God, as one reserved for them after they were dead, and sometimes even as earned already in their lifetime.[17] But plainly it would be out of the question for these personal relations to be at all intimate except for a very few, and even for them they would only exist during the term of the natural life of

[16] See *Summa c. Gentiles*, i. 44 *seqq.* ; *Summa Theol.* p. I. qu. 14; cp. *Studies in the History of Natural Theology*, p. 246.
[17] Cp. W. Warde Fowler, *Roman Ideas of Deity*, c. 5.

their object. Nor probably was it in the design of those
who at various times have inaugurated or promoted the
deification and worship of men who " exercise authority
and are called benefactors " [18] that the devotion which
was to find expression in it should have much or anything
to do with the deeper emotions of the worshipper's personal
life. A ' god ' of this kind, although certainly a person,
is not the kind of God to satisfy those among ourselves
who would most earnestly proclaim their need of a ' personal God.' For not only would he probably seem to them
unworthy to be called God at all, but he would have too
slight and external a connexion with the personal life
of his worshippers to meet the demand which a ' personal
God ' is supposed alone capable of supplying.

We turn to the claim to be considered as a personal
God of such a deified hero, when conceived as after his
death raised above the vicissitudes of mortal life, hence-
forth to be related to his fellowmen no otherwise than as
the recipient of their worship. It must be borne in mind
that I am not now speaking of a sage or prophet or founder
of a religious community, whom his followers honour as
a God, but only of the ruler, the conqueror, or the pioneer
of civilization, who is reverenced in gratitude for external
benefits which he is understood to have conferred upon
posterity. If the departed giver of these good gifts is
realized in any fullness by the imagination, he will enter
the company to which the gods of the various pagan
mythologies belong ; although we may not share the belief
of Euhemerus that these were all originally real men who
had been deified after their death.

No other nation known to us has placed at the service
of religion for the construction of such a mythology so

[18] Luke xxii. 25.

powerful a creative imagination linked with so sound an understanding and so fine a sense of form and beauty as have found expression in the poetry and sculpture of the ancient Greeks. Thus it is from a consideration of the Gods of Greece that we shall best learn whatever a mythology may have to teach us respecting the meaning of Personality as applied to an object of worship.

Now the contrast between two types of God acknowledged by the Greeks, that of the ' mystery God ' represented by Dionysus and that of the Olympian represented by Apollo, is familiar to modern students of classical antiquity. Already recognized by Hegel,[19] it has more recently been made by Nietzsche, in his essay on *The Birth of Tragedy*, the basis of a whole philosophy of art. A very few words will serve to explain the nature of this contrast sufficiently for our present purpose. The ' Olympian Gods ' are described in the well-known words of Coleridge [20] as " the intelligible forms of ancient poets, the fair humanities of old religion." They are human forms of superhuman beauty and majesty, revealed through the sculptor's or the poet's art to the admiring contemplation of their worshippers but abiding themselves in their glorified existence above the " smoke and stir " [21] of mortal life. On the other hand, the ' mystery God ' is human rather as an influence intimately felt in the emotional fellowship of an initiated company, who are swayed and rapt out of their separate everyday selves by a common enthusiasm, in which they put on the attributes of the divinity who inspires them and perform in their own persons superhuman acts—as when the Bacchæ of Euripides rend asunder the cattle upon the hills in

[19] *Phänomenologie d. Geistes* E b (*Werke*, ii. pp. 522 ff).
[20] *Piccolomini*, ii. 4.   [21] Milton, *Comus* 5.

their frenzy.[22] The 'mystery God,' though not incapable
of apparition as a glorified man or of representation by
an image in human shape, yet makes his presence more
characteristically known in the sacramental food or drink—
Dionysus, for instance, in the fruit of the "grief-assuaging
vine"[23] by participation in which his worshippers are made
one with him—in the sacred plant or animal, or again
in the celebrants of his mysteries, who, as they accomplish his rites, are changed from their own likeness into his.

I am not here concerned to examine this contrast of
the Olympian and the mystery God, or to inquire how far
it is actually illustrated by the history of Greek religion.
It is enough to say that we certainly find in Greece and
elsewhere the two distinct attitudes towards the object
of religious worship to which we have just called attention,
and to point out that the consideration of the difference
between them is instructive in regard to the meaning of
the demand often made in the interest of Religion that it
should be directed towards a 'personal God.'

For we can scarcely fail to observe that, while the
Olympian God seems to be regarded as possessing 'personality' in himself more properly than the 'mystery
God,' just because of his remoteness and distinctness from
his worshippers, it is rather the 'mystery God' the relations of the worshippers to whom possess that intensity
of warmth which makes us ready to describe their religion
as 'personal religion.' His *personal* relation to them
is all the closer in that he is not, like the 'Olympian,'
distinct from them ; because in the communion of his
holy things they become one with him and he with them.

---

[22] Euripides, *Bacchæ*, 735 *seqq.*
[23] τὴν παυσίλυπον ἄμπελον, Eur. *Bacch.* 772. The English epithet
is that in Professor Murray's translation.

Now whatever the origin of an Olympian God may have been, he has already, as Olympian, ceased to be a purely tribal deity. Whatever the special claim which a particular city or family may have upon him, he is thought of as a power belonging to all mankind, so that it is natural to identify with him any God, even though he be the God of a quite alien people, to whom like functions are attributed. The very fullness with which the personality of the Olympian God is imagined tends to make personal sympathy and, still more, personal intimacy out of the question between the worshipper and such a different kind of person from himself as the God he worships. The revolt of Euripides against the inhumanity of these Gods of his people was the direct consequence of the full humanity with which the poetical imagination of that people had invested them ; for it was this that made it possible to judge of the deeds related of them in legends handed down from ancient and barbarous times, as though they were the actions of real men, to which the standards of a more civilized age could be plausibly applied. The like treatment could not have been meted out, for instance, to beings without a definite human personality, such as were the divinities of the Roman State before the Latin poets had identified them with the Gods of Greece and told of them the stories previously attached to the names of the personages of Hellenic mythology.

Thus we see that faith in a ' personal ' God is not (as is sometimes hinted) merely another name for anthropomorphism in theology ; for a thorough-going anthropomorphism may have the effect of removing the God thus conceived far from the possibility of exhibiting the personal sympathy and attracting the personal devotion the need of which makes men demand a ' personal God ' to worship. The Epicurean Gods, splendid beings dwelling in the intermundane spaces, the effluxes from whose majestic forms strike upon our senses in sleep, who care nothing for us, know nothing of us—these Gods are the direct descendants of the Olympians. The only worship which could be directed to them was not prayer, for in no sense do they control our destinies, but the willing tribute of admiration paid to beings so greatly superior to ourselves. And, however far we may rightly rank the Aristotelian conception of Godhead as Perfect Intelligence above the Epicurean notion of it as a peculiarly fortunate and enduring combination of atoms, yet the only reason for worshipping Aristotle's God would be of the same kind as might be alleged for worshipping those of Epicurus —the disinterested admiration of what is supremely beautiful and excellent.

We may apply to worship paid for such a reason those words of the poet :—

> The worship the heart lifts above
> And the heavens reject not ;
> The desire of the moth for the star,
> Of the night for the morrow,
> The devotion to something afar
> From the sphere of our sorrow. [24]

But we must remember that, if the heavens reject it not, it is because they know nothing of it ; though certainly a disinterested worship of this sort proves the worshipper to be of no ignoble spirit, yet it is not what those have in mind who insist that religion at its best demands a ' personal God.'

If we turn from the ' Olympians ' to the ' mystery

[24] Shelley, ' To ——.' (" One word is too often profaned."

Gods' we find indeed that, as we have seen, they offer greater opportunities of personal religion, just because the God does not remain so remote from his worshipper, but also that there is present in this kind of religion an opposite tendency, which may be said to be present also in every kind of mysticism, a tendency to lose the personality of the God in that of his worshipper. In the language of the popular theological antithesis of transcendence and immanence to which I referred above, the Olympian God is too *transcendent*, the 'mystery God' too *immanent*, to be precisely what is meant by a 'personal God.'

Where, then, shall we look for an example of what is really meant by a 'personal God'? We shall plainly be most likely to do so with good hope of success in the one historical religion of which, as we have seen, Personality *in* God (though not, until quite modern times, 'the Personality *of* God') has been a recognized tenet—that is to say, in Christianity. I think it must be admitted that here it has been found easier than elsewhere to secure what may be called a 'personal religion' without a mystical dissipation of the personality of its Object and to attribute personality to that Object without removing it to a distance from the worshipper too great to admit of genuine sympathy and devotion.

I can only indicate here very briefly how in my judgment this result has been obtained. It is due, as I take it, in the first place to the fact (for a fact I do not doubt it to be) that the Christian Church has worshipped as God a real historical person, of whose life and character it has preserved a genuine record ; and that, as presented in this record, he is one beyond question able to make upon men of various races and belonging to various types

6

and tenets of civilization an impression of moral and spiritual supremacy so united with an extraordinary personal charm as to arouse in them a genuine sentiment of personal love and devotion. The control exercised by the record upon the imagination on the one hand has prevented particular groups or generations of Christ's followers from so fashioning or refashioning his figure in their own likeness that it should be irretrievably lost to those of another habit or temper of soul ; and on the other hand the conviction of real objective individuality which it has imposed has hindered for the most part, even among the many mystical schools which have from time to time appeared in the Christian Church, the loss of all sense of his distinctness from and transcendence of the souls which he has notwithstanding been held and felt to indwell.

To say what I have just said is to say that the success of Christianity in maintaining a doctrine of Divine Personality is due to its peculiar doctrine of Divine Incarnation ; for, though there are many doctrines of Divine Incarnation beside the Christian, it will be found to be on the special features which distinguish the Christian doctrine from others that the characteristic Christian view of Personality in God depends : and these features are recognizable in the everyday piety of Christians as well as in the theology of the Christian schools. In contradistinction from the doctrine of the Incarnation the doctrine of the Trinity has often, no doubt, been by unspeculative Christians rather reverenced as a sacred formula than felt to be part of their own faith as individuals. Yet this doctrine has also been instrumental in assisting the sense of Divine Personality even in the religious life of ordinary Christians ; for it has enabled the personal relation between Christ and the God whom he called his Father, with which the Gospels have familiarized them, to be regarded as a relation *within* the life of God himself, yet without sanctioning at any rate the tendency observable in most doctrines of Divine Personality —for it cannot be denied that this tendency has at times made itself felt even in orthodox Christian Churches— to introduce into the Godhead a clash of moral attributes fatal to that whole-hearted devotion to a single ideal of life which monotheism is especially concerned and qualified to promote.

But although, as we should expect, it is from the one historic faith which has insisted on the importance of affirming the presence of Personality in God that we can best learn what is meant by a ' personal God,' it is, of course, as we have already indicated, not the only faith whose adherents would usually be considered, and would in some cases consider themselves to be, in the same sense as Christians, worshipping a ' personal God.' I am now thinking only of faiths professed by civilized men to-day. Concerning the meaning of the expression as applied in these I will venture to add a few words, although I am profoundly sensible how difficult it is to feel at all sure that one has not missed the significance which religious and theological language may bear to those to whose traditions and fellowship one is oneself a stranger ; a difficulty of which we are constantly reminded by the mistakes made by others in their discussion of beliefs and practices with which any of us chances to be' acquainted from within. Even the most learned student of religions other than his own must experience this difficulty ; and I, to whom Hebrew and Arabic, Sanskrit and Pali are unknown tongues, have no claim to be called a student of Judaism or Mohammedanism, Hinduism or Buddhism. I do not indeed suppose that it is necessary, in order to enter into the spirit of a religion, that one should be able to read its Scriptures and its doctors in their original languages. A man may be a very good Christian without Greek or Hebrew, and a very bad Christian with both. But for the merely external study of a religion it must be a serious disqualification to be constantly driven by ignorance of the idioms used by its chief interpreters to second-hand sources of information concerning it.

The religion most closely akin to that Catholic Christianity to which my recent observations referred is, no doubt, Unitarian Christianity. Here the Personality *of* God (and not only Personality *in* God) is certainly held and insisted upon. God is worshipped as the Father revealed by Jesus, and the attitude of Jesus towards God is taken as the great example of true religion. God is thought of as a Being having the ethical character attributed to him by the tradition of Christendom, to a share in the inheritance of which Unitarian Christianity regards itself as possessing a legitimate claim ; and if certain features of this character—that, for instance, of an extreme severity to sinners which does not shrink from their eternal punishment—are frankly discarded, it is held that the retention of these is inconsistent with the main trend of the teaching of Jesus and with the general impression made upon the reader of the Gospels by the record of his life, which is thought of as the grand illustration of the type of life acceptable to God. We are not, of course, here concerned with any differences between Catholic and Unitarian Christianity except such as relate to the doctrine of Divine Personality. In respect of this doctrine we see that both conceive of God as a Being with whom personal relations are possible : but that for Unitarian Christianity such relations are not as for Catholic Christianity rooted in a like relation within the Godhead itself ; and the historical personality of Jesus not being itself an object of divine worship, the control which the record of that personality exercises in Catholic Christianity over the religious imagination is only exercised indirectly in so far as the thought of God actually present to the minds of Unitarian Christians is one inherited from predecessors who with less qualification or hesitation sought their clue to the divine character in that attributed in Scripture to the Founder of their religion.

In the next place one naturally thinks of Judaism, which stands in the direct line of descent from the religion out of which Christianity sprang, and with which it preserves a more complete and obvious continuity than the sister creed. Though Jewish theology has never, I believe, made use in describing God of any word exactly corresponding to Personality, and has ever offered a resolute opposition to the Christian doctrine with which the term as employed in theology was at first associated, of a plurality of Persons in God, few would hesitate to describe Judaism as a religion with a personal God. Long before the rise of Christianity the prophets of Israel had succeeded in a task which the Greek philosophers had failed to accomplish, or indeed had scarcely attempted. They had maintained a close connection between the universal and spiritual religion to which they had attained and the religious institutions of their nation. The personal relation of the tribesman to his tribal God was preserved as the basis of piety towards the one God of all, who had chosen one family out of all the families of the earth to be his prophet to the rest.[25]   This piety, in which the piety of Christianity is rooted, is the treasure of Judaism.

The tendency which existed at one time among the Jews, a tendency of which Christian theology itself is to a great extent an outcome, towards a doctrine of a plurality of persons within the divine nature, met, after the development of Christianity had rendered it suspect, with repression, and ultimately with extinction.[26]   The fear of 'making God too much a man,' [27] a fear stimulated by aversion to the Christian doctrine of the Incarnation, combined with the influence of Aristotle on the thought of mediæval Jewish thinkers, such as Maimonides, in emphasizing the distance between God and man, may have imposed a greater restraint upon developments of personal religion, which in Christianity were at once encouraged and directed by the ascription of Godhead to its historical Founder.   But it would be absurd to deny that a religion has a personal God which has ever taken as its ideal the great Lawgiver to whom his God 'spake face to face as a man speaketh unto his friend.' [28]

Of Mohammedanism, the other great religion of the world belonging to the same historical group as Christianity and Judaism, I take it that one might more reasonably hesitate before answering the question whether it conceives God as personal or no.   It is certainly true that anthropomorphic language is used of the God of Islam and that

[25] Cp. *Problems in the Relations of God and Man*, pp. 208 foll.

[26] See *Jewish Encyclopædia*, s.v. 'Elisha ben Abuyah'; Oesterley and Box, *Religion and Worship in the Synagogue*, c. ix.

[27] M. Arnold, *Stanzas in Memory of the Author of 'Obermann,'* Nov. 1849 ; of Goethe : ' For he pursued a lonely road, His eyes on Nature's plan, Neither made man too much a God, Nor God too much a man.'

[28] Exod. xxxiii. 11.

in the teaching of the Arabian prophet he is certainly not conceived pantheistically or as immanent in his worshippers. But it would seem that the tendency of that teaching is to reduce the personal relations which can exist between man and God to the lowest terms, to those, namely, which may exist between a slave and a master of absolutely unlimited power. Still this *is* a personal relation, and on the whole it would seem best to describe the God of Mohammedanism as a personal God, while remembering both that Personality is not expressly reckoned among his attributes and that, when the Moslem aspires after a more intimate kind of piety than his canonical scriptures suggest, he seems to pass at once to a pantheistic mysticism wherein the personal distinction between the devotee and his God tends to disappear altogether. But in speaking at all of Islam, I occupy the room of the unlearned and speak subject to correction by those better informed.

Concerning the great religious systems of the farther East I will only here make one or two remarks with an apology for their inevitable superficiality. It would seem, speaking generally, that while the European mind is apt to associate with the word ' person ' and its derivatives the thought not only of distinct individuality but even of a mutual exclusiveness between persons—a mutual exclusiveness, however, which as existing between God and his worshipper is in every profound religious experience found to have been done away—by Indian thought distinct individuality is comparatively little emphasized. Hence to the European Indian conceptions of the Supreme Being seem to lack the definite personality which is suggested by the ordinary religious language of Christians, Jews, or Mohammedans about God. On the other hand, religious emotion or meditation probably plays a far larger part in Indian life than in European ; and this is certainly personal religion. So that if we may say that the God of much Indian worship is not what we should usually call a ' personal God,' we must take care not to imply by this that the Indian's religion is not his personal concern, for nothing could be less true. Moreover the important and widely prevalent type of Indian piety known as *bhakti* is admitted to be devotional faith in a personal God [29] : while Buddhism, which originally perhaps acknowledged neither God nor soul, has produced in the worship of Amitabha, the ' Buddha of the Boundless Light,' the ' Lord of the Western Paradise,' a form of piety which has seemed to some scholars too similar to the Christian to have originated except under Christian influence.[30]

With these observations I bring the historical portion of my course to a close, hoping that it may have prepared us by a study of what has been actually meant by Personality when applied to God to inquire further into the reasons for so applying it, to discuss the difficulties which beset the application, and to form a judgment as to its validity.

Before entering on this inquiry, however, it will be desirable to endeavour, by asking ourselves how we should distinguish Personality from certain related conceptions, to make as clear to ourselves as is possible what we have in mind when we employ the word. It is this problem which will occupy us in the next two Lectures.

[29] See G. A. Grierson's article on ' Bhakti-marga ' in Hastings' *Encyclopædia of Religion and Ethics*; cp. J. N. Farquhar, *The Crown of Hinduism*, p. 332.

[30] See A. Lloyd in *Transactions of Congress for Hist. of Religion*. Oxford, 1908, vol. i. pp. 132 ff.

LECTURE IV

PERSONALITY AND INDIVIDUALITY

MY purpose in the present Lecture is not, as in the two preceding, to examine the past history of the word Person, but to ascertain the meaning which it now bears for us by trying to answer the question how we should distinguish the conception for which it stands from certain others to which it would seem to be closely related. With this end in view we shall find it convenient to orientate ourselves, as it were, by taking as our starting-point a provisional definition ; and I know of none better adapted to this purpose than that old one attributed to Boethius, to which in my survey of the word's history I have already so often referred : *Persona est naturæ rationabilis individua substantia.* It would be generally allowed, I think, that by a *person* we mean a *rational individual,* or, if we prefer to put it so, a *concrete individual mind.* I have chosen this latter phrase as leaving open an alternative of which many would embrace one side and many the other. If we think that, in order to be concrete—that is, to exist upon its own account and not as a mere characteristic or attribute of something so existing—a mind must be *embodied,* then we shall think that a person must be an *embodied mind* ; if, on the other hand, we think that a mind can thus exist upon its own account unembodied,

then we shall think that a person need not have a body.
Thus those who are persuaded that the departed after the
dissolution of their bodies continue to exercise mental
activities undoubtedly regard these discarnate spirits as
persons, and as the same persons that they were when
we knew them in the body.

It may, indeed, be noted here in passing that some who
have believed that individual souls survive the dissolution
of the body have held that a disembodied spirit is not a
complete person, so that only when soul and body have
been reunited at the resurrection is the personality to
be restored which was suspended at death. This is, for
example, the view of St. Thomas Aquinas.[1] Nevertheless
it would probably be true to say that those who maintain
this view think of the life of the disembodied soul after
death as a *personal* life and are ready (e.g. in their invocation of the saints) to address them as persons.

I am of course aware that to some the very admission
of the possibility that a mind, personal or other, could
exist apart from a body will seem to involve so groundless
and improbable an assumption as to put any one who
makes it out of court. I hope in the second series of these
Gifford Lectures to take an opportunity of describing
more fully my attitude towards the problem of the relation
of Personality to what may be variously regarded as its
physical basis, condition, expression, or vehicle. But for
the present I shall content myself with the following
observations. In view of the fact that, within that part
of our experience which no one regards as illusory, Per-

---

[1] See *Summ. Theol.* I. qu. 29, art. 1 and qu. 75 art. 4. The
Master of the Sentences (iii. 5 § 5) held that the disembodied
soul was a person : but this was one of the points upon which his
authority was not generally followed.

sonality is normally associated with a material organism, we are, I think, bound to ask ourselves whether there may not be grounds for supposing this association to be necessary in every case. But I do not think that the grounds which may be alleged in support of this supposition are so overwhelmingly strong as to make the counter-hypothesis unworthy of consideration by reasonable men, and I therefore hold myself justified in adopting at this stage a description or provisional definition of Personality which leaves the question open.

A person, then, is, by our definition, *individual* ; but it would usually be held that not all *individuals* are *persons*. That it is no easy matter to say what we mean by an individual will not be disputed by any one who recollects the controversies which have been carried on in the schools of philosophy about the *principium individuationis*, the principle of individuality, or the notorious difficulty which biologists have found in deciding what constitutes an individual organism. The remarks which I am about to offer for your consideration have no aim so ambitious as would be that of attempting to solve these celebrated problems. They will do little more than indicate some outstanding facts as to the use of the word ' individual ' as well in common speech as by philosophers, especially in relation to and in distinction from the word ' person.'

' Atom ' and ' individual ' represent the same Greek word ; but the former (when used with any strictness) is usually taken to imply an impossibility of *physical*, the latter an impossibility of *logical* division. Thus there is nothing in the traditional way of using the word ' individual ' which is inconsistent with admitting that an individual may be composite in origin, or susceptible of disruption into several individuals ; but these then

would not be *instances* of the original individual, they would
only be several individuals, whether of the same or of
any other kind from the first, taking the place of one
which had ceased to exist. Nor is there anything to
prevent an individual being made up of distinguishable
individuals of a different kind—e.g. an individual nation
of individual men, or an individual organism of individual
cells, or an individual river of individual drops of water.

The general term ' man.' is not the name of an individual,
because there are many *men*, each of whom is *a* man ; but
' Socrates ' *is* the name of an individual because there
are not and cannot be in this way several Socrateses,
each of whom is *a* Socrates. Of course there may be several
men called *Socrates*, but they do not constitute a class
characterized by participation in a common ' *Socrateitas*,'
as the Latin Schoolmen said, of which each would afford
an instance. In the technical language of elementary
logic it is only *equivocally* that the name is applied at
once to the philosopher and to the ecclesiastical historian.

. A ' person ' is by our definition not only an individual
but an individual *substance*. That is, we should not call
anything which exists only as an *attribute* of something
else a *person*, in the sense we are now trying to fix. No
doubt there are senses of the word ' person,' and those
earlier senses than the one we are studying, in which it
signifies something which is not a substance but an accident—for example, an assumed character or a legal qualification. But in the sense in which ' person ' is equated
with ὑπόστασις a person must be a substance, not an attribute, and moreover an *individual* substance. For a personal name, such as Socrates, is not the name of a *kind*
of substance, whereof there may be many instances, but
of an *individual* substance of which there can be no

instances. Here a certain temptation to sophistry offers itself, which we shall do well to note as we pass and so to avoid yielding to it. ' Person ' itself (it may be objected) is after all a common term ; it is therefore the name of a kind of substance and applies to many such substances. I am *a* person as I am *a* man, or *a* lecturer, an instance of the universal ' person ' of which every one of my hearers is an instance too. And on the other hand *a* man or *a* lecturer no less than *a* person must be an individual substance. Is there anything to distinguish ' person ' in this respect from such other appellations as I have mentioned ? I am of course assuming that by ' person ' we mean a rational *individual* or an *individual* mind. If *person* were a mere synonym for ' human being,' of course it would be a common or general term like any other, but I think that it is not usually employed as a mere synonym for ' human being,' and that we could not substitute it for this latter term on all occasions, but only in certain special contexts.

Now if everything real is individual, and if every description (as distinct from a mere designation) of a thing must be in general terms, it follows that, unless we carefully bear this in mind, we shall be at the mercy of any sophist who says either that, since we can only know what is real, there must exist an individual corresponding to every description that embodies knowledge, or that, since every description must be in general terms, what is described must always be what logicians call a ' universal.' The former type of sophism has been so often discussed that we are more likely to be on our guard against it than against its fellow. It may take the form either of ascribing an individual existence to a universal in abstraction from its particular instances, or of denying to the universal the common nature or character which individuals share, any reality except as a name on our lips or a thought in our minds. I need not dwell on the difficulties into which such views must bring us ; they are sufficiently indicated by a reference on the one hand to the celebrated argument of the ' third man ' brought in antiquity against a crude statement of the Platonic theory of Ideas [2] ; and on the other to the question which Plato represents Parmenides as asking of the young Socrates when the latter had suggested that the universal was perhaps a notion in the soul : ' Is it a notion of *nothing* ? ' [3]

But the fellow-sophism to this is, as I said, less familiar and therefore perhaps more dangerous. I will therefore deal with it at somewhat greater length.

Just as there is a temptation to take that which is not individual either for an individual or for a figment, so there is an opposite temptation to treat that which is individual, because described in general terms, as a universal. And we may yield to this temptation, as to the one before mentioned, in two distinct ways. We may point out that such words as ' individual,' ' person,' ' self ' and so forth are themselves common predicates ; that as Socrates and Plato are alike men, the one no more or no less than the other, so they are both alike individuals and persons and selves. Thence we may be induced to attempt a short cut to idealism, by way of the reflection that the object of knowledge turns out on inspection at close quarters to be nothing but thoughts ; since universals, if not mere thoughts of yours or mine, at least exist as such only in the medium of thought. This short cut is not unfamiliar to students of philosophy—I will

---

[2] See Alex. Aphrod. on Aristotle, *Metaph.* A. 990 b 15 *seqq.*
[3] Plat. *Parm.* 132B.

admit that I once thought it would take me whither I
wanted to go—but I am convinced that he who trusts
himself to it will have cause to remember the proverb
' More haste less speed.'   This is one form of our sophism.
The other is this : We ask what seems more undeniably
real, substantial, impenetrable than the individual, and in
particular than the individual that each of us knows most
intimately, I *myself*.   Yet you call yourself *I* as justly
as *I* do ;   *self* means you just as well as me :   and in the
end ' self ' will turn out to me a mere appearance, like
the gleam upon the water or the rainbow's end which
shifts "for ever and for ever when " we " move," 4 so
that we can never come up with it and grasp the bright
thing which to a child's inexperienced eyes it seems so
easy to suppose that we shall reach, if we do but walk
steadily forward in a certain direction.

It is no part of my intention in these remarks, as some
of my hearers may perhaps suspect, to suggest that there
is some being inaccessible to thought ;   still less that in
such an impenetrable shrine is concealed what is of highest
and most enduring worth.   Such a view would be entirely
alien to my own way of thinking.   However imperfect
what we call our knowledge may be, I should contend
that it is, so far as it goes, an apprehension of Reality ;
not merely an apprehension of something with which
Reality puts us off, as it were, while remaining in itself
inaccessible to us.   No doubt we may often find ourselves
in presence of something which we cannot describe, because
the description of it would exceed our actual powers of
comprehension and expression ;   but the mere fact that
we can say nothing about a thing does not for me

4 Tennyson, *Ulysses*.

imply that it passes all understanding ; it may be only
that there is nothing about it to say.

It was not, then, because I wished to insinuate a doctrine
of the Unknowable that I spoke of the necessity of guarding
against the sophism which would turn the individual
into a universal no less than against that other sophism,
with the exposure of which we are all familiar, which turns
the universal into an individual. It was rather because
I desired to insist that reality is throughout individual
and universal ; not in part one and in part the other ;
but both alike throughout and at every point. In words
of Goethe which Hegel quotes to emphasize this truth :—

> Natur hat weder Kern noch Schale,
> Alles ist sie mit einem male.
>
> Nature has neither kernel nor shell,
> She is all at once one and the other as well ! [5]

Everything that is real, then, is unique, this thing and
no other. But just because it is thus unique, it fills a place
of its own in a system of Reality in which it has its being ;
it is describable by way of relation to and distinction from
other things, other elements in that Reality : so that a
full description of it would state its relation to and its
distinction from every other such element or part of the
whole. This double aspect which belongs to all that is
real is manifested most conspicuously and unmistakably
in *persons*. The person, the rational individual, is not
only recognized by others, but recognizes himself as unique
and individual, just because he is aware of something
beyond himself, however vaguely conceived, a background
against which he himself is, as it were, set alongside with

[5] Goethe, *Gott und Welt* (*Jubiläums Ausgabe*, ii. p. 259). Quoted
by Hegel, *Werke*, vi. p. 276.

what is not himself ; an encompassing world within which he and other things from which he distinguishes himself are alike included. This background or encompassing world is potentially infinite since, however we may attempt to envisage or picture or describe it, as soon as it is thus envisaged or pictured or described it is at once found to be itself embraced within something yet more comprehensive, and so on for ever. We may see this truth illustrated by all those myths of the origin or creation of the world which tell of a transaction requiring a world already made in which it could take place, and so provoke the further question, Whence came the beings or things, whatever they may be, which are represented as taking part in the transaction ? a question which in its turn leads on to some further story and yet further question, in a series to which only the exhaustion of the myth-maker's fancy can set a period.

At this point a question of some importance suggests itself for consideration. When we say that the double aspect of all that is real is most unmistakably manifested in *persons*, which are individuals conscious of themselves as such, is this because the individuality of persons is an individuality more perfect than that of individuals which are not persons, or only because here and here only is there revealed to us who are persons what is in fact the true and inward nature of all individuals whatsoever ?

With regard to this question I shall here content myself with a reference to the doctrine of Leibnitz. It is well known that in the view of this philosopher the reality of the world consists in an infinite multitude of ' monads ' or individual substances which, as he picturesquely put it, " have no windows "—that is to say, admitted no influences from without ; so that all that is done by, or happens to, any monad is part of the necessary development of its own nature ; although among all these coexistent lines of development there is what he called a pre-established harmony, the effects of which we are apt to mistake for the effects of mutual interaction among the monads.[6] It is not, however, of the ' windowlessness ' of the monads or of their ' pre-established harmony ' that I wish to remind you now. It is rather of the fact that, although Leibnitz, while considering all souls to be monads, did not consider all monads to be entitled to the designation of souls, yet it was undoubtedly the personal soul as apprehended by itself that served him as his starting-point in construing the nature of the monads. That there could be beings possessing the genuine individuality which the personal soul attributes to itself and yet not exhibiting that consciousness which is the characteristic activity of the personal soul—this became intelligible to him by means of the experience which the soul has of the continuity of its own development through and across periods of subconsciousness and unconsciousness, during its continuance in which we can attribute to it no activity but that of *petites perceptions* [7] which do not rise, in the metaphorical phrase familiar to us in modern psychology, above the threshold of consciousness. I think we may borrow from Leibnitz here an answer to the question upon which I have just touched. What the personal soul is conscious of being in itself, this it is conscious of being because it is it to a certain degree of perfection ; were other individuals this to the same degree, they would be also conscious of being it, and so would be self-conscious individuals or persons. There is, then, a genuine identity between the individuality which

[6] See his *Monadologie*.   [7] See *Nouv. Ess.* ii. 1, § 13, *Monadol.* § 21.

is self-conscious and which we call personal and that
which we, who are persons, recognize in other things to
which we do not give the name of ' persons.' It is that
kind of identity to which we give the name of *development*
or *evolution* ; where we recognize the same nature or type
under a succession or series of forms so related that each
exhibits the nature or type in question more adequately
than its predecessor.

Individuality from the first is characterized by independence—relative independence at least—of other
individuals ; but, as it appears to us in *things*, we find
ourselves in every case tempted to ask whether it is not
something which *we* are attributing to them, which is
defined by *our* purposes only, and which another spectator
might define quite otherwise. We desire to correct *our*
view of it by a view of it which shall be the thing's own ;
but this, just because the thing is not conscious, and
therefore has no view of itself, we cannot do. In the
case of organisms which we should not dignify by the
name of persons we find something more like what we
are looking for ; but it does not satisfy us ; for, as the individuality of the mere *thing* seemed to need in order to
determine it a mind which it did not itself possess, so
does even that of the organism. For although in its
action and (in the case of animals) in its feeling it affords
a principle of determination other than *our* purposes, it
still does not determine *itself* as we determine our own
individuality by our own self-consciousness. In the
case of a *person*, the individual may be said to determine
himself by his thought of himself. If even here the principle
which has guided us so far does not seem to be completely
realized ; if we are liable to self-distractions out of which
we can only imperfectly recover ourselves by the effort

of self-consciousness ; if our power of grasping in thought
what we are seems limited on the one side by physical
conditions, which we find already given, and on the other
by an ideal of which we are conscious that we fall short
—all this is only to say that such 'personality' as ours is
not the highest form of individuality possible, although
highei than any we attribute to beast oi plant or inanimate
body. Our inquiries have brought us up against a controversy intimately connected with our main subject in
this course of Lectures, a controversy on the terminology
of which I have already commented, but the further
examination of which I expressly postponed. I refer
to the difference between Mr. Bosanquet and Lotze which
is expressed by the former's ascription of Individuality
and denial of Personality to the Absolute, as contrasted
with the assertion of the latter that Personality belongs
unconditionally only to the Infinite.[8]

Let me before going further take note of an historical
circumstance which may prove of some use to us as a
guide-post in the mazes of the inquiry upon which we
are entering. Most readers of the two philosophers I
have named, Lotze and Mr. Bosanquet, if suddenly asked
which of the two stood nearer in this matter of the individuality and personality of the Absolute Reality to the
position of historical Christianity, would probably reply
without hesitation that it was Lotze. I do not say that
we may not ultimately see reason to endorse this opinion.
But at first sight we may well hesitate to do so.

For, so far as the terminology goes, it is not Lotze but
Mr. Bosanquet that agrees with the tradition of Christian
theology in calling God an *individual* but not a *person* [9] :

8 See above, Lect. I, pp. 18 f. ; II, pp. 52 ff.
9 The agreement of Mr. Bosanquet with the traditional theology

that God is *individual* in the logical sense, as man (for example) is not, so that there cannot be several individuals

of Christendom would not end here, if we were able to assume (as I think we may) his agreement with Mr. Bradley's pronouncement (*Appearance and Reality*, p. 528) that " it is better, on the whole, to conclude that no element of Reality falls outside the experience of finite centres," and could then argue that the supreme experience must be possessed ~~by~~ the supreme activity of thought exercised by *persons* ; since certainly no ' centres ' less than such as (to use Mr. Bradley's expressions) ' imply ' or ' entail ' personal souls can be supposed capable of possessing that experience or exercising that activity. But I do not doubt that both Mr. Bradley and Mr. Bosanquet would reject this inference from their premises. The very ' finitude ' attributed to the ' centres ' outside of whose experience, it is held, no element of Reality can fall is inconsistent with attributing to *them* such possession and such exercise. The Absolute, though appearing in finite centres, and probably only there, is itself neither a finite centre nor an aggregate of such ; for all ' finite things ' as Mr. Bradley says (*A. and R.* p. 529) " are there transmuted and have lost their individual natures." I have thought it worth while, however, just to mention a possible misuse of the principles of these two philosophers to establish a position which they would repudiate, because I feel that nothing in their writings presents greater difficulty than their language concerning an ' experience ' which, though it is the supreme Reality, yet belongs to none of those ' centres of experience ' in which alone it is described by Mr. Bradley, usually indeed as 'appearing,' but sometimes as ' realized,' as though it were not infinitely more real than they. It is no doubt true that Mr. Bradley, at any rate, often insists that the appearance of the Absolute in finite centres is ' inexplicable ' —a phrase which suggests not merely that it is an ultimate feature of Reality, but that it is one which excites our surprise, so that we do not rest in it as being the most natural thing in the world, but desire an explanation and are baffled by our failure to find one. Is it possible that in their anxiety to point out the inadequacy of our religious and theological phraseology to express the ultimate truth of things (an inadequacy which no one would deny) both Mr. Bradley and Mr. Bosanquet have done less than justice to the contribution made towards the revelation of the nature of the supreme Reality by the religious experience to which that language owes its origin ? See esp. Mr. Bradley's *Appearance and Reality*, pp. 226, 527 ff. ; *Truth and Reality*, pp. 349 ff., 420 ff. ; and Mr. Bosanquet's *Principle of Individuality*, pp. 303 ff. ; *Value and Destiny*, pp. 253 ff.

who are all alike Gods as there are many individuals who are all alike men ; as also in the sense that there cannot be said to be any act of his in which only a part of him is concerned—this would be affirmed by any accurate exponent of Christian doctrine. And, as we saw in the third Lecture, the *personality of God* (as distinct from the acknowledgment of *persons in God*) is affirmed by no Christian creed or confession of faith which has not so far departed from the normal type as to abandon the doctrine of the Trinity in Unity.

No doubt Mr. Bosanquet and Mr. Bradley also have been at pains to make clear that they do not consider the Absolute to be another name for God.[10] The God of religion, they say, is or may be thought of as standing in a personal relation to his worshipper ; and they would, I think, be inclined to add that there are aspects of Reality which of course fall within the Absolute but are ignored by religion or, if not ignored, are regarded by it as antagonistic to God. We shall have to return to the question of the relation of these two conceptions, God and the Absolute. But for the present I do not think it affects what I have said above about Mr. Bosanquet's agreement with Christian theology. For he would probably be quite ready to concede that in the theologians' account of the Trinity in Unity we have less a description of God as the Christian worshipper conceives him in the actual practice of his religion than a description of a philosophical speculation (though one no doubt suggested by the history of religious experience within the Christian Church) concerning the nature of the Supreme Reality or, in Mr. Bosanquet's own terminology, of the Absolute.

[10] See Bradley, *Appearance and Reality*, pp. 445 ff. ; *Truth and Reality*, c. 15 ; Bosanquet, *Value and Destiny*, pp. 255 f.

What is it, then, we may ask in the respective views of Lotze and of Mr. Bosanquet which causes this closer agreement of the latter than of the former with the traditional theology of Christendom to strike one as something which one would not have expected ? The answer to this question will, I think, throw light upon that conception of Personality the application of which to God, the Supreme Reality, we have proposed to ourselves to discuss.

For this answer is to be found in the *ethical* implications of this conception of Personality : and of these we have not as yet spoken, except incidentally.

Now in the first place, if we cast back our thoughts to that history of the word *person* which I traced in a previous Lecture, we shall see that the original associations of the word were with the performance of functions in social intercourse. We see this alike in the case of the *persons* in a drama and the *persons* at law who are the subjects of rights and duties. We do not wonder, then, that the thought of Personality cannot easily be disconnected from that of social conduct or, in other words, from the sphere of Morality.

We shall, I think, bring this fact home to ourselves if we raise the question whether a self-conscious individual supposed to stand altogether outside that sphere could naturally be called a person. Let us take two instances to illustrate what I mean : one from a contemporary novelist, the other from an ancient philosopher. The adventurous fancy of Mr. Wells has, in the ' Martians ' of his romance *The War of the Worlds*, familiarized his readers with the picture of a rational and scientific animal who is imagined as sharing the intellectual but not the moral nature of mankind. A stranger to the

desires and pleasures of sex and of nutrition, the Martian
is equally a stranger to the moral emotions which, in their
simplest and most universal shape, are connected with
the satisfaction of those desires and the enjoyment of
those pleasures.

Now we may not unreasonably doubt whether, if the
Martians were wholly without morality, they could have
organized the invasion of this planet which is the theme
of Mr Wells's story. That there must be ' honour among
thieves ' if they are to form successful gangs, is the familiar
teaching both of proverbial philosophy and of the
Republic of Plato.[11]   And the same line of thought
would suggest that Mr. Wells's Martians must after all
have had at least those rudiments of a moral sense which
were necessary to ensure their efficient co-operation.

But, however this may be, I think that we should in
speaking of one of the Martians as described by Mr. Wells
hesitate to call him—or it—a *person*. For with such a
being what we call personal relations would be impossible
for us ; and it is by the possibility of such relations that
we judge of the presence of personality in others. It
is just what constitutes the nightmare-like ghastliness
of these creatures of Mr. Wells's imagination that they
have some of the attributes we associate most closely
with personality, and yet, for lack of that moral community with us which makes personal relations possible
are not really persons. The horror which they inspire
is an intensified degree of that which in real life is excited
in us by the maniac who has not indeed, like the fabled
Martians, the intellectual capacity of a human being, but
at any rate presents (as they do not) the outward form of
man, and yet not withal the opportunity of human fellow-

[11] Plat. *Rep*. i. 351 c.

ship which that form seems to promise.   And the maniac it would certainly seem unnatural to describe, except with some apology, as a *person*.

To my other—very different—instance of a self-conscious individual who is thought of as standing outside of the sphere of morality I have already referred in an earlier Lecture [12] ;   and so I will do no more now than mention it.   It is God as described by Aristotle.   To God, according to the express statements of that philosopher, ethical predicates are inapplicable.   He enters into no reciprocal relations with other beings, although the desire to attain to his supreme excellence is the cause of the movement of universal nature ;   for he himself, by reason of his very perfection, can have no concern with or knowledge of anything that is less perfect than himself—and all things except himself are that.

We saw before that such a being is not at all what those who attach importance to the recognition of a ' personal God ' are thinking of when they use that phrase :   for since there is no possibility of personal relations with him, he is not in any natural sense a person, any more than the maniac or the Martian.   The denial of personality is in these three very various cases based upon the same negation which may be made about them all, namely that they are outside the sphere of morality, which is the sphere of personal relations ;   so that personal relations with them there cannot be and persons they cannot properly be called.

Now the Absolute of Mr. Bosanquet's and of Mr Bradley's philosophy also transcends the spheɪe of Morality, although in a somewhat different sense from the God of Aristotle.   For in the view of Mr. Bosanquet

[12] See above, Lecture III, pp. 73 ff.

and Mr. Bradley the moral life of human beings and of any other beings (if such there be) who progress from a more imperfect to a more perfect state of existence under the impulse of aspiration after an ideal which is not yet realized, does not fall altogether outside of the Absolute Experience ; on the contrary, it is wholly comprehended within it, although only as transmuted, one may say, beyond all recognition. For, whereas Morality is unfulfilled aspiration, we have here satisfied fruition.[13] And whereas Morality involves external relations to other beings to whom the moral *person* owes duties, and from whom he claims rights, there is nothing beyond the Absolute. Thus in this philosophy the Absolute transcends the sphere of Morality, and therefore cannot be called a Person.

On the other hand, Lotze does not deny Personality to the Infinite because he holds that what we are compelled to regard as the highest conceptions, of which conceptions the Good (that is, the morally good) is one, lose all reality and become empty abstractions except as referred to a Person ; while to him the description of the Supreme Reality as a " Living Love that wills the blessedness of others," [14] does not, as to the Engl sh thinkers with whom I have contrasted him, appear inconsistent with that freedom from all want or dependence which must belong to that Supreme Reality. Rather, so he thinks, it satisfies a deep-seated demand in our nature to find that what has supreme reality has also supreme value ; and this he would certainly have refused to find in an Absolute like Mr. Bosanquet's, our conception of

---

[13] See Bradley, *Appearance and Reality*, pp. 201 f., and pp. 436 ff. ; Bosanquet, *Value and Destiny*, pp. 138 ff.

[14] *Microcosmus*, ix. 5 § 7, Eng. tr. ii. p. 721.

which is reached by the application of a criterion the
" proper name " of which is non-contradiction.[15] For the
present we will bring to a close this account of the difference between Lotze on the one hand and Mr. Bosanquet
on the other which expresses itself in the attribution to
the Ultimate Reality of Personality by the former, and
by the latter of Individuality but not of Personality. We
have compared with both a third view, namely, that
embodied in the traditional theology of Christendom.
This theology agreed, as we saw, with Mr. Bosanquet
as against Lotze in affirming *individuality* but not *personality* of the Supreme Being : and in finding Personality
included within the nature of the Supreme Being, but not
predicable of it. On the other hand, Lotze is at one with
this same theology in his teaching, which Mr. Bosanquet
would be unable to endorse as it stands, that the Supreme
Being is a " Living Love that wills the blessedness of
others," although he does not carry his agreement so far
as to represent this will to bless *others* as rooted in an
eternal activity of love between *persons* who are not
other than the Supreme Being, because their distinction
from one another falls within its unity, and yet are not
(like the persons who in Mr. Bosanquet's doctrine also
fall within the unity of his Absolute) transitory and
finite manifestations of an eternal and infinite Reality.

On the problems suggested by the comparison and
contrast of these views there remains of course much to
be said : and I hope to return to them hereafter. But
what I have said will perhaps be sufficient for our
immediate purpose, which was only to illustrate the

[15] The expression occurs in a review by Mr. Bosanquet in *Mind*
(October 1917) of Prof. Pringle-Pattison's *Idea of God*. See *Individuality and Value*, pp. 44 ff. (cp. Bradley, *Appearance and Reality*,
p. 537).

distinction of the notion of *personality* from that of *individuality* and the relation of the one to the other.

In the next Lecture I shall pass to the distinction of the notion of *personality* from and its relation to another, to which as well as to *individuality*, of which we have just been speaking, reference is made in the Boethian definition of *person*, namely the notion of *rationality*.

LECTURE V

PERSONALITY AND RATIONALITY

In my last Lecture I took as a provisional definition of Personality the celebrated formula found in the Christological treatise traditionally attributed to Boethius: *Naturæ rationabilis individua substantia*; and I endeavoured to give some account of the relation of the notion of *personality* to that of *individuality*, which enters into this description of its essential nature. I now desire to fix your attention upon another notion which also appears in the same description as an element in Personality, that namely of reason or *rationality*. As we previously inquired in what respect the *individuality* of a *rational* being differs from that of any other, so now we will attempt to discover how *reason* is modified by being manifested in a *personality*. But I do not desire by using this expression to commit myself to the implication that Reason in fact exists except as the activity of personal minds.

This inquiry will lead us straight to that part of our discussion in which we shall be concerned with the *motives* that can be alleged for and the *objections* that can be brought against ascribing Personality to God. For in examining the discrepancy which we shall presently have to consider between what, as rational and common to

all persons or rational beings, takes no account of the
distinction of persons, and what on the other hand distinguishes one person or rational being from another, we
shall find ourselves dealing with a fact which is the principal inspiration at once of the demand for a personal God
and of the reluctance of many—especially among philosophers—to admit the legitimacy of this demand. This
I will describe for the moment by a name which, as I hope
eventually to show, is in truth inappropriate, but which
will notwithstanding serve better perhaps than any other
to suggest at the outset the problem which I have in mind.
I will call it ' the irrationality of the personal.'

It will, I think, be found most convenient in dealing
with this subject not to draw any hard and fast line
between the general treatment of it and the special investigation of its bearing on the question of Divine Personality,
which is the principal topic of these Lectures.

It will not be denied that many instances may be given
of the use of the word ' personal ' in our ordinary speech
—and it is never safe for the philosopher to neglect the
testimony of ordinary speech—to express what, at least
in contrast with something else to which in the context
it is opposed, we regard as *irrational*. Thus we may
speak of a ' personal prejudice ' which prevents a man
agreeing to some .plan or approving of some appointment
against which he can bring forward no argument based
on grounds of *reason*. No doubt such a ' personal prejudice ' is always susceptible of an explanation ; it may,
for example, be due to some unpleasant association, some
instinctive physical repugnance, or what not ; but we
should not consider these to be in the proper sense *reasons*
for rejecting the plan or refusing to sanction the appointment ; though they may be the *causes* of the prejudiced

man's acting as he does. On the other hand, we might say quite naturally that it was a *reason* for not appointing So-and-so to a certain post that he would not get on with some colleague who had a *personal* prejudice against him. But the reason here would not be the man's who had the 'personal prejudice,' but somebody else's who was taking that prejudice dispassionately into account.

One can without any difficulty find many similar instances of the use of the word ' personal ' for what is, in some particular connexion, to be *discounted* (like the ' personal equation ' in a scientific observation or experiment) before a result can be attained which is fit to form part of the common stock of experience which we call *science* in the widest sense of this word. We sometimes contrast *History* with *Science* as dealing with individuals and for the most part with *persons*—while science is concerned only with universals, classes, generalities, and so forth. But historians are constantly attracted by the aim of making History *scientific* and so adding it to the common store of which I have just spoken. The attempt to do this necessarily tends towards the subordination of the *personal* element or its resolution into what can be represented as intelligible from principles applicable to *any person* under the circumstances of *this* one. Thus to the generalizing reason, which is the very breath of what we call Science, Personality is, as it were, a surd ; it can at best be represented by a series of characteristics which can never be completed, so as to constitute *that very person*, and not merely a *person of just that kind*.

But one may go further. Not only does there thus seem to be something in Personality which refuses to be rationalized by what one may call the scientific understanding with its method of generalization ; there may even seem to be something in it irrational from a more strictly philosophical point of view. In my first Lecture, when I was attempting to describe the circumstances which just now specially invited to an investigation of the notion of Personality, I described the embarrassment caused by that notion to the philosophy of an important school of thought, which in recent times has predominated in this country; and I promised that the true reasons of this embarrassment would become more evident at a later stage of our discussion. It is to these reasons that I desire now to call attention.

It was, as I said before, the peculiar task of the school in question to expose the failure of the empirical philosophy which it found in possession and to give such an account of the human mind as would render intelligible its capacity for the very kind of knowledge regarded by that philosophy as the authentic type of genuine and valuable knowledge—that knowledge, namely, which goes by the name of Natural Science. It recalled attention to the relations or principles of synthesis which Kant had designated as ' forms of sensibility ' and ' categories of the understanding,' and showed that, apart from these relations or principles of synthesis, the objective validity of which, since the knowledge of them could not be traced to sense-perception, the empirical philosophy could not consistently affirm, there could be for us no *nature* and therefore no *natural science* at all.

To recognize this was to acknowledge a unity of consciousness, a ' spiritual principle,' as Green called it, apart from the presence whereof to them all the several sensations, which the empirical philosophers had held to be the sole constitutents of our experience, would each have vanished for ever before another came and so could never have given rise to the perception even of a single object, much less of a world of objects.

There is more than one problem concerning the nature of such a ‘ spiritual principle ’ as this which might be raised.   But there is only one which I now desire to discuss. And that is the problem of the relation of such a ‘ spiritual principle ’ as Green, for example, contended that we must recognize in knowledge to what we call *personality*.

At first sight, indeed, it might seem that it was just of our personality that Green was speaking.   I am a person, not a thing nor yet an animal ; for an animal, although conscious, lacks (as we suppose) the capacity to distinguish itself as a permanent consciousness from what to us who observe it are its *successive* sensations.   And it is just because I am thus not a thing, nor merely an animal, but a *person* that I am aware in myself of this enduring self, which has sensations but is not any one of them nor all of them together, but something of quite another nature than theirs, which is for ever establishing for itself con-nexions between sensations, and so exhibiting them as factors in its own perception of an enduring world.

But, as one looks closer, it is plain that what Green is thinking of is not personality as I distinguish *my* personality from that of any of *you*, but rather the activity which goes on in all minds that think or reason and which, so far as they perceive and reason correctly, must be the same in all.   And this does not seem to be what we commonly mean by personality.   It seems, indeed, to be a principle of unity in experience, as personality also is, but a *different* principle, combining experiences in a different order and dividing them into groups on a different plan.

Of these two principles one is the principle which combines premises with the conclusions which follow from

8

them, the thought of causes with the thought of their effects, the members of series with what comes next to them in mathematical or logical order. It distinguishes logical priority from temporal, mere sequence from necessary connexion, one kind of subject or department of knowledge from another, and so forth. It holds together in one system the experience of all rational beings ; one such being has no more right in it than another, though one may, so to say, through greater or less vigour of mind, or more or less abundant opportunity, be able to make more or less use of it than his fellows. It is this principle of which Green is, I take it, usually thinking when he speaks of his ' spiritual principle ' in experience. No one would deny to this principle the name of *Reason*.

The other principle combines and disjoins experiences on quite a different plan. It combines all sensations, perceptions, thoughts which I call *mine* together, as *mine*, no matter how little logical or generally intelligible connexion they may have with one another. It divides all sensations, perceptions, thoughts of *yours* from all of *mine*, no matter how closely they may resemble mine. If, by communication through speech or writing or otherwise, my thoughts are conveyed to you, or yours to me, according to this principle they must be reckoned twice over, as yours and as mine, although their content be identical. Now we must not ignore the fact that a person's thoughts and actions are at any rate no less *personal* when they are guided by reason, and from grounds which all thinking men would understand and approve, than when they are most whimsical and capricious or depend upon considerations of purely private concern. But we are apt to use the word *personal* most often as an

epithet for motives or interests which are *merely* personal
—that is, where the explanation of them lies in connexions
determined only by the second of the two principles I
have just described and not in connexions established
by the former.

It is with the word *personal* here as with the phrase
' *association of ideas.*' When we reason we may of course
be said to ' associate ideas,' though to explain reason
by the association of ideas, as a famous school of thinkers
attempted to do, is to put the cart before the horse.
But a quite natural instinct has tended to appropriate
the phrase to those cases where the ' association ' of ideas
implied by an action is not what we should usually call
rational, but depends upon some individual habit or
private memory, as when (to take a trivial instance) a
man waking in the night at an hotel feels for the switch
of the electric light not where he had found it when about
to turn it off on going to bed, but in the place corresponding
to that of the switch in his bedroom at home. Here, to
account for what he does, he must revert to an ' association
of ideas ' which is *not* rational ; and it is in the same
way just for what is *not* rational in men's proceedings
that we often use the word *personal*, because we seek the
explanation of them in their *personal* history and not in
any system of connexions to be found in the great world
which is common to us all—*in mundo majore sive communi*,
as Bacon quotes from Heraclitus.[1]

In this way there springs up an antithesis of the *personal*
and the *rational*, which will deserve our close attention.
But in attending to it we must constantly bear in mind

[1] *Novum Organum*, i. 42 ; the original saying of Heraclitus is
quoted in Sext. Emp. *adv. Math*. vii. 133 (Heraclitus, Frag. 92,
ed. Bywater, Diels *Vorsokratiker*, p. 66).

that it will mislead us if we forget that only in the minds of *persons* do there take place movements of thought from ground to consequent, from cause to effect, from premises to conclusion or *vice versa*, such as are determined by principles of *reason* ; that it is only minds in which we suppose such movements of thought may take place that we should describe as *personal* ; and lastly, that the world wherein we trace the connexion which we call rational is a world of which persons are a part and, to us at any rate, the most interesting part. Thus, as I hinted before, the expression ' irrationality of the personal ' upon which I fixed as conveniently suggesting the problem with which I am now concerned is not really an appropriate one. For it is *persons* only that *reason*, and *reasoning* beings only that are *persons* ; and Reason is not unconcerned with persons though it is not concerned with persons only. Yet the *personal* principle of unity or organization in experience does appear to be distinct from the *rational* ; and in cases where the latter affords no ground for a particular connexion, but we find one in the former, we come to institute a contrast and opposition between them which suggests that irrationality is characteristic of what is *merely* personal.

This contrast and opposition we have next to observe at a higher level of experience than that to which we have so far been going for our examples. We have now to observe it as it appears in the sphere of Morality. And here we shall have the great advantage of seeing it emphasized in the ethical systems of two great philosophers, by whom moreover it is so exhibited as to display those theological bearings for the sake of which we are now studying it. These two great philosophers are Kant and Fichte.

It is, as is well known, the doctrine of Kant that nothing can be morally right but what can be regarded as law universal, as obligatory, that is to say, upon all rational beings. This does not, of course, mean that every one's duty is the same as every one else's ; that what is right for the judge is right for the criminal, what is right for the parent right for the child, what is right for the physician right for his patient. But it does imply that every one's duty is always what would be any one else's under those circumstances. Every *personal* interest and *personal* preference must be discounted in ascertaining what is *right*. The presence of a personal inclination to what is right makes it possible that what seems to be a morally right action is after all due merely to this inclination and not to the consciousness that it is our *duty*. Thus the absence of inclination or the presence of positive repugnance to a certain course which is notwithstanding adopted becomes the one certain test of genuine morality : for the consciousness of duty alone could have moved us to act thus clean contrary to our liking. And so Kant comes sometimes to use language such as could provoke the celebrated epigram in which the poet Schiller laughed at the notion of our never fulfilling the moral law except when we do so with horror.[2]

Now in Kant's use of the words *personal* and *personality* there is certainly an ambiguity ; or perhaps it would be more correct to say that he does not clear up an ambiguity involved in our ordinary use of the words, now for what is private and peculiar to this or that individual, now for knowledge and morality, which distinguish human beings not only from inanimate things but from the lower animals ; for these, although they possess life

[2] *Die Philosophen* (*Säkular-Ausgabe*, i. p. 268).

and consciousness, we do not call persons because they lack that capacity. Hence he sometimes calls by the name of Personality that very rational nature in virtue of which we can will to do what we see to be right for all who share that nature, whether we as individuals, with private feelings and interests unshared by our fellows, chance to like it or not ; sometimes, on the other hand, that from which in ascertaining the universal laws of morality we have to abstract is called by him ' the *personal* distinction between rational beings.' 3 It is the use of the word *personal* in this second connexion which corresponds with that employment of it of which I spoke before which contrasts the *personal* with the *rational* ; although every one would allow that rational beings within our experience are personal, nor should we call any beings personal which we did not take to be rational.

The ambiguity which, as we have just seen, was left in Kant's use of *personality* in respect of ourselves, reappears in his theology. The representation of moral duties as commanded by God he approves,4 although we are always to remember that we can only legitimately regard them as commanded by God because we are independently conscious of their obligatoriness ; we cannot otherwise ascertain them to be commanded by God, and then regard ourselves as in consequence obliged to perform them. Nor does his approval of this way of representing them appear to be merely a concession to the demand for an imaginative representation of what

3 *Grundlegung der Metaph. der Sitten,* 2 Abschn. (*Werke,* ed. Hart. iv. p. 281). For the use of Personality to mean the rational nature see *Kr. der pr. Vern.* 1 Th. 1 B. iii. H. pts. (Hart. v. p. 91). Cp. *Rechtslehre* (Hart. vii. pp. 20, 36).

4 See *Rechtslehre* (Hart. vii. pp. 24, 137) ; cp. *Die Religion innerhalb. d. Gr. d. bl. Vern.* Vorrede zur 1 Ausgabe (Hart. vi. p. 100).

is strictly unimaginable For he holds that *reverence*, which is our proper attitude towards the moral law, can only be felt towards *persons*,[5] and this would seem to suggest that the representation of moral laws as divine commands may be something more than an imaginative personification. Nor do I suppose that to Kant himself it was no more than this. But he could have scarcely developed the theistic implications of the sentiment of reverence as, for example, Martineau does in his *Types of Ethical Theory* and its sequel *A Study of Religion*.[6]

For the principles of the Critical Philosophy, which debarred the human mind from any knowledge of things as they are in themselves, combined with that stern aversion from the least compromise with sentiment in matters of conduct which was so characteristic of Kant's moral temperament to hinder him from admitting the legitimacy of that personal intercourse with God in the experience of which—or at least in the desire for it—the affirmation of Personality in God is founded. Hence, although while he could not in mature life bring himself, except when it was his official duty as Rector of the University of Königsberg, to take part in public worship [7] he could nevertheless allow of it as the expression to one another by the members of the congregation of a common resolution to order their lives according to the Moral Law [8] ; for *private* prayer as distinct from such a resolution

5 Kr. der pr. Vern. l.c. (H. v. p. 81).

6 Or as my lamented and honoured teacher, the late Professor Cook Wilson, did in a paper of marked originality, which made a great impression on those who heard it read at Oxford, and which I hope may hereafter be made public, when the return of peace shall have set his literary executors free to carry out the pious task of giving to the world what he has left behind him.

7 See Stuckenberg, *Life of Kant*, p. 354.

8 *Die Religion*, etc., Allg. Anm. (H. vi. p. 297).

on the individual's part, to which when alone he would
not need to give outward expression, he could find no
room at all. He held that a man who was properly
instructed in the nature of Morality—as bound up with
the autonomous freedom of the individual will, which yet
in willing made no account of its individual distinction
from other rational beings—could not but be ashamed
to be found by a stranger upon his knees alone.[9] Such
an attitude would imply at once a superstitious neglect
of the limits of human experience, as though God could
be sensibly present, and an immoral attempt to claim
divine aid in the performance of our duty otherwise than
by the right attitude of will which alone could deserve
such aid. Nor was there a place left in Kant's religion
for any love of God other than the cheerful performance
of his commandments ; any more than in his ethics he
could ascribe moral value to any love of our neighbour
other than the practical love shown in the cheerful performance of our duty towards him.[10]

We find thus that Kant ascribes moral value solely
to the Good Will, which, although the capacity for exercising it constitutes the essence of our personality, yet
abstracts altogether from the features that distinguish
one person from another, and belongs in common to all
rational beings. We find also that, in close connexion
with this aspect of his teaching, he eliminates from his
theology everything suggestive of the possibility of a
communion with God that could bring into play any part
of our nature except this same Good Will, which wills
only what can be law universal for all rational beings,

9 *Die Religion*, etc., Allg. Anm. (H. vi. p. 294 *n*.); cp. *Tugendlehre*,
I B. I Aboh. I H. pts. iii. Art. § 12 (H. vii. p. 243).
10 *Kritik der prakt. Vern*, I Th. I B. iii. H. pts. (H. v. pp. 87, 88).

and takes no account of what is peculiar to this or that individual, save as an external circumstance affecting the special mode in which the Good Will is exhibited in a particular instance.

But it is in Fichte that we find this same point of view adopted with a full realization of its paradoxical results and a vehement insistence on the necessity of accepting them which are absent from the elder thinker.

Thus he says : " The utter annihilation of the individual and submission thereof in the absolute and pure form of reason, or in God, is most certainly the final end of finite reason." [11]   It is true that he admits that this end cannot be attained in any finite time, and that it is the error of mysticism to treat it as though it could be.   " I am never to act," he says again, " without having first referred my act to this conception " of duty.   " Hence there are no indifferent acts at all."   " It is absolutely immoral," he tells us, " to take care of our body without the conviction that it is thus trained and preserved for moral activity—in short, for conscience' sake. Eat and drink for the glory of God. If any one thinks this morality to be austere and painful we cannot help him, for there is no other." [12]   Like Kant, he insists that the 'love of our neighbour ' which is a duty cannot be a love of the feelings. He adds, indeed, that it would be wrong to suppose that therefore it requires no internal affection, but merely

[11] *Sittenlehre*, § 12 ; *Werke*, iv. p. 151 (Eng. tr. p. 159).

[12] *Sittenlehre*, §§ 13, 18 ; *Werke*, iv. pp. 155, 216 (Eng. tr. pp. 164, 227). Signor Croce agrees with Fichte in holding that from the moral point of view there can be no indifferent acts ; but he gives to what he calls the ' economic ' character of all actions an independent value always distinguishable from, though always presupposed by the ethical.   See Wildon Carr, *Phil. of Croce*, pp. 128 f. Kant, *Tugendlehre*, Einleitung, § 10 (*Werke*, ed. Hart. vii. p. 213), admits the existence of *adiaphora*.

external conduct towards him, for no act can be moral which does not proceed from an inner disposition. It is not sufficient to act, for example, as if we loved our enemy, no matter how much we may hate him in point of fact. " I must love him : that is to say, must believe him capable of reform." [13] Now, whether or no it is possible to love an enemy whom one does not believe capable of ceasing to be one's enemy, it is surely hard not to feel that to believe a man capable of reform is a very different thing from loving him in any natural sense of that word.

It is only the logical sequel to such statements as I have quoted that God should become for Fichte nothing else than the Moral Order of the universe, beside which there is no God. [14]

Now I do not wish to deny—I would rather insist upon —the attraction of this vigorous type of ethical doctrine, exemplified by the two great thinkers of whose teaching I have reminded you, to any one who has at any time heard in the depths of his soul with a full understanding of its unconditional claim upon his obedience the august voice of Duty, and has cried with all his heart to that ' stern daughter of the voice of God ' in the words of the poet :—

> The confidence of Reason give,
> And in the light of Truth thy bondman let me live. [15]

If, as Fichte implies in one of the passages which I have just cited, and as " the spirit of self-sacrifice," of which Wordsworth speaks in the same poem, may suggest to generous and enthusiastic souls, any appeal for a fuller

---

[13] *Sittenlehre*, § 24 ; *Werke*, iv. p. 311 (Eng. tr. p. 326).
[14] *Ueber den Grund unseres Glaubens an eine göttliche Welt-regierung (Werke*, v. pp. 186 ff.).
[15] Wordsworth, *Ode to Duty.*

recognition of a claim for consideration on the part of what we should call the personal feelings of individuals were but a declension from the true standpoint of Reason, at which it is our privilege as *persons* to be able to take up our position, we could scarcely without shame allow ourselves to join in such an appeal. But we may with a good conscience so join, if we do it in the profound conviction that these ' personal feelings ' have themselves an intrinsic worth to which the rigorism of Kant and Fichte does not do full justice ; that it is this intrinsic worth of what is sacrificed to duty which makes the value of the sacrifice—as the hand cut off, the eye plucked out, in the Gospel saying,[16] are things not contemptible but most precious ; and that a Moral Order in which persons are sacrificed to what is itself impersonal is really robbed of that claim to reverence which only when envisaged as God, as a Being with whom persons can stand in personal relations, it can in full measure possess.

Moreover when we ask ourselves whether we could be content with the ideal which Fichte, while admitting it to be unattainable in any finite time,[17] confesses to be in his view the ideal to which our moral aspirations point, must we not hesitate to reply in the affirmative ? Must we not admit that the picture of a moral character which should be the mere embodiment of indifferent Reason would be unlovely and unvenerable ? Morality, though claiming to be the rule of *life* according to reason, when it is thus set in sharp opposition to all that is *personal*, tends itself to assume a strange resemblance to what we call *mechanism*. Now mechanism, though the work of Reason, is *merely* mechanical just because Reason does

---

[16] Mark ix. 43, 47.
[17] *Sittenlehre*, § 12 ; *Werke*, iv. p. 151 (Eng. tr. p. 157).

not any longer *live* in it, so that for any fresh initiative we should have to resort to a new act of Reason from without, and take the watch back to the watchmaker.

Thus, if it is the element of seeming irrationality in what is personal that makes it difficult, as we see from the example of Fichte, to attribute Personality to God, it is the absence from Reason, when divorced from Personality, of what makes Reason a possible object of religious reverence which excites our discontent with the representation of God as an *impersonal* Reason.

Now it is precisely because, as Fichte points out, Morality, conceived as he conceives it, implies an ideal proposed to a finite being which is yet unattainable in any finite time, that later thinkers have objected to Fichte's view of Morality as the essential feature of the supreme system of Reality. They hold the *absence of contradiction* to be our one criterion of the fitness of any features of our experience to persist unchanged as an element of that supreme system.[18]   And so in their view neither Morality, which, by the admission of its great champion, has a contradiction at its heart, nor yet Personality, which as the subject of Morality is always in Morality striving to be that which yet it cannot be without ceasing to be Personality, can assert a claim to final and ultimate reality.[19]

Such is the position taken up, for example, by Mr. Bosanquet. The Absolute of Mr. Bosanquet's philosophy may be said to be, like Fichte's, an order or system which determines the true mutual relations of all things, and therefore, among the rest, of all persons, but which is

[18] See Bradley, *Appearance and Reality*, p. 136 and *passim*; Bosanquet, *Individuality and Value*, p. 46 and *passim*.

[19] See Bradley, *Appearance and Reality*, p. 173 ; Bosanquet, *Value and Destiny*, pp. 136 ff.

not itself a person or persons. It differs from Fichte's in that it cannot be called a *moral* order ; since it is not in Morality that its true nature is most perfectly exhibited. The " proper name " of the principle or spirit of this system is, as Mr. Bosanquet tells us, ' non-contradiction.' [20] The name of a Moral Order might indeed seem to be a more inspiring designation for it than this negative and highly abstract phrase. But, on the other hand, it is easier to translate ' non-contradiction ' by Love than so to translate ' Morality ' which seems at first, as is shown by the interpretations placed by Kant and Fichte upon the Gospel precept to love one's neighbour, to leave no room for much that the word *Love* must naturally suggest. Thus Mr. Bosanquet can represent his philosophy of life as fundamentally the same with that of the great poet of mediæval Christendom. But though this identification, to which he often recurs, is plainly very near to Mr. Bosanquet's heart, I find it impossible not to think that there is really a wide difference between Dante's view of the world and his own, a difference which is very closely connected with the absence from Mr. Bosanquet's theology, if theology we may call it, of the notion of Divine Personality.

Mr. Bosanquet would probably regard the obvious unlikeness between the two as due rather to the use by Dante of a traditional phraseology and imagery which for us of the modern world has no longer the significance that it had for him, than to a real divergence in his own view from the fundamental convictions which found expression in the *Divine Comedy*.

I think myself that some of what Mr. Bosanquet would

[20] See a review by Mr. Bosanquet of Prof. Pringle Pattison's *Idea of God*, in *Mind* (October 1917).

thus consider to be unessential to the deepest meaning
of Dante belonged in fact to the substance of Dante's
faith, and that the failure to recognize this is the cause
of what I venture to regard as Mr. Bosanquet's mistake
respecting the relation of his own philosophy to the poet's.
But upon this I shall not dwell at present ; we shall find
ourselves returning to the subject later on in other connexions. For the present I am concerned only with
Mr. Bosanquet's account of the true system of Reality
which makes it more than a merely *moral* order, but which
still leaves it, though embracing persons and determining
those mutual relations in and through which they possess
their personality, yet itself without personality of its
own. And here I would call your attention to a remarkable passage in the Gifford Lectures on *The Principle of
Individuality and Value* which, unless I am greatly mistaken, reveals, as it were by accident, the defect in this
account. " We might "—so we find Mr. Bosanquet
saying—" compare the Absolute to . . . Dante's mind
as uttered in the *Divine Comedy*. . . . The whole poetic
experience is single and yet includes a world of space
and persons." [21]   Is it not clear that this analogy would
naturally lead up to the conception of a *personal* Absolute ?
For the mind of Dante to which the Absolute is here
compared is certainly a *personal* mind. No doubt it is
not fair to press too far an analogy admittedly introduced
only to illustrate a particular point. And so I will resist
the temptation to do more than ask whether in Dante's
introduction of himself among the characters of his
Comedy we may not find an analogue to that personal
intercourse with human souls which Religion ascribes
to God, but which it seems to philosophers of Mr. Bosan-

[21] *Individuality and Value*, p. xxxvii (in abstract of Lecture X).

quet's school impossible to ascribe to the Absolute, because human souls are included within the Absolute. And no doubt one would not have been tempted even to put this question if Mr. Bosanquet had happened to choose the mind of Shakespeare instead of the mind of Dante for his comparison. But in that case, too, the inclusive mind would still have been personal, although in none of his plays is Shakespeare himself a *dramatis persona.*

The denial of personality to the system within which we finite persons are included, not only as respects some particular aspect of our being, but wholly and throughout, wherein, to use familiar words, ' we live and move and have our being,' [22] in such accounts of its nature as we have just been reviewing, presupposes in truth that contrast or antithesis of Personality and Reason to the consideration of which this Lecture has been devoted. Just because the supreme system, which the authors of these accounts are endeavouring to describe, is to be the complete expression of Reason, it can *include* but cannot itself *possess* Personality. Reason is indeed the characteristic constituent of Personality ; but there is always in Personality something which falls short of the universality of Reason, and therefore it cannot without self-contradiction be ascribed to the *universal* Reason ; for so to ascribe it would be to speak in effect of a *particular universal.* Particulars must always be particulars *of* a universal ; but the universal itself is by definition not a particular.

On the other hand, a rejoinder may be made to this argument, and this rejoinder will presuppose the same antithesis as did the argument to which it is a reply. The thought of the universe as a whole, as a single system

[22] Acts xvii. 28.

wherein we " live and move and have our being," primarily presents itself, both in the history of mankind at
large and normally in that of the individual, as a *religious*
thought, and is associated with the characteristically
religious emotions of awe and reverence.[23] Such thinkers
as those I have instanced in this Lecture as denying
Personality to this Supreme System, Fichte and Mr.
Bosanquet, have certainly no intention of dissociating
these emotions from that thought. But I am not satisfied
that such dissociation is not in the long run inevitable,
unless our relation to the universe is conceived as essentially
of the same nature as our relation to a person ; and that
it is not in fact merely postponed by the circumstance
that the language in which the philosophers who deny
personality to the Absolute find themselves driven to
speak of it is permeated by the suggestion of that which
they explicitly deny.

It will no doubt be said that, when such thinkers deny
Personality to the Absolute, they do not intend to assimilate it to what is confessedly *less* than personal—for
example, to a force like electricity—but to emphasize
the necessity of regarding it as free from the limitations
of finite Personality, as *more* than personal. And I should
most certainly not hesitate to allow that, if we may
ascribe Personality to God, it must be only in a sense
which will admit of a great difference between what we
call Personality in ourselves and what, for want of a
better term, we call Personality in him. What, however,
I think even the most cautious maintainers of Divine
Personality must assert against such a critic of their
view as Mr. Bosanquet is the capacity of finite persons

[23] Cp. Royce, *Problem of Christianity*, ii. 8, and my *Group Theories
of Religion*, pp. 188 f.

for what can only be called a *personal* relation to the Supreme Reality—and therefore the presence in the Supreme Reality of whatever is necessary for the existence of such a relation thereto.

It will throw, unless I am mistaken, some light upon this matter if we inquire why the man in the street is disposed, if told of the idealism of Berkeley, to dismiss it with a kind of incredulous contempt as a visionary paradox, while a report of the speculations of physicists as to the electrical constitution of matter he is ready to receive with surprise indeed, but yet with respect. I think that this difference of attitude towards two doctrines which might at first sight seem to be equally subversive of ordinary preconceptions is to be thus explained. Berkeley seems to treat our everyday experience of a material world as an illusion, while the physicist is taken to be merely telling us that, while genuine enough as far as it goes, this same everyday experience has brought us but a very little way in the knowledge of what we are dealing with ; so that, if we knew more about it, we should find it to be something very different from what it strikes one as being at first sight. I am of course well aware that Berkeley insists that he is denying nothing to which the senses bear witness ; and on the other hand, I do not forget the difficult problems which may be propounded about the relation of the theories of physicists to the sensible facts on which they are supposed to be based. But I am now speaking only of the impression made by these two types of speculation upon the ordinary man on his first acquaintance with them. I do not think that it can be denied that it is on the whole such as I have described. It is then because, rightly or wrongly, Berkeley is thought to aim in his argument at proving that we are *mocked* in our deep-seated conviction of being constantly, as we say, ' up against ' a world of bodies which are *there*, independently of us, whether we are aware of them or not, while the physicists, without casting any doubt upon the reality of this world, do but concern themselves with the discovery of further facts about it, with which we have no particular business, that the teaching of the former is at once repudiated, but that of the latter accepted without demur.

This difference of attitude on the part of the ordinary man towards Berkeley and the physicists respectively in regard of the material world, may help us to understand a like difference of attitude on the part of the ordinary religious man toward two distinct kinds of theological speculation which agree in proclaiming the inadequacy of the anthropomorphic imagery implied in the common language of religious devotion. The ordinary religious man, at any rate among ourselves, is, one may say, perfectly willing to allow that the nature of God must infinitely transcend the reach of his understanding, and that any description he can give of it undoubtedly falls so far short of what it truly is, that from the standpoint of a fuller knowledge, it would seem scarcely to convey any information at all. Hence if, on other grounds, he is disposed to accept, for example, the doctrine of the Trinity set forth in the Athanasian Creed as authoritative, he will not be deterred from doing so and regarding it with veneration merely by the fact that it very likely conveys to his mind no distinct idea, or by inability to say what difference it would make to his conduct or to his religious feelings if he had never known it. But, if a view like Mr. Bosanquet's were put before him, I feel little doubt that he would interpret it as dissolving what he had taken for an experience of reciprocal intercourse, as with another person, between himself and God into *illusion*, and would regard it as leaving him no real God at all, just as the Berkeleian philosophy is commonly interpreted as leaving us no real material world at all. On the other hand, just as the physicist is taken, even where his speculations seem most remote from our everyday apprehension, to be merely telling us that the real material world is very different, when you come to know it better, from what it seems at first sight, so a theology like that of the Athanasian Creed may discover as many mysteries as it pleases in the nature of God so long as it does not deny that God is real, as a person is real with whom we may enjoy a reciprocal personal intercourse.

It is upon the possibility of this reciprocal intercourse that the whole question turns. A child will offer sweets from its pocket to an elder friend with the intent to give him the pleasure the like offer would give to the child himself. He may feel disappointed that his sweets are not appreciated, or baffled by the inexplicable pre-occupations which divert the attention of his elders from his own concerns; but, whatever momentary distress these things may cause, he is sure that he has to do with a real person, who, however strange his tastes and pursuits may be to the child's apprehension, can answer the child and understand him and perhaps care for him. It would be a very different thing if he came to find that there was not really any person there at all, that he was no more in communication with any one other than himself than when talking to himself and consciously 'making believe.'

So too, in the course of the religious development of our race, we may not only come to say ' No ' to the question

put by the prophet in God's name, ' Thinkest thou that
I will eat bull's flesh and drink the blood of goats ? '[24] but
may even doubt whether we can suppose that the thanks-
giving and vows which the Psalmist would have us offer
in their place will be accepted by God exactly as a mighty
king might accept them. Yet it is fallacious to infer
that because there is in one sense no limit to the process
in which we lay aside in turn every imaginary picture of
God as inadequate to his infinite perfection, therefore a
transformation which leaves no Being to whom we can
intelligibly ascribe a reciprocation of our personal address
to him is but a further extension of this same process.
There was after all a true instinct in the tradition which
saw in Spinoza, ' God intoxicated ' as he has been called
(and only a very unsympathetic reader of the last book of
his *Ethics* can deny his claim to the epithet), the great
standard-bearer of atheism. For when he said that,
while we could have an intellectual love of God and God
could love himself in our love of him, yet God could not
be said to love *us*, he did, after all, condemn the religious
man to the doom of Ixion, who found in his embrace not
a goddess but a cloud.

No, it will be replied, this similitude does not do justice
to those whom you are criticizing. Ixion's cloud lacked
all that made the goddess desirable ; but in the Absolute
Mr. Bosanquet would have us acknowledge all that piety
seeks in God and more. I do not know whether I am right
in detecting a certain distinction here between the views
of Mr. Bosanquet and Mr. Bradley. It appears to me
that on the whole Mr. Bosanquet, though holding that
to think of a God with whom we could be in personal
relations is to think of a merely finite being and not of

24 Psa. l. 13.

the Absolute, yet finds in the contemplation of the Absolute the satisfaction of his religious aspirations, while Mr. Bradley dwells rather on the thought that philosophy must recognize the God to whom religious devotion is directed to be not the Absolute but, like all else in our experience, an appearance of the Absolute. God, he would say, the object of religion, must be finite, and therefore cannot be the Absolute ; but Religion is a real experience ; there is an intercourse between oneself and God ; yet neither in oneself nor in God can one find ultimate reality ; both are appearances of that which is ultimately real, but it, the Absolute, transcends them both. We have here suggested to us the thought, which is urged upon us also by writers of a very different school to Mr. Bradley, of a ' finite God.' By recognizing that God is finite it has seemed to many that we can escape from the difficulties which came to light in considering the relations of Personality to the supreme system of Reality. God is a person, so that personal relations with him are possible ; but he is not the supreme system of Reality ; for he and we are alike included within it. It is to the consideration of this suggestion that I propose to devote my next Lecture.

LECTURE VI

THE DOCTRINE OF A FINITE GOD

THE subject of this Lecture was, it will be remembered, to be the conception—now so frequently in one shape or another brought to our notice—of a *finite* God, which it is sometimes thought will satisfy the claims at once of Religion and of Metaphysics. For a finite God, we are told, can be a person, in personal relations with ourselves ; but since he is admitted, as finite, not to be the Infinite and all-inclusive Reality to which philosophers have in recent times given the name of the Absolute, the difficulties of ascribing personality, with its implication of finitude, to the Absolute, which by definition is not finite, are at once removed. This conception appears, as I have said, in several forms. To one—which I may conveniently associate with the name of Mr. Bradley— I referred toward the close of my last Lecture. Here God is not the Absolute, but (like every separate object of experience) an *appearance* of that Reality which, when we speak of it not as it appears but as it is in its undivided harmonious unity, we call the Absolute. We may in the end find this the most intelligible form of the doctrine of a finite God ; but it is not the form of it which to most people the phrase would immediately suggest.

More familiar perhaps is a form of the doctrine in

which the all-inclusive Reality, however designated, is regarded as an aggregate of spiritual beings, fundamentally and ultimately distinct from one another, to one or more among whom is ascribed a vast superiority over the rest, which fits it (or them) to be worshipped by the rest. A single Supreme Being of this sort may even be considered—as by Dr. Rashdall, who has in several of his works [1] elaborated a view of this kind—as the original source from which all the other beings derive their existence. Such a God is said to be *finite*, as being limited both by the other beings who through his own will have come to coexist with him and also by the necessities of his own nature, which is described, after the analogy of what we call our own original and natural endowment, as something which he finds *given*, and as setting to his activity a bound which it cannot pass. Other writers—for instance Professor Howison [2]—would make the other beings beside God not merely coexistent but coeternal with him ; and here too we must, I think, suppose the world in which he and they coexist to have a nature of its own which determines that of the beings which it includes ; this nature could, however, not be described as the nature of that " firstborn among many brethren " [3] who is called God rather than as the nature of any other member of the universal society.

One of the most brilliant of contemporary novelists has lately presented to us [4] as a ' new religion,' challenging the allegiance of all who desire to prove themselves equal

[1] See *Personal Idealism*, pp. 369 ff. ; *Contentio Veritatis* (1902), pp. 34 ff. ; *Theory of Good and Evil*, ii. pp. 238 ff. ; *Philosophy and Religion* (1909), pp. 101 ff.
[2] *Limits of Evolution and other Essays*, p. 359.
[3] The phrase is used of Christ, Rom. viii. 29.
[4] In *God the Invisible King*, by Mr. H. G. Wells.

to the demands of our time, yet another version of the
doctrine of a finite God. The God of Mr. Wells is an
object of personal loyalty and devotion. He is also
in some sense, as the phrase goes, ' immanent ' in us,
and not merely another than we, standing in external
relations with us. But he is not the all-inclusive and
ultimate Reality. He is not one with that ' Veiled Being,'
nor does our knowledge of him throw any special light
upon its nature. There is a genuine religious experience
open to individual human beings of which this God is
the object ; but such experience has merely a racial not
a cosmic significance. I venture to think that the chief
interest of this latest Gospel lies not in its philosophical
value, nor even in its capacity of exerting a practical
influence on men's lives, but in the appeal of its author
to certain personal experiences of his own, as authenti-
cating the creed of which he has proclaimed himself the
apostle. I would therefore call attention to a fact of
some importance about these personal experiences as
described by Mr. Wells, which ought not to be overlooked
in passing judgment upon the doctrine which they are
alleged to support.

It is an essential feature of this doctrine that the God
whom it invites us to accept as our ' invisible king ' does
not in any way claim to be the author or indwelling Spirit
of Nature. But the book in which the new religion is
propounded is not, as it happens, the first in which its
prophet has related the personal experiences in which
his God revealed himself to his soul. They had already
been described in an earlier confession of the author's
faith, published under the title of *First and Last Things*.
But the account of them there given leaves no doubt
that Mr. Wells was then without suspicion that it was

any other being than the Spirit immanent in Nature with whom he had enjoyed communion. It is clearly only as the result of subsequent reflexion upon difficulties which (as he is well aware) are no novelties in the history of theology that he has come to hold a different opinion ; although it would seem that, by a common psychological illusion, his later judgment has coloured his memory of the original experiences.5 Mr. Wells is not unconscious of the kinship between his speculations and those of the thinkers of early Christian times who distinguished the Author of Nature as a being of wholly different character from the Author of the Gospel. In the light of his earlier record of the mystical experiences upon which he founds his belief, we may see in these experiences a confirmation of the contention which is the theme of Tertullian's great treatise against one of those thinkers—the celebrated Marcion—the contention that, whatever the difficulties of reconciling the moral attributes of God with the phenomena of nature, we can never consistently mean by God less than that being whose witness is, in words which I quoted in another connexion, in my first Lecture, *totum quod sumus et in quo sumus* : our whole selves and our whole environment.

I feel convinced that when once a stage of intellectual development has been reached at which the question of the relation of God to the Absolute would arise, no conception of God which takes him for less than the

---

5 See *First and Last Things* (1908), p. 50. In a revised edition of this work, published 1917, Mr. Wells adds the significant note : " So in 1908. Since then I have cleared up a certain confusion between God as the Master of the Scheme and God as the Presence in the Heart. That is the chief intellectual difference between this and its successor in 1917, *God the Invisible King.*" I had not seen this note when I wrote the words in the text.

ultimate Reality will satisfy the demands of the religious consciousness. And this is so because it is, I think, in principle true from the first that what men have sought in religion is always communication with that which is supposed or suspected to possess within itself the secret of our life and of our surroundings, and therefore to exert over us and them a mysterious power which we shall do well to enlist upon our side.

Wherever this hidden power may be conjectured by primitive men to reside—in whatever queer-shaped stone, or totem animal, or initiated wizard, or vanished founder of their tribal customs—it is dislodged from one abiding place after another as knowledge is increased and the horizon of the worshippers' interests widens, and at last we discover that it is after all nothing less than the ultimate Reality wherein " we live and move and have our being " [6] that we are inquiring ; this which we have been seeking throughout. Now it is, I suppose, precisely because in Religion we seek to place ourselves effectively in touch with what nevertheless must, it would seem, already include us within itself that a philosopher like Mr. Bradley can find in it a necessary and essential contradiction which forces us, when we apply to the criterion of non-contradiction, to regard it as, in the end, *appearance* only. The other forms of the doctrine of a ' finite God ' fail, I will venture to say, just because they abandon the attempt to identify God with the Absolute, and in so doing abandon the quest which *is* Religion. But what I have called Mr. Bradley's form of the doctrine invites a more detailed discussion, for here we find what we miss in the rest, a clear recognition that to abandon that quest must be in the long run the ruin of the

[6] Acts xvii. 28.

very thing which it is intended by this strategy of retreat to save from destruction at the hands of Philosophy.

It is indeed true that all genuine religion involves a paradox, even if we do not care to call it a contradiction. On the one hand religious worship is ever full of the insistence upon the vast distance between the divine majesty and the worshipper who humbles and prostrates himself before it ; and yet, on the other hand, it is of the essence of Religion that this vast distance is annihilated ; that the worshipper comes to live in God and God in him ; so that it is not to himself but to God in him that he attributes the acts wherein he expresses the life which through his religion he is thus enabled to live.

It is true also that it is not Mr. Bradley's intention by his formula that in Religion we have only Appearance to reduce Religion to an illusion. For in the language of his philosophy every object of experience is ' appearance,' so that it is in its appearances that the Absolute Reality lives, moves, and has its being. Religion can, I think, have no interest in maintaining that it can establish communication with a Reality which does not appear ; and certainly the Christian Religion, which is committed to the doctrine of a Logos, which was in the beginning with God, and was God,[7] cannot deny appearance to be essential to ultimate Reality.

Thus with Mr. Bradley's philosophy of Religion indeed, especially as it has found its latest expression in the chapter ' On God and the Absolute ' in his *Essays on Truth and Reality*, I should, for my own part at any rate, feel that I am in essential agreement. Nevertheless certain doubts of its complete adequacy remain in my mind. The nature of these will appear from some further

[7] John i. 1.

comments which I propose to offer upon it, in the course
of which I shall also point out what I take to be the relation
of Mr. Bradley's philosophy of religion to that of Mr.
Bosanquet. For, near to one another as these two eminent
thinkers are, not only in their general view of the world
but also in the terms which they employ in speaking of
the relation of Religion to the Absolute Experience, yet
I think that on a near inspection there will be found to
be between their respective attitudes toward Religion
an important difference which will repay our study.
These discussions will bring us to close quarters with
the antithesis of Divine Immanence and Divine Transcendence which has played a considerable part in recent
theology, and to which I promised in my first Lecture
that I would call attention.

I will begin the observations which I wish to make on
Mr. Bradley's philosophy of Religion by quoting the
following passage from the essay ' On God and the Absolute,' to which I have just referred.

"Whatever ideas," says Mr. Bradley, "really are
required in practice by the highest religion are true. In
my judgement their truth is not contradicted by metaphysics, so long only as they will not offer themselves
as satisfying our last intellectual demands. And exactly
how religious truths are to be in the end supplemented
and corrected, I would repeat that, as I understand the
matter, metaphysics cannot say. Within the outline
which it takes for real there is room for all truth and all
truth assuredly is completed. But the answer in concrete
detail is beyond the finite intellect, and is even beyond
any mere understanding." [8]

I do not think there is anything here said with which

---

[8] *Essays on Truth and Reality*, p. 433.

I should not agree. If any objection can be taken to Mr. Bradley's statement, it would not come, I take it, from the theologians who insist on what they call the ' personality of God ' as a religious truth, and whose position, in the context of the passage I have quoted, Mr. Bradley is criticizing. They would be probably in most cases quite willing to admit that in our most intimate communion with God our vision of him must still be proportioned to the measures of our creaturely nature, which, however highly exalted, must remain creaturely and other than the uncreated nature. They would, at least if they were Christian theologians, find no fault with the wonderful stanzas with which the *Paradise* of Dante ends ; yet whoever will place the words of Mr. Bradley which I have just quoted by the side of those stanzas will, I am convinced, be surprised to see how closely the thought of the philosopher echoes that of the great Christian poet :—

> Veder voleva, come si convenne
> L'imago al cerchiò, e come vi s'indova.[9]

In my third Lecture, when I was dealing with the history of the application of the word ' person ' to God, I showed that this application was first made in the theology of Catholic Christianity, wherein the personal communion with God which found expression in the recorded language of a historical person, Jesus Christ, was affirmed to belong to the eternal nature of the Supreme Being. This being so, the problem which Dante has in mind in the lines which I have just quoted, the problem traditionally known as that of the two natures in Christ, involves the problem which Mr. Bradley is considering in the passage

[9] *Parad.* xxxiii. 137–8.

I cited above. So far as the demand that God should
be 'personal' is a genuinely religious demand, it is the
demand for an assurance that the possibility of such a
relation to God as is exemplified in the Godward attitude
of Jesus is no vain dream, but is rooted in the fundamental structure of ultimate Reality.

Dante could not see what he wished without a flash
of supernatural illumination :—

> Ma non eran da ciò le propice penne
> Se non che la mia mente fu percossa
> Da un fulgore, in che sua voglia venne.[10]

So, too, Mr. Bradley ends his essay on God and the
Absolute with the confession that we need a new religion,
which philosophy has it not in its power to supply, though
he doubts whether any religious doctrine will be " able
in the end to meet our metaphysical requirement of
ultimate consistency." [11] What we want is "a religious
belief founded otherwise than on metaphysics, and a
metaphysics able in some sense to justify that creed."
Whether a 'new' religion is really required for such
justification of this demand, or only a more thorough
and courageous acceptance of an old one is a matter on
which much might be said, but which cannot be discussed
here : for apologetic is not the business of a Gifford
Lecturer.

I have already observed that there seems to me to be
a certain difference in the attitudes towards Religion
taken up by Mr. Bradley and Mr. Bosanquet respectively,
and have suggested that we should find it instructive to
note where it lies. Mr. Bosanquet does, unless I mis-

---

[10] *Parad.* xxxiii. 139-41.
[11] *Essays on Truth and Reality*, p. 446.

construe him greatly, conceive it possible to make the
Absolute the object of religious devotion. In this I
should so far be in sympathy with him that I should even
insist that the object of religious devotion cannot, when
once the question is raised, be held to be less than the
Ultimate Reality.[12] But Mr. Bradley seems to imply that,
not only for the less philosophical, but even for those
who share his own metaphysical convictions, there is still
room for an ' exoteric ' religion which may involve the
consciousness of a personal God. His words suggest
that the absence of a generally recognized religion which
might fill this place without being in flagrant contradiction with those convictions is to him a matter for regret.
How far I am right in interpreting his attitude thus I
am not sure. But should it turn out thus, then I should
find myself more in sympathy with his philosophy of
religion than with Mr. Bosanquet's, in so far as it
evinces a keener perception of the permanent and universal
value of elements in the religious consciousness, with
which it appears to Mr. Bosanquet, unless I greatly
mistake his meaning, comparatively easy to dispense ;
and consequently a greater sense of the grave loss which
may attend the inevitable depreciation of these in view
of their failure, in the judgment of both philosophers
alike, to satisfy the metaphysical test for admission to
a place in the system of ultimate truth. A kindred
difference between the two thinkers in their respective

[12] I do not know how far this impression may be due to the fact
mentioned by Mr. Bosanquet in the Preface to *Individuality and
Value* (p. vii) that in his first course of Gifford Lectures he has
not "sharply distinguished between God and the Absolute." But
I think that he could scarcely have found it possible to forbear
doing so were there not some truth in what I have said of his
attitude in the text.

attitudes toward the question of a future life will engage
our attention when I come, as I hope to come in my
second course of Lectures, to the consideration of that
question as part of the problem of finite personality.
According to Mr. Bradley the " belief in God as a
separate individual " seems to many (though not to all)
religious minds to be required for practical religion.
" Where truly that belief is so required," he says, " I
can accept it as justified and true ; but only if it is supplemented by other beliefs which really contradict it." [13]
With this statement, again, I should certainly have no
quarrel ; for I am sure that the consciousness of standing
in a personal relation towards God, however we may
picture it, is never, at any rate where it is the form of
a genuine experience, the consciousness of standing in
such a relation towards a ' separate ' individual. There
is ever present a sense at least of God's privity to the
thoughts and intents of our hearts which we could not
admit in the case of a truly ' separate individual ' as
tolerable, even if conceivable.[14]   In Mr. Bradley's treatment of the subject there sometimes seems to be too little
distinction drawn [15] between two contrasts : the contrast
of a ' personal God ' with the Absolute—that is, the ultimate
system of Reality, within which God and his worshipper
and everything else that is real must be embraced—and
the contrast of a God personally distinct from his worshipper with a God who is ' the indwelling Life and Mind
and the inspiring Love ' [16] both of the universe which he
makes and sustains and also of the finite soul.   But the

[13] See *Truth and Reality*, p. 436.
[14] See *Problems in the Relations of God and Man*, pp. 147–8.
[15] See, however, p. 436 *n*.
[16] *Truth and Reality*, p. 436.

two contrasts are not, I think, the same contrast, and should be discussed separately.

For of the former contrast it seems sufficient to say that in no religion that I know of is the nature of God held to be exhausted in a personal relation to his worshipper. Religion may demand that this relation be regarded not as merely figurative or illusory, but as real, and as no less real than the worshipper's own personality or than his personal relations with his fellow-men ; this, however, is not to say that there is in God nothing beyond his relations to us. Indeed, to suppose this would surely be highly unsatisfactory to the religious emotions, which, on the other hand, respond readily to that profound saying of Anselm [17] that God is not only that than which no greater can be conceived, but is also greater than anything which can be conceived.[18] " If I am forced to take reality," says Mr. Bradley, " as having . . . only one sense . . . nothing to me in this sense is real except the Universe as a whole : for I cannot take God as including

[17] *Proslogion*, c. 15.
[18] It is noteworthy that the traditional theology of Christendom has described God as *wholly* personal (for there is no God beside the three persons of the Trinity), but has not treated personality as the primary attribute of the Supreme Being. I do not think that it can be said of any standard expression of this theology, whatever be the case with certain modern Christian theologians, that it " takes personality as being the last word about the Universe " (see Bradley, *Truth and Reality*, p. 451). I venture to think that Mr. Bradley's observation about ' polytheism ' on p. 436 confirms a suspicion to which other passages in his writings have given occasion, that he has allowed a certain impatience to hinder him from doing justice to the real significance of the doctrine of the Trinity. I do not of course at all suggest that, had this not been so, he would have found it solve all difficulties ; and probably the inconsiderate assertions of certain theologians to this effect have had a powerful influence in deterring him from a more careful study of it.

or as equivalent to the whole Universe. . . . But if . . .
I am allowed to hold degrees in reality . . . God to me
is now so much more real than you or myself that to
compare God's reality with ours would be ridiculous." [19]
I will confess that, in the sense in which we may rightly
speak of degrees of reality, and of God's reality being
greater than yours or mine, I should not attribute a
higher degree of reality to the " Universe as a whole " than
to God ; for it is, as I take it, only in God that the Universe
is a whole.   I will content myself with saying that among
the ideas which (to quote Mr. Bradley) " are required
to satisfy the interest and claim " of the religious consciousness, and therefore must be true, I am compelled
to reckon that of the ultimate reality of its object ; but
that this does not for me mean that in the personal relation
to that object, which is another ' idea ' (if we are to use
this phraseology) required for the same purpose, we
apprehend the whole of its nature ; nor is it, I believe,
an ' idea ' in any way required by the religious consciousness that we do so apprehend it.

I pass to the other contrast, that between a ' separate
individual ' and an indwelling Spirit. As I said before,
this contrast seems to be insufficiently discriminated by
Mr. Bradley from that last mentioned. He does, indeed,
recognize that they are distinct by pointing out that
even a ' higher inclusive will ' than the will of an individual
human being, if it be one ' which can say " I " to itself,'
such as that of the State or of some vaster society (no
matter how vast we imagine it) must still be " finite." [20]
It seems to be implied in this remark that the Absolute
could not say ' I ' to itself ; no doubt because the Absolute
is not confronted by any thing that is not itself.   I have

[19] *Truth and Reality*, p. 448.   [20] Ibid., p. 436 *n*.

already reminded you [21] of Lotze's criticism of this implied view. My own criticism would take a somewhat different form, but I will reserve it till a later and more constructive stage of my argument. But certainly there is nothing in the incompatibility of 'personality' with absolute reality, even though we should admit this, which involves the incompatibility of 'personality' with what is nowadays often called 'immanence.' That there is an essential contradiction between the two I do not admit, and should appeal with confidence in support of my contention to the religious consciousness, which, so long as the nature of the absolute or ultimate Reality is reserved for the cognizance of metaphysics, Mr. Bradley admits to be in religious questions the final court of appeal. I do not think that in religion God is ever regarded as having a purely exclusive or separate personality; wherever he is regarded as a person, this is not felt to exclude his indwelling. I could call here as a witness Mr. Wells, who in his recent summons to thinking men to adopt his new religion, insists that its God must be a person without it ever occurring to him that this must exclude his indwelling in his worshippers. But I would prefer to point out that to no one who has been brought up to think of the Holy Spirit as a Person should it seem strange to regard the notion of a 'person' and that of an 'indwelling spirit' as mutually consistent.

Of course it is not only in religion that we find ourselves in a difficulty, if we attempt to regard the complete mutual exclusiveness of human souls " each in his hidden sphere of joy or woe " [22] as of the very essence of

[21] See supra, Lect. IV. p. 106.
[22] Keble, *Christian Year*, Twenty-fourth Sunday after Trinity:
    ' Each in his hidden sphere of joy or woe,
      Our hermit spirits dwell and range apart.'

personality. Nowhere is there a fuller consciousness of the Personality and of the distinction from one another of the persons concerned than there is in love. Yet just here, in proportion to the greatness and the depth of the love, such mutual exclusiveness is transcended and done away.

It would be of course absurd to suppose that this thought is unfamiliar to Mr. Bradley. Few philosophers have shown themselves more keenly alive to the lessons to be drawn from this region of experience. Never unregardful of the significance of poetry for metaphysic, he has lately told us that he finds himself " now taking more and more as literal fact " what he used in his youth " to admire and love as poetry." [23] It is not for lack of appreciation of the importance of the experiences of saint or lover that he would regard the paradox of those experiences as proving their failure to make good a claim to ultimate reality. It is rather because of that principle of his logic which has led him to call all ' relations ' unintelligible because they are relations and not something else. If one is not convinced by his reasoning upon that subject, one may venture also to deny that any inconsistency or contradiction is involved in saying that in Religion we have communion with a personality which is more perfect than our own, just because our personalities do not exclude it as the personality of any one of us excludes that of any other of our fellow-men.

The ' immanence ' of God, if we are to use this now familiar expression, is certainly a doctrine with which the religious consciousness cannot dispense. But the same is, to my mind, true of the complementary doctrine of his ' transcendence.' It is necessary, however, to

[23] *Truth and Reality*, p. 468 *n.*

scrutinize somewhat more closely the sense in which this term is used.

There is a transition of thought—and, as it seems to me, a fallacious transition of thought—in the philosophy of Herbert Spencer of which we are reminded by an unfortunate ambiguity sometimes to be found in discussions of Divine Transcendence.   Spencer starts, as is well known, from the position which is called Realism. He holds that the onus of proof lies upon any one who denies to physical objects a reality independent of any perception or consciousness of them by human or other minds.   But he ends by finding the ultimate and genuine reality of things to be unknowable by any mind whatsoever.   Here what begins by being ' outside of ' or ' external to ' our minds, in the sense of having an existence independently of our thinking or being aware of it, gradually slips into being ' out of mind ' in the sense which that expression bears in the proverbial phrase ' out of sight out of mind,' where it means in fact that we do not think of it at all.   But what is thus maintained at the end is just the reverse of what was maintained at the beginning.   The physical world is not an idea in our minds ; it is that which we perceive, of which we think.   Our perception, our consciousness gives itself out, so to speak, as perception and consciousness of a reality which, whether ultimately independent of mind or no, is at least independent of the act of perception or consciousness of it, since this act presupposes it. Such is the first position, the position of Realism.   On the other hand, according to the final position, that of Agnosticism as we may call it, the physical world is really something of which we can never be aware as it really is ; what we are aware of is always something else than what it really is ; for it is merely a ' phenomenon ' which, as it appears, is not independent of our consciousness.

I do not now propose to criticize the transition of thought here involved, but only to show that what is in principle the same transition has introduced a parallel difficulty into theology. When God's transcendence is opposed to his immanence, we sometimes begin by meaning merely that in our religion we have to do with something more than ideas or emotions of our own, which, whatever value or practical efficacy they may possess, are not ideas *of* anything or emotions excited *by* anything beyond our own individual or racial life. We intend to deny that, so far as we speak of a God or gods, we are merely *personifying* certain moods or emotions, as poets *personify* passions or virtues, to which they yet do not by any means intend us to ascribe an independent being like that of another real person, as real as ourselves. But we must be careful not to let *this* kind of transcendence pass over under our hands, as it were, into a transcendence which severs God altogether from the religious consciousness, in and through which alone we know him, and treats him as an unutterable mystery, of which we can say nothing that is true. A God thus transcendent has nothing to do with Religion. That sense of something beyond the reach of scientific knowledge, in which alone Herbert Spencer could recognize a legitimate form of religious consciousness,[24] can be called Religion at all only in virtue of that last rag of intelligibility which is left to the Unknowable, when we describe it as the ultimate ground of all that we can know, and are (doubtless in company with Spencer himself) stirred as

[24] See *First Principles*, cc. 2, 5 ; see esp. p. 113 ; *Ecclesiastical Institutions*, c. 16 ; see esp. pp. 841 ff.

we think of this by the characteristically religious emotion of solemn awe.

I said just now that only in and through the religious consciousness do we know God; and I think that a discussion of this phrase, the like of which is frequently to be found in the writings of Mr. Bradley, will assist us in defining the meaning of the transcendence which, if I am not mistaken, is always ascribed to God in Religion, and that even where God cannot be said to be conceived as personal.

Si magna licet componere parvis, I will here illustrate this matter of our knowledge of God from our knowledge of a poet or of a musical composer—of Shakespeare, for instance, or of Beethoven. Would it not be true to say that we could only know Shakespeare as a poet or Beethoven as a musician in and through our poetical or musical experience? Had we no appreciation for poetry, no ear for music, we could know nothing of Shakespeare as poet or of Beethoven as musician. We might know a number of facts about them—the dates of the chief events in their life, of the editions of their works, or what not—we might even be learned in their autographs or in their bibliography, but, if their poetry or music waked in us no emotions, we should still be strangers to the poet or the musician. Moreover, our knowledge of the poet or musician could never go beyond our appreciation of his work; for only by an æsthetic activity, secondary no doubt and stimulated in us from without, but still one which echoes, as it were, the mightier activity of the creative mind whose works we study, can we understand at all a work of art. Yet we know that this activity is not the primary activity of creation, that it is stimulated by and dimly echoes another; we can make

no mistake about that.   It is easy to make the application of the parable.   It is true to say that only in and
through a religious experience have we any knowledge
of God ; what are called ' arguments for the existence
of God ' will never prove to those who lack such an experience the existence of God, but only at most the need of
assuming, in order to account for our experiences other
than religious, a designing Mind, or a Necessary Being,
or an Absolute Reality.   But the religious experience is
ever an experience of a Reality distinct from and unex-
hausted in the experience as *mine*.   And where there is
religious experience present, the arguments which apart
from it prove the existence of something which is yet
not God are informed with a new significance.

No doubt here as elsewhere the parable will fail at
certain points.   The æsthetic activity by means of which
we appreciate a work of art, though stimulated by that
work, is initiated by ourselves in each particular case,
and not by the personality of the artist, the existence
of which is notwithstanding presupposed in the whole
process.   But, on the higher level of religious experience,
the initiation of our experience in every case is referred
to its object.   Thus, to take an example, St. Paul, when
he speaks of his converts as having known God, corrects
himself at once—" or rather are known of God." [25]   Again,
there are facts about Shakespeare and Beethoven which
may be said to have nothing to do with their art.   Not
only do such facts fail by themselves to help us towards
the knowledge of what the men to whom they relate are
as artists, but, if we know those men as artists through
appreciation of their art, this knowledge of them as artists
throws no light upon these facts, which yet no doubt

[25] Gal. iv. 9.

may come to be interesting as associated with men who have become so much to us in other ways. But, on the higher levels of Religion at any rate, we cannot regard anything as thus disconnected from God. To the religious man the experiences which cannot bring the irreligious to God are transfigured by his religion. The heavens, which the irreligious astronomer can sweep with his telescope and find no God there, are to the religious man telling his glory and showing his handiwork.[26] He may not be able to see God in all things, but he cannot but believe him to be there. The statement, in which recent philosophers of very various schools in this country have concurred, that ' God is not the Absolute ' must, I am sure, if seriously taken, make nonsense of Religion ; and the reasonings of Mr. Bradley, though they deserve, like all that comes from him, the greatest respect and attention, have not convinced me that a new religion could conceivably be found which could, if it knew itself to be the neighbour of a metaphysic that openly made that statement, live alongside of it on any terms but those of declared hostility.

So far as concerns the demand of the religious consciousness for an immanent God, a demand on the importance of which I am wholly at one with Mr. Bradley, I see nothing in this inconsistent with a demand for a God with whom we can stand in personal relations. I would express this latter demand thus rather than as a demand for a ' personal God.' For I do not think that Religion is concerned with the nature of the divine self-consciousness, except so far as this may be involved in the reality of our personal relations with God : so long as these are not regarded as figurative or illusory, we have no religious

[26] Psa, xix. 1.

interest in hesitating to confess without reserve that God's thoughts are not as our thoughts nor his ways as our ways.[27]

Again, I am convinced that Religion cannot, when once it has reached the stage at which the question has become intelligible, give any but an affirmative answer to the question whether God is the Absolute. I see no more, if also no less, difficulty in allowing that the Absolute may be the object of personal religious devotion than in allowing that the Absolute may be the object of metaphysical speculation ; and I should say that the existence of Religion (in some of its highest manifestations), and the existence of Philosophy prove that the Absolute can be, because it is, both the one and the other.

But, just because neither Religion nor Philosophy can consent to admit itself to be an illusion, both are bound to recognize that the activity in which the Absolute is known or worshipped is not and cannot be something which falls outside of the Absolute, for if it were this, the Absolute would not be the Absolute. Hence, philosophy can use in the person of Apollo those words of the hymn which Shelley puts into his mouth :—

I am the eye with which the universe
Beholds itself and knows itself divine.[28]

And Religion—even, and especially, that very religion by which the representation of divine worship as a personal relation has been most seriously taken—can find itself driven to recognize in the Spirit which expresses itself in the 'worshipper's personal love and devotion to

[27] Isa. lv. 8. See Bradley, *Truth and Reality*, p. 436 *n.*
[28] Shelley, *Hymn of Apollo.*

God as to a Father nothing less than an integral factor in the very life of God himself.

This is by no means, however, as perhaps has sometimes been too hastily assumed, an end of our difficulties. If our worship of God is regarded as a divine activity, where is there room for that sense of infinite distance between the worshipper and that which he worships which has no doubt predominated in certain forms of religion more than in others—I suppose that Islam stands especially for it among the great historical faiths—but which seems to have a place in all higher religion, and may give even to the profoundest consciousness of union with God its keenest poignancy, as the adoring soul measures by her own infinite unworthiness the infinite love of the divine Bridegroom, who has so joined her to himself that she and he are no more twain but one spirit ? [29]

I shall pass in the next Lecture to the consideration of the problem thus presented to us. We may call it the problem of Creation. For the term 'creation' calls up the thought of the origination by God of something outside of himself and of quite different nature ; it is just in virtue of this thought that it differs from other metaphors such as those of 'procreation' or 'emanation' which suggest rather a unity of substance between the produced and the producer. Is there, then, I shall go on next time to inquire, any reason for retaining the metaphor of 'creation,' as expressing something which the other metaphors do not express, but which needs expressing, or should we do well to discard it as a relic of anthropomorphic mythology, and one perhaps fraught with danger to a right estimate of our spiritual dignity ? It is to this problem that we must now turn.

[29] See 1 Cor. vi. 17.

LECTURE VII

THE PROBLEM OF CREATION

At the end of my last Lecture I said that our next subject would be the problem of Creation; not, however, the problem of the creation of the material universe, but that of the creation of spiritual beings. We were to ask whether the relation of our spirits to God is better described as *creation* or as *generation* or *emanation*. All such phrases, as used in this connection, of course involve metaphor; the question is which of these metaphors will best express what we want to express. The outstanding distinction is that between a metaphor which, like that of *creation*, lays stress on the *difference* of nature between God and our own spirits, whose relation to him is compared to the relation of a manufactured article to the craftsman who has fashioned it, and metaphors which suggest rather an *identity* of nature such as exists between the child and its parent, or the river and the spring from which it flows.

Scholasticism, meaning by this name the philosophy accepted by the Latin Church as providing a speculative background for her theology and a terminology in which she can approximately express it, has, I believe, been compendiously defined by one of its critics as the philosophy which denies the divinity of the human spirit.[1]

[1] I owe the knowledge of this epigram to Prof. J. A. Smith.

The intention of such a definition is of course to emphasize the difference between this way of thinking, which represents the activity of the ' finite spirit ' even at its highest and best as still to the end distinguishable from that of God, and a way of thinking which is concerned to insist rather upon the identity of human thought, so far as it is free from error, with the divine. This latter way of thinking may be conveniently illustrated by the doctrine of Malebranche that we ' see all things in God,' no less than by the absolute idealism of Hegel and others in more recent times ; although Malebranche would no doubt have subscribed to theological propositions for which the contrasted view, attributed above to Scholasticism, has usually been considered to afford a more congenial setting.

We have in the last Lecture criticized the position that recognition of divine *immanence* is inconsistent with recognition of divine *personality*. The stress laid by such representatives of idealism as I have just mentioned on the identity of our spiritual nature with the divine tends —though the tendency is not always prominent—to a denial not only of Divine Personality but of any sort of Divine Transcendence, except it be that of the part by the whole. I will take as an emphatic statement of this denial the following words of an eminent thinker of the present day, Signor Benedetto Croce. It is noteworthy that this writer finds the position of Hegel, with whose general view he is much in sympathy, unsatisfactory in that he has left an opening for an interpretation of his teaching which would make it lend support to faith in a God who should not be *merely* immanent in nature and man. " We can well think God," says Signor Croce, " in nature and man, *Deus in nobis et nos,* but certainly

not a God *outside* or *prior to* nature." [2] I am not sure
that the expressions ' outside ' and ' prior ' here, with
their implication that they express the only possible
alternatives to *Deus in nobis et nos*, do not beg certain
important questions ; but I will not dispute about this ;
I will only take the sentence, as I think it is meant, for
an uncompromising repudiation of Divine Transcendence
in any form, unless indeed it be merely in that of transcendence of the part by the whole. The Italian philosopher does not shrink from the consequences of such
a repudiation. For we find him expressly rejecting the
claim of Religion to stand by the side of Art, Philosophy,
Natural Science, and Mathematics as an independent and
permanent form of the theoretical activity of Spirit.
It is, he tells us, to be resolved into Philosophy [3] ; and
Signor Croce is at pains to make it clear that this means
for him something quite different from the resolution
of Philosophy into Religion.

This view of Religion as in fact a rudimentary form of
Philosophy certainly follows naturally enough from the
repudiation of divine transcendence. But it is as impossible for those who know from within what Religion is
to admit this view of it as it would be for a poet to see
in his art, or a mathematician in his science, an activity
which will have done its work when it has detached the
soul from absorption in sensual pleasures or the mind
from preoccupation with particular sensible objects and
so prepared the way for morality in the one case or for
metaphysics in the other. I am far from denying the

[2] *Saggio sullo Hegel* (ed. 1913), p. 137 (Eng. tr. p. 201).
[3] See *The Task of Logic* in Windelband and Ruge's *Encyclopædia of the Philosophical Sciences*, i. Eng. tr. pp. 210; cp. *Estetica*,
I. c. 8 (Eng. tr. p. 104).

intimate connexion of Religion with Philosophy. I should allow that it is normally in connection with Religion that the interest in Reality as a whole, which is the characteristic interest of Philosophy, first takes shape in the human mind.[4] I should hold also that this interest does not obtain its full satisfaction while there is not found in the whole that which Religion seeks there—that is to say, while Philosophy and Religion are at odds or at least not on terms of friendship with one another. But I should insist that there are data of religious experience which, while (like all data of experience) they are the concern of Philosophy, and cannot rightly be withdrawn from her criticism, have a distinctive and specific character, and cannot be adequately described as a symbolical or mythical representation of ideas which Philosophy—at any rate in that intimate and indissoluble union with History which is ascribed to it in Signor Croce's system—possesses more securely in a purer and truer form. Signor Croce is accustomed, like Mr. Bradley, to use language which suggests that it is especially the doctrine of a ' personal God ' which resists assimilation by Philosophy and must eventually be abandoned by any one honestly desirous of understanding the world in which he finds himself. But I venture to think that *all* Religion, and not only that which asserts or lays stress on Divine Personality, implies an object which is not *merely* immanent, though it certainly also implies one not *merely* transcendent, and must therefore reject the formula accepted by Signor Croce, *Deus in nobis et nos*, when explicitly offered as a sufficient description of that with which it has to do. It

---

[4] See Royce, *Problems of Christianity*, ii. 8, and my *Group Theories of Religion*, pp. 188 f. Cp. supra, Lect. V, p. 128 ; and infra, Lect. X, pp. 214 ff.

would be of course desperately untrue to history to deny
that faiths which, in our common way of speaking, may
be said to lack a 'personal God' are notwithstanding
fully entitled to be called forms of Religion. Yet, as
the third Lecture of this course will have shown, I am
disposed to regard the express affirmation of Personality
in God as something quite other than a survival of the
crude anthropomorphism of primitive religion. It is
rather the correlative, whether we call it the cause or the
effect or both at once, of a fuller development in the
believer of a sense of his own individual personality.
This is sometimes concealed from us by a misinterpre-
tation of the fact that in our part of the world it has often
been among the highest minds—great poets and great
philosophers—and among those of lesser calibre most
sensitive to the movement of thought around them—that
we observe a tendency to rebel against belief in Divine
Personality and to fall back upon a conception of the
Object of Religion from which this feature is eliminated.

This fact points to the danger which lies for religion
in a onesided development of an aspect the appearance
of which is itself a mark of progress. It will be, I think,
found that in India, where there has been less progress
in this direction, but where, on the other hand, the complementary sense of divine indwelling has been less thrust
aside by the impact of material interests, what may be
called advanced religious thought shows on the whole a
theistic bent. Thus we note in liberal movements origin-
ating among men bred in Hinduism a tendency towards
sympathetic approximation to Unitarian Christianity—
that is to say, to the very form of European religion
which, as we saw, is historically associated with the
doctrine not merely of Personality *in* God, but of the

Personality *of* God ; or, to put it another way, in which the ascription of Personality to God is not blurred or balanced (whichever may be thought the more appropriate word) by the confession of three Persons within the unity of the Divine Nature. There are of course other circumstances of a more external kind, which have favoured the approximation of which I have been speaking ; but I do not think my diagnosis of its deeper significance is wholly mistaken. And if it is not, it will confirm my previous statement that a certain tendency on the part of advanced religious thought in Europe to minimize the doctrine of Divine Personality is to be explained not so much by anything intellectually unsatisfying or unphilosophical about the doctrine itself as by the sense of a need for reaffirming other elements in Religion which are in danger of disappearance in the hurry and complexity of our civilization. Yet it may be in truth a no less urgent necessity of our spiritual well-being that in our religion the self-assertive individual personality in ourselves should shock and clash against another personality than that we should be able from time to time to go on leave, as it were, from the fighting line of our everyday life into the refreshment of a mystic reverie, where what makes up the greater part of our daily life is left behind and forgotten as though we had passed into another world.

The interest for our purpose of the thoughts suggested by Signor Croce's rejection of any transcendence in God other than the transcendence of the part by the whole, together with his consequent denial to Religion of any independent place in human life by the side of Philosophy, whereof it is, according to this view, no more than an immature form, has led us to stray somewhat aside,

11

though not, I hope, altogether unprofitably, from the main theme of my present Lecture, namely, the problem of the best metaphor—*creation*, *generation*, or *emanation*—to use in expressing the relation of our own spirits to the Divine Spirit. What has been said, however, may suffice to indicate the inadequacy of such a doctrine of God as Signor Croce gives us, which makes him *merely* immanent. We shall do violence to deep-seated instincts of our nature and deprive of significance a whole range of religious experience no less if we suppress that sense of a distinction of nature between God and ourselves which finds expression in the metaphor of ' creation ' than if we are deaf to those lofty claims and aspirations of the human spirit which find utterance in the counter affirmation of kinship with the Highest made in such words as that Greek poet's whom St. Paul is said to have quoted to the Athenians, "τοῦ γὰρ καὶ γένος ἐσμεν": " For we are also his offspring." 5

Now I think it may fairly be said that, of the metaphors which lie ready to our hand for expressing the relation of the Divine Spirit to ours, that of *creation* harmonizes best with the sense of a distinction of nature between ourselves and God, those of *generation* or *emanation* with the sense of a community of nature, a kinship, between us and him. Of the two latter *generation* would seem so far preferable to *emanation* for the purpose which either might serve, in that the latter suggests a process more wholly unconscious and involuntary than the former. We are thus left with two metaphors, *creation* and *generation*, and they seem both to be required in order to express the complex relation involved in our religious experience,

5 Acts xvii. 28.

A combination of the two, in which they are not merely used alternately with one another but an attempt is made to unite in an intelligible manner the two aspects of religious experience which they respectively express, is found in the doctrine of a *Mediator*, which, though it is more important in Christian theology than in that of any other religion, and certainly assumes in Christianity its most highly developed and probably its most defensible form, is yet by no means a doctrine peculiar to Christianity. While it is no doubt true that the identification with the Mediator of the historical Founder of that religion has powerfully contributed to keep the doctrine alive and effective in Christianity as it has not been kept alive or effective elsewhere, it is perfectly possible to maintain it apart from that identification. We may here recall Gibbon's celebrated gibe that the doctrine of the Logos was " B.C. 200 taught in the School of Alexandria, A.D. 97 revealed by the Apostle St. John "[6] and the often-quoted passage in Augustine's *Confessions* which tells how, before he had accepted Christianity, he had learned from the books of the Platonists the same doctrine as is contained in the Prologue to the Fourth Gospel concerning the divinity and the creative and illuminating agency of the Word, but did not find it there taught that " the Word was made flesh." [7] It is interesting to compare Coleridge's statement [8] that he held this doctrine philosophically " while in respect of revealed religion " he " remained a zealous Unitarian." These references, indeed, are all to Neo-Platonic speculation. But, though it is true that the use there made of the notion of a Mediator is more nearly akin than what can

---

[6] In the table of contents prefixed to the *Decline and Fall*.
[7] *Confess.* vii. 9.   [8] *Biog. Lit.* c. 10. (ed. Shawcross, i. p. 137).

elsewhere be found to the Christian dogma, over the presentation of which of course the speculations of the later Greek philosophy exerted no small influence, it would not be difficult to illustrate the notion from other quarters. Our present concern, however, is with the notion itself. In this way of expressing the matter, *identity* of nature with God, and therefore the metaphor of *sonship* which aims at suggesting this, is appropriated to the Mediator ; the *difference* of nature and the corresponding metaphor of *creatureship* to the individual human spirit. The relation of the Mediator to the individual human spirit may be said to be that of archetype.

The individual human spirit is conscious, especially, though not exclusively, in its religious experience of its *incompleteness* ; and it can only find satisfaction in a larger spiritual life than that which it can as an individual call its own. This larger spiritual life is at first that of a society, of which the individual feels himself to be a member ; but no function in a finite society can ultimately exhaust the infinite capacities of which he is aware in himself, and which he can only conceive to be fulfilled in the infinite and absolute life of God.

It is just in this point that St. Paul's conception of our membership in the body of Christ " in whom dwelleth all the fullness of the Godhead bodily," [9] goes beyond that contained in the exposition by Plato in his *Republic* [10] of the necessary identity of structure between the Soul and the State.[11] The principle there laid down by Plato, a principle, I am convinced, of fundamental importance, is restricted in its application by Plato's envisagement of the society which is the Soul writ large under the forms

[9] Col. ii. 9.   [10] See esp. *Rep.* ii. 368 c. ff. ; iv. 435 c. ff.
[11] Cf. *Problems in the Relations of God and Man*, pp. 227 foll.

of a Greek city-state. St. Paul, no doubt, in his turn
had his attention concentrated on the moral and religious
activities of the human spirit to the comparative neglect
of others. But the principle on which he was insisting,
rather indeed as a preacher than as a philosopher, with a
freer use of metaphor and much less of argument than we
find in Plato—the principle that the larger inclusive Spirit,
whose traits are seen, as it were, in miniature in those
of each human Soul, is no other than the one Divine Life
—this principle may rightly be regarded as the comple-
ment of Plato's, though indeed it is implicit in Plato's
requirement that the rulers of his state should behold
" all time and all existence " in the light of the one supreme
Idea, the Idea of the Good.[12]

But it is not this aspect of St. Paul's teaching about
the ' body of Christ,' in which it supplements the Platonic
doctrine of the identity of structure in Soul and State,
to which I now specially wish to call attention. To
this I shall return in my second course of Lectures, in
which I hope to deal with human personality in the light
of the theological conclusions reached in the present
series. The feature of the Pauline theory which primarily
concerns us now is its introduction of a Mediator. The
body of which those are figuratively described as
' members,' who do what in the apostle's judgment all
men are called upon to do—this body is called the body,
not of God, but of Christ. It is of course beyond question
that, in the view of St. Paul himself, it was of the very
essence of his message that the Christ of whom he speaks
had actually appeared as a man among men in the person
of his elder contemporary, Jesus of Nazareth. It was
in virtue of this fact, as he took it to be, that he had a

[12] See *Rep.* vi. 484B, 486A, 504D, ff.

gospel to preach, and not merely a theological theory to propound. But for the moment it is not our business to examine into the truth of Paul's belief in the exalted nature of Jesus ; we have to do at present only with the conception of the 'body of Christ' altogether apart from any doctrine of the Incarnation of the Mediator in a particular historical person.

The thought of St. Paul (and I am especially thinking of the *Epistle to the Colossians*, and taking it to be his) seems to be that though the larger and inclusive life in which that of any individual man or woman must find its completion is the life of God (and for St. Paul there can certainly be no more than one God), yet it can only find this completion in the divine life when that life is poured out, so to say, into a person who, while thus sharing the divine nature, is yet distinguishable from God. The distinction from God which Religion implies remains to the end ; but the difference of the created nature from the divine is transcended through the intimate union (symbolized by that of the members of a body with its head) with a Spirit essentially one with God, though distinguishable from him, the archetype of the created spirits, who obtain in their union with this Spirit what is described as a sonship, not, like that Spirit's own, by nature, but by adoption.[13] I think that this is a true account of St. Paul's meaning in its upshot, but it must of course be remembered that we are not here interested in the question, important enough in its own place, how far St Paul himself had thought out the issues of his own view. In the above analysis the subsequent dogmatic development of the Pauline speculations has been borne in mind, and on the other hand I have deliber-

[13] See Rom. viii. 15, Gal. iv. 5.

ately neglected their historical relationship to ideas which were current in the intellectual environment of the apostle himself, but have to a great extent lost their significance for us to-day. I do not, however, reckon among these obsolete ideas the doctrine of a Mediator. I consider it, on the contrary, a contribution of permanent value to our understanding of the nature of the spiritual world.

Two possible criticisms of this view may probably occur to my readers : one that to seek light from this doctrine is to fall back from Philosophy to Mythology ; the other that any doctrine of mediation, if seriously taken and consistently followed out, will break down, because involving us in a *regressus ad infinitum*.

In order to meet the former of these criticisms, it will be desirable to consider somewhat carefully what we mean by Mythology, and what service Mythology of any kind can render to philosophy. The latter criticism will be discussed afterwards. The question at present before us is not whether myths may not be used for what we may call rhetorical purposes in philosophical as well as in other kinds of literature ; for there can surely be no reason for debarring the philosophical writer from the employment of this kind of device on occasion ; but whether myths are ever, and if ever, under what conditions, the appropriate vehicle for philosophical reflection which could not be better expressed in some other form.

There is a celebrated observation of Aristotle [14] that the lover of myths is in a sense a lover of wisdom or philosopher : ὁ φιλόμυθος φιλόσοφός πώς ἐστιν. Another reading of this saying was formerly current, which ran

[14] *Metaph.* A. 982 b. 18.

thus : φιλόμυθος ὁ φιλόσοφός πώς ἐστιν : "The lover of wisdom is in a sense a lover of myths." There can be no doubt that the former reading is correct, and that Aristotle regarded Mythology as an immature form of Philosophy, wherein the same impulse to wonder which at a more advanced stage of intellectual development sought satisfaction in such speculations as his own contented itself with an infantine diet of marvellous stories. But the false reading, according to which the philosopher himself is still a lover of myths, though it does not agree with the context of this passage, may nevertheless bear a good meaning of its own. It was probably in a recollection of the myths of Plato that the misunderstanding of Aristotle's remark originated ; it might well seem natural enough that the pupil in philosophy of one who had interwoven so many immortal tales with his philosophic discourse should mention the love of tale-telling as characteristic of the philosopher.

What relation, we shall find it profitable to ask, did the myths of Plato bear to his philosophy ? I will ask you to allow me to state dogmatically the answer which I should be disposed to give to this question. I think that with him the myth is not concerned, strictly speaking, with the same subject-matter as Philosophy, but rather takes the place of History, where a historical question is asked, but the materials for an historical answer are lacking.

How did the world come into being ? How did society begin ? What will happen to our souls after death ? It is to such questions as these that Plato offers replies in the form of myths. Philosophy cannot answer such questions, any more than it can tell me where I dined this day last year or where I shall dine this day next year.

For an answer to the former of these two inquiries I should consult my personal memory or my journal ; and if I wished for information about something that happened before I was born, I should seek for it in the history books. But if what I want to know must have happened at a time whereof there is no record extant, what can I do ? The best I can do, says Plato, is to frame a myth, a story which, if not the truth, will at any rate be like the truth.[15] But this cannot merely mean that it is to be like what actually occurred, for *ex hypothesi* I do not know what did occur, and hence cannot tell what would be like it and what not.

What it means for Plato, however, is not doubtful. It means that the myth is to be in accord with those conclusions as to the general nature of things which I derive not from History but from Philosophy. Just as you could not tell me where and on what I dined this day last year, but could confidently assert that it was not in fairyland and not on nectar and ambrosia, so too we are sure that whatever took place in the unrecorded past must have been consistent with what we know to be the eternal nature of Reality ; whatever we have reason to think is incompatible with that eternal nature of Reality we have reason to think did not occur in the past and will not occur in the future. Thus when Socrates in Plato's *Republic* has to lay down a law for the stories of gods and godlike men which can be tolerated in his model State, he rules out all such as violate the philo-sophical axiom that only what is good can be divine.[16] Stories, on the other hand, which attribute good actions to the gods may be told, for such, though perhaps not true, are like the truth ; whatever was done by God must have

[15] See *Rep.* ii. 382D.   [16] See *Rep.* ii. 379 ff.

been good, whether it was just that particular good action or another. So, too, the myth of Er at the end of the same Dialogue is frankly fiction as to its details ; but it is, in Plato's judgment, ' like the truth ' in so far as it represents the good and evil in human characters as working out their consequences in a rise or fall respectively in the scale of being. That life is and always must be the scene of moral judgment, of this Plato is convinced ; and therefore if we would weave stories about the future which is hidden from us (perhaps for the reason that it is not yet made) we must not allow ourselves to suppose things governed by any other principle, or we shall assuredly be disappointed.

A philosophic myth, then, after the fashion of Plato, is a story told about individuals, where memory and history and prophecy (if such a thing there be) have failed us, so that we do not know from these, the only possible sources of information about individual facts in the past and future, what was or what will be the fate of the individuals about whom we are curious. It is a story thus which is quite likely to be untrue—nay, even quite unlikely to be true in detail, but which is in the Platonic phrase ' like the truth,' because it is controlled by our knowledge, obtained through Philosophy, of that fundamental nature of the universal system which any particular event falling within it must of necessity exemplify. It thus illustrates our philosophical knowledge without adding to it, and gives the outline of the historical fact, which is unknown in detail, because it belongs either to a forgotten past or to an unforeseen future (I do not here inquire whether the future can ever be foreseen) or again, to a present beyond our ken.

But, if this be a true account of the part played by

myths in the Platonic writings, there is another feature
of the myths actually found there which deserves our
attention. All the principal Platonic myths may be
said to relate to the Soul. Some concern the past or
future of particular souls—such are those in the *Phædrus*
and in the last book of the *Republic* ; while of others the
theme is the origin of the World Soul (as in the *Timæus*)
or (as in the *Protagoras* or in the third book of the
Republic) of the community, in which, as we may learn
from the second book of the latter Dialogue, we find writ
large the same story as is set forth in lesser characters
in the souls of its members.

Now why is it that the philosophical myth as employed
by the thinker who has made most use of it, and who is
also the greatest thinker that has ever made use of it,
is so closely associated with the Soul ?   We shall find that
the answer to this question will help us to see why we
should not be surprised to find a conception useful to us
in our present inquiry—such as that of a Mediator—
lending itself to illustration by a myth, and will also
perhaps throw some light on our main problem of
Personality.

The Greek word which we translate Soul, the word
$\psi v\chi\acute{\eta}$, is certainly not equivalent to Personality. It
has a much wider range of denotation, and is used of
life in plant and animal and of the universal Life which
' rolls through all things " [17] no less than of the intellectual and moral life of human beings.

At the same time it may, I think, be said that, so far as
regards Plato at any rate, it is to the human soul, to which
we should attribute personality, that he goes for his clue
to the nature of Soul elsewhere. We need not accept

[17] Wordsworth, *Tintern Abbey.*

too literally the account in the myth of Er of the rebirth
of human souls in the forms of those animals which ex-
hibit the qualities that had distinguished them in their
lives as men and women ; but I do not think we can be
wrong in taking it to hint at least at a fundamental kinship
between all forms of life, which will justify us in tracing
everywhere within the world of living beings the likeness
of what we know more intimately as it appears in our
fellow-men and in ourselves.[18]   And it is distinctly taught
in the *Philebus* [19] that, just as our outward frames are built
up out of elements which are found on a larger scale in
the world around us, whence the stuff whereof they are
made was originally taken and is during life constantly
replenished ; so also our reason testifies to the presence
of a vaster reason " in the nature of Zeus," the divine
Soul of the World, whence alone we can suppose ours to
derive its origin and maintenance.   Thus to say that all
the Platonic myths relate to the nature of the Soul is to
say that they relate to a nature which we know most
intimately in a personal form, and are thus almost constrained to construe elsewhere on the analogy of our own
personal life.

Moreover in Plato's philosophy it is Soul which is the
source of all motion, the active principle of the whole
cosmic process.[20]   The Idea or Form of the Good is indeed
the supreme principle of explanation, in the light of
which it is the aim of the philosopher to view all reality
as one harmonious system ; but it is in and through Soul
that this and all the Ideas, Forms, or eternal natures,
among which the Idea or Form of the Good is pre-eminent
as the sun among the lesser lights of heaven, initiate and

[18] Cp. Nettleship, *Lectures on Plato's Republic*, pp. 333, 364.
[19] See *Philebus*, 29A ff.   [20] See *Phædrus*, 245 D, E.

carry forward the creative process which is the history
of the world. Not that the Ideas are (to quote
Berkeley in his latest and most Platonic mood) " creatures
of the soul of man "—or, we may add, of any super-human
soul conceived on the analogy of the soul of man. Rather
they are, as the same philosopher goes on to tell us,
" innate and originally existent therein, not as an accident
in a substance, but as light to enlighten and as a guide to
govern "—" not figments of the mind, nor mere mixed
modes, nor yet abstract ideas in the modern sense, but
the most real beings, intellectual and unchangeable and
therefore more real than the fleeting, transient objects
of sense." [21]

I added just now to my quotation from Berkeley the
words ' nor of any superhuman soul conceived on the
analogy of the soul of man,' because I think it important
to remember that, if we find it unsatisfactory to regard
Goodness, Beauty, and Truth as ' mere ideas ' in our
modern sense, inhering in the mind, ' as an accident in
a substance,' it will not be less unsatisfactory to regard
them as ideas of this kind in God's mind, so far as we
take the Divine Mind to be related to its thoughts and
notions no otherwise than as our minds are related to
our thoughts and notions. This difficulty is recognized
by the scholastic theologians, who attempt to obviate
it by the help of their doctrine that whatsoever God is,
he is that not in virtue of a nature which he possesses
or in which he shares, but in his own right and, as it is
put, substantially. Thus Socrates may be wise and good,
but we could not say that he *is* wisdom and goodness,
only that he has some share of them. He may, indeed,
not always have been wise and good, he may not

[21] *Siris,* § 335.

always remain so, but wisdom and goodness are still what they are whether he or another order his ways according to them or not. On the other hand, when we call God wise and good we mean more than this. We mean that he is himself the wisdom and the goodness of which we are speaking ; there is no wisdom or goodness beyond him in which he shares. We cannot conceive him apart from wisdom or goodness, nor, if we believe in him at all, can we think of wisdom and goodness apart from him.

It is probable that Plato did not identify God with the Form or Idea of the Good, but rather regarded him as a Soul, informed by that Idea, which was the source of all the glorious order and harmony which we find in the universe ; but, as a great Platonic scholar, Professor Burnet of St. Andrews, has lately observed, it was in this distinction of Plato's between God and what was acknow- ledged to be the Highest, a distinction which the modern theist does not make (though Mr. Bradley, it is true, holds that he cannot become a philosopher without making it), that we must seek the principal source of those controversies which the Church Councils of the fourth century of our era were summoned to decide.[22] I feel myself convinced that the maintenance of the Platonic distinction can never prove in the long run satisfactory to the religious consciousness. The God whom we worship must be the Highest, must be what Plato called the Idea of the Good ; but this Good must not, as in the Platonic tradition (which Plotinus also followed), be something in its innermost nature above and beyond even the most exalted kind of Soul. The best Soul, the divine Spirit, which moves and works in the world, and is the source

[22] Burnet, *Greek Philosophy from Thales to Plato*, § 255, p. 337.

of what is good in the human souls, which derive their origin from it, must be essentially one with the Highest ; even in its innermost nature the Highest must possess that spiritual life of which our personality is but a faint and imperfect likeness.

I have been dwelling on the teaching of Plato respecting the Soul, since it was in speaking of the Soul that, as we saw, he found himself led to that use of myths in connexion with philosophical speculation which is so characteristic of his writings. But I should not have dwelt on that teaching at such length did I not in the main accept it and hold that he was right in recognizing the doctrine of the Soul as the meeting-point of the Universal and the Individual, of Philosophy and History, where therefore Philosophy requires to be reinforced by History, and therefore, failing genuine history, by Myth, which, as we have seen, is in Plato's view the surrogate of History, showing what the historical fact might have been, within the limits imposed by that eternal nature of things the outlines whereof Philosophy has ascertained.

Now this sphere, in which the philosophical myth is in place, is also the sphere of Religion. In teaching Greek philosophy one has often to bid one's pupils beware of allowing the religious associations of the word ' soul,' as employed in our everyday language, to confuse them in studying what the Greeks have to say of ψυχή. Nevertheless those very associations of the word ' soul ' with Religion, which may in certain circumstances prove misleading, have their roots in the fact that it is just in the experience which we call religious that we become most intimately aware of the nature of the Soul, as the meeting-point of the Universal contemplated by Philosophy with the Individual which is the subject-matter of History. In Religion we are not content (and I believe, though I cannot now go in detail into the reasons for my belief, some of which I have attempted to give elsewhere,[23] that this discontent is most strongly marked in the highest forms of Religion) to treat what is historical as a mere illustration of the universally valid, or again the universal as a mere abstraction from the historically real. Nor are we even content, with some who would do neither of these two things, to keep the eternal truth of Philosophy and the individual fact of History for ever apart, as the concave and the convex in the circumference of the circle are apart, never meeting though for ever inseparable. It is indeed possible to follow a distinguished philosopher of our own day, to whose sentiments on this subject I have already referred, and whom I had in mind in what I have just said, I mean Signor Benedetto Croce, in treating Religion on this very ground as no genuinely distinct form of spiritual activity but as a naïve confusion of the infinite with the finite, of the universal with the individual, from which Philosophy, in substituting itself for it, has withdrawn all reason for existing. But this view, which sees in Religion nothing but an imperfect and inferior kind of knowledge, does not, as I have already said, stand in need of refutation for any one who knows for himself from within what Religion is. It would be as idle to seek a valuable account of Religion from a man who does not know this, even though he be as acute a thinker as Signor Croce, as it would be to go for a theory of art to a certain person—an able and in some ways highly cultivated man—who professed himself unable to see what excellence could be attributed to portraiture

[23] See *Studies in the History of Natural Theology*, p. 30.

besides that of such a likeness to the original as we are
content to look for in a photograph.

It is, then, where we can least afford, while contemplating the universal form and nature of Reality, to
dispense with considering it in relation to the historical
and individual Reality whereof it is the form and nature,
that the philosophical myth may provisionally take the
place of a history which we have not at hand in memory
or on record. This will be where the Soul (which must
certainly here be personal Soul, for only personal Soul
can philosophize) is occupied in the task which was
prescribed to it long since by the Delphic oracle,[24] of
investigating its own nature. And not only in ancient
Greece, but here and everywhere, it is the influence of
Religion which most often drives us to undertake such
an investigation.

It is easy to see that a genuine ' revelation,' in that
legitimate sense of ' revelation ' in which it is used of the
historical and individual element in religious knowledge
as contrasted with the element which is rather philosophical and universal (for in another sense we must
acknowledge all religious truth to be a revelation),[25] would
render the device of a myth unnecessary here.[26]

I have dwelt so long upon the nature and function of
the philosophical myth because there can be no doubt
that the conception of a Mediator is one which certainly
lends itself to embodiment in such a myth and hence may
be too hastily dismissed as merely mythological.

It seemed, therefore, worth while to make an attempt
to show, by means of the discussions we have just

---

[24] Γνῶθι σεαυτόν.
[25] Cp. *Problems in the Relations of God and Man*, pp. 48, 58 ff.
[26] Cp. Plato, *Phædo*, 85D.

completed, that conceptions which call for a myth to bring out their significance for the life of individual souls are not to be ruled out of court in such an investigation as that upon which we are now engaged. What I understand by the doctrine of a Mediator, apart from any mythical elaboration, is this, that religious experience in its most complete form presupposes a twofold relation of the soul to God, to which the phraseology of that doctrine gives a more satisfactory expression than any other which we can find. We may most conveniently illustrate this by comparing that phraseology with other language that has been employed in describing the implications of the religious consciousness. To one factor in that consciousness, the sense of kinship with the Highest, the lofty language of Stoicism gives an utterance which may sometimes rise into sublimity ; but there is another mood which at least alternates with this in Religion, to which the unqualified claim to divinity which that language makes is repellent and even absurd. This mood sometimes takes its revenge even in Stoicism itself by intense and sometimes even morbid scorn of that side of humanity which is akin not to God but rather to the beasts that perish. On the other hand, there is a language of grovelling self-abasement in which this mood itself is found sometimes to pour itself out, which is no less repugnant to souls that cannot forget " that imperial palace whence " they " came " [27] and feel that servility does not become the " children of the Most High." [28]

Where the conception of a Mediator is introduced and the individual human being conceives himself as created by God through the instrumentality and in the likeness

[27] Wordsworth, *Ode on Intimations of Immortality.*
[28] Psa. lxxxii. 6

of the Mediator, and as adopted to be God's child, not in his own right, but only as united with the Mediator, who is God's Son by nature, it is possible to reconcile and combine the two religious moods of which we have spoken and which may be said to occupy the opposite poles of the religious consciousness. The consciousness of nothingness before God is justified as befitting the creature in the presence of the Creator, but is redeemed from servility and baseness by the consciousness of divine sonship ; while the unlovely pride which tends to spring up in one who holds, like the Stoics, that God has no advantage over the wise and good man except in his longer continuance,[29] is checked by the sense of devout gratitude for the free gift of adoption, both towards the Father who adopts, and towards the Son the Mediator, in and through whom the adoption takes place.

In all this, even if the play of imagination be not further encouraged, there is metaphor and even myth employed ; but the conception of our relation to God, in accordance with which the metaphors are selected and constructed, is one which (if I am not mistaken) satisfies better than any other which can be suggested the competing demands of the religious consciousness. Herein lies its justification as a religious doctrine ; and it is a sufficient justification. It is scarcely necessary to add that, if the interpretation put by the Christian Church on certain occurrences should be admitted, genuine history would then to a certain extent supersede myth in this case ; but it would be to a certain extent only, for it is obvious that, to use for the moment Christian phraseology, the pre-existent and the ascended life of Christ could not be

[29] See Seneca, *Ep.* lxxiii. § 13, *de Providentia*, i. § 5. Cp. Zeller, *Stoics, Epicureans, and Sceptics*, Eng. tr. p. 254.

described except in a mythical fashion. No doubt, as I have suggested above, the conviction that one is here availing oneself not merely of myth but of genuine history, has caused a conception by no means peculiar to Christian theology to persist in that theology with an intensity and practical efficacy to which it could scarcely otherwise have attained.

I shall dwell at far less length on the second objection which I mentioned earlier in this Lecture as brought against the notion of a Mediator, in addition to that of being mythological. This was the objection that if once we admit a mediator, we shall find ourselves committed to a *regressus ad infinitum*. I must reply to this that here, as in some other instances in which this objection has been alleged to be subversive of quite indispensable notions (I am thinking especially of Mr. Bradley's criticism of Relations) [30] it will prove on closer inspection to be an unsubstantial phantom. Where there is a significance in mediation between two terms which cannot be found in any further mediation between the mediating term and either of the extremes there is nothing to drive one to continue mediation *ad infinitum* ; and in this present instance this would seem to be the case. The conception of a Mediator corresponds, if there be anything in what I have just put before you, to a genuine demand of the religious consciousness, which does not repeat itself *ad infinitum*. I am of course aware that there are certain facts in the history of Christian dogma which might appear to contradict this assertion. Into the detailed consideration of these I cannot now go, but must content myself with the following observations. In the case of some of these we have to do with fallacious subtleties

[30] *Appearance and Reality*, c. 3.

corresponding in the sphere of religious speculation and devotion to the subtleties which in logic have sometimes arisen from the vain attempts to explain indispensable conceptions in terms of something else. In the case of others, again, I should admit that there may be and certainly is mediation elsewhere in the religious life than in the fundamental relation of the soul to God (for example, the truth about this or any other matter may be communicated to one man by another), but that here again in these genuine cases of mediation there is no need whatever to proceed *ad infinitum*.

The doctrine of a Mediator has, then, supplied us with a means of uniting the thoughts which were respectively symbolized by the metaphors of *creation* and of *generation* as descriptions of the origin of our spirits from God. In their separateness and in their actual finitude they are creatures of God and not sharers in his nature ; but in their totality and ideal completeness, in their archetype (as we may say), they are sharers in it, they are ' begotten of God,' [31] and in their historical development, through an identification of themselves with the archetype which comes to pass in time (and which need not always take the form of an explicit acceptance of such a formula as we may find the best for expressing the facts), they become conscious of their divine nature as belonging to them not in their own right but as mediated through their archetype. Every soul which thus becomes conscious of her divine nature at all will express it in terms which, at least in part, may be called mythological. But we must remember that what we find taught in these matters in the writings of thinkers who avoid obviously mythological language very often differs from the teaching

[31] 1 John v, 18.

which we find in religious creeds not by being less mythological but only in being more prosaic.

The description and mutual reconciliation of those facts of religious experience which I have described as at first sight mutually inconsistent and so requiring to be harmonized by the help of this conception of a Mediator will, I think, be found to involve, when worked out into a theological doctrine, the recognition of a twofold Personality in the Divine Nature. For we have to express a consciousness of personal communion with God felt on the one hand to be a communion of spirit with kindred spirit, of Son with Father, and yet on the other to belong as such not to the individual in isolation and imperfection, but in the ideal and archetype of his nature, as completed in a society of which he may be a member not only in respect of a part of his capacities but of his whole being. Here the personal communion itself, as belonging to the true nature of God—and in nothing less than this can the aspiration of the religious consciousness find satisfaction—implies a personal distinction within that nature ; while the individual further distinguishes his own separate and imperfect personality from the ideal personality which is thought of as eternally distinguishing itself from God in the communion which is the consummation of the religious life. No doubt such a belief as that of Christianity in the incarnation of this ideal personality, this divine Logos or Mediator, in the historical Jesus, if it introduces certain not inconsiderable difficulties of its own, also gives to these thoughts a content on which the mind and heart can feed, which is lacking while they remain in the region of speculation or are associated with figures purely imaginary, or again with spiritual realities which do not possess full personality, such as a

Nation, a Church, or a Law. It is thus easily explicable
that the doctrine of a Mediator should be more prominent
in Christianity than elsewhere, and might easily be mistaken for a mere inference from a certain interpretation
of historical facts which cannot here be assumed. But
in truth it is, as was said before, a doctrine which may
appear, and has appeared, in contexts other than Christian ;
while it must not be forgotten that Christianity itself,
in its identification of the Logos or Mediator with Jesus,
sees in his earthly life as a man among men no more than
one stage of the manifestation of the Son of God, who is
known by his Church in her theology and her worship
" not after the flesh " [32] but after the spirit as risen and
ascended and as the head of his ' mystical body,' the
ideal society of redeemed Humanity.

So far, in distinguishing the individual soul from that
in which it seeks completion, and which may be described
in religious language as the eternal Son of God, I have
spoken merely of the individual soul as imperfect, not
as *evil* or *sinful*. The consciousness of Sin introduces a
new complication of our problem. For the existence of
evil, and in particular of moral evil or sin, is held by some
to be the greatest of all difficulties in admitting the presence
of Personality in God, by others as a proof that God must
be distinguished from the Absolute. To the consideration of this most difficult topic I shall turn in my next
Lecture.

[32] 2 Cor. v. 16.

LECTURE VIII

THE PROBLEM OF SIN

AT the end of the last Lecture we found ourselves confronted with the fact of our consciousness of *Sin*, which seems to make it impossible to regard our souls as differing from the divine Spirit merely as parts differ from the whole, or even as the lower grades of one nature differ from the higher. Even the metaphor of *Creation*, which was invoked to express one pole of our religious consciousness, is not entirely adequate to describe the sense of alienation from God which we call the consciousness of *Sin*. We are, in the phraseology of Christian theology, not creatures only, but fallen creatures. There is that in us which cries out not merely for improvement and completion but for correction and forgiveness. This consciousness of Sin may not be, and is not, equally vivid in all men, or at all times, or under all circumstances. It may be intensified and fostered by a tradition which makes much account of it, weakened and discouraged by one which ignores it. But no one who has really known it can be content with theories which confound it with the consciousness of incompleteness or finitude, such as may be present where there is no thought of self-reproach, and where to entreat forgiveness for our lack

184

of what it in no way behoves us to possess would seem inappropriate and absurd.

This distinction between the consciousness of Sin and that of incompleteness or finitude is not to be treated as negligible because there is a possibility of mistaking even in ourselves particular instances of mere incompleteness for instances of Sin and particular instances of Sin for instances of mere incompleteness. We can distinguish blue from green well enough, although we may sometimes be in doubt whether a particular shade of colour is green or blue.

It is by no means my purpose in this Lecture to enter upon a general discussion of that which Carlyle has called [1] " a vain interminable controversy touching what is at present called Origin of Evil," a controversy which, as he adds, " arises in every soul since the beginning of the world ; and in every soul that would pass from idle Suffering into actual Endeavouring must first be put an end to." I am only concerned here with the question of the bearing which the consciousness of Sin, of moral evil, in ourselves may be thought to have upon the conception of Divine Personality.

As I hinted at the end of my last Lecture, it may be argued in two ways from two opposite points of view that this consciousness is not really compatible with the recognition of Personality in the infinite and absolute Being. This is contended in one way by those who would deny Personality to the Supreme Being, in another by those who attribute Personality to the God of Religion, but refuse to identify the God of Religion with the Absolute or Ultimate Reality.

I will first call your attention to the former way of

[1] *Sartor Resartus*, ii, 9,

stating the difficulty and ask you to examine the supposed incompatibility of the existence of Evil with the affirmation of Personality in a Being who is conceived to be the Cause of the Universe.

There is no doubt that, in the ordinary course of events, if something has taken place which we think ought not to have happened, and it seems probable that it is due to human activity, we ask : ' Who is to blame for this ? ' This would be our first question did we find a corpse with marks indicating that death was due to violence. If, however, on further investigation it is found that the cause of death was not a murderous assault by a human being but a stroke of lightning, we cease to inquire who is to blame. There was in that case no *personal* agency concerned in bringing about the sad occurrence ; and with the elimination of *personality* there is eliminated also all possibility of praise or censure. If death from lightning could be considered as in literal fact what it is called in the language of English law, an ' act of God,' moral predicates would become applicable to it, and, the world being such as we find it, if the whole course of events is to be attributed to a person or persons, we must, it is said, consider that person or those persons as deficient either in goodness or in power. But if we refuse to suppose personal agency concerned at all in the production of that great majority of events which cannot be referred to human volitions, we get rid (so it is sometimes supposed) of any need to assign *blame* for the presence of Evil in the universe at all ; and the controversy about the origin of Evil falls to the ground.

I question, however, whether we are not here in danger of slipping into the very common error of taking for granted that an argument valid within a restricted field must of necessity be no less valid when extended to the whole universe of reality. For the purpose of the coroner's jury it is sufficient to have ascertained that a person found dead was not killed by any one within the jurisdiction of the law of the land ; so that, even though the death were undoubtedly due to human agency, it may no further concern the law, if that agency—suppose it that of a belligerent enemy—is uncontrollable by any power at the disposition of the court. Hence we see ' the act of God and of the King's enemies ' often coupled together in legal documents. The judicial chronicler or historian has a less restricted range ; his judgment is not limited by a jurisdiction, and he will appraise human agency wherever it is found. But where he finds none such— where an event is traceable to the activity of irrational animals or to the forces of inanimate nature—there he recognizes a limit to his function of distributing praise or blame. Yet this no more debars a further question arising about these events, if there be reason to think a personality other than human to be concerned in their production, than the necessary silence of the law of any country respecting the responsibility of that country's enemies for their acts of war renders those acts immune from moral censure.

And, do what we will, such further questions must inevitably arise. We may be rightly on our guard against transferring in a naïve and uncritical fashion predicates applicable to members of a society of human beings to the ultimate Ground of all existence. But in the long run we cannot avoid the question of the significance to be assigned to our moral consciousness in the formation of our general view of the world. It has been an unfortunate circumstance that what is known as Kant's moral argument [2] for the existence of God—upon which that philosopher relied as a sufficient basis for Religion after the overthrow of the old metaphysical proofs which he believed himself to have brought about by the discussions in his *Critique of Pure Reason*—was expressed by him in an awkward and unimpressive form which has led to less than justice being done to the thought which underlies it. No one of course has insisted more strongly than Kant that absolute disinterestedness is the very hall mark of genuine morality ; and when we find him going on to contend that there must be a Moral Governor of the Universe to award happiness to the virtue which deserves it, it is easy to think that he has fallen, perhaps in consequence of a timid deference to established tradition, from the height of his great argument to the level of a crude theological utilitarianism like that of Paley. But in fact the more we emphasize the independence of the moral consciousness upon considerations of private advantage, the more we exalt the " manifest authority " (to use Butler's famous phrase [3]) of the Law which speaks in us by the voice of conscience, the more difficult is it to find intellectual satisfaction in regarding that voice as one crying in the wilderness of an alien world, whose course is in continual contradiction with what we should expect in a realm wherein its authority should be recognized and obeyed.

We may appreciate to the full the heroic temper which inspired Huxley's doctrine of ' ethics ' as running counter to ' evolution,' [4] and which has since found eloquent

[2] See *Kritik der praktischen Vernunft* I. Th. II. B. II. Hpts. V. (*Werke*, ed. Hart. v. pp. 130 ff.) ; *Kritik der Urteilskraft*, § 87 (*Werke*, ed. Hart. v. pp. 461 ff.).

[3] *Second Sermon on Human Nature.*

[4] In his Romanes Lecture on *Evolution and Ethics.*

utterance in Mr. Bertrand Russell's description of the
" free man's worship." 5 Who can but admire the spirit
of men who thus resolve, like Louis Stevenson's " old
rover with his axe " 6 to enlist in defence of a cause acknowledged to be noble with clear foresight of its inevitable
defeat ? We may even acknowledge that perhaps only
by means of such Promethean defiance of the powers
that be could Religion be purified from the spirit of the
facile—one may even say the smug—acquiescence in the
arrangements of Divine Providence which had characterized much of the popular and some of the philosophical
theology of an age against which we are still in revolt,
though its heyday is now long past. But surely we
must yet admit that a world which can produce a hunger
and thirst after righteousness and yet nowhere contain
the means of satisfying them is a world fundamentally
incoherent and irrational. If, then, we pass a moral
judgment upon the world to the extent of seeking a solution
of the problem of the existence of Evil therein, we are
not merely carrying out the consequences of a previous
assumption, which we need not have made, that the Cause·
of all things is personal and so liable to be judged as such.
We are asking a question we must needs have asked
even though that assumption had not been made at all.
Thus I do not think that we can get rid of the burden of
the problem of the existence of Evil, especially of moral
evil or Sin, simply by denying personality to the Supreme
Being.

If this be our conclusion, and if our religious experience
be found to imply as its foundation a personal relation

5 Reprinted in his *Philosophical Essays* (1910) and in *Mysticism
and Logic* (1918).
6 In his Fable of ' Faith, Half-Faith, and No Faith at all.'

to God, we may perhaps be led to think that a view which
gives due recognition to this relation is so far from especially finding the existence of Evil a stumbling-block that,
if it imparts to the sense of Sin a peculiar poignancy, it
also provides it with a more intelligible setting than any
other view. The whole cycle of ideas which we connect
with such words as Probation, Judgment, Atonement,
Repentance, Forgiveness, may perhaps be expressed
in terms which avoid the acknowledgment of a personal
relation between the individual sinner and that (however
we may describe it) by which he is tested and put in his
place, with which he may know himself to be in harmony
or out of harmony, and upon whose resources he must
draw for any recovery or improvement. But they will
gain infinitely in significance, will strike home with a
vastly increased sense of reality, when they are translated
into the language of a personal relation to a Spirit wherein
" we live and move and have our being,"[7] and yet in the
drama of our existence distinguish ourselves from it, in
order to be able to unite ourselves again with it by an
act of free and voluntary self-surrender. The *possibility*
of Sin is after all involved in freedom to choose the good ;
and it would seem meaningless to find a new problem in
the *reality* of what is already understood to be in a true
sense *possible*.

To avoid any misunderstanding, I would here repeat
that I am only attempting to meet the objection to the
admission of Personality in God which is drawn from the
existence of moral evil. I am not pretending to discuss
the whole problem of Evil ; and I am quite well aware of
many points in what I have just said on which the critics
might join issue with me. Thus one critic might challenge

7 Acts, xvii. 28.

my reference to freedom as begging the question so long debated between the partisans of Liberty and Necessity ; another my assumption that the sense of Sin is not an irrational survival of primitive superstition, altogether without the value in the interpretation of Reality which I have attributed to it. Others, again, might dispute my right to take for granted that even in the ultimate Reality, in the Absolute, the discords and seeming contradictions of the world of appearance are laid to rest ; while, on the other hand, the followers of Mr. Bradley or Mr. Bosanquet might contend that I had overlooked the failure of Morality, when tried by the criterion of ' noncontradiction,' [8] to make good a claim to ultimate reality.

In reply to such strictures I can only say at present that I am by no means insensible to the importance of these various issues which I may seem to have left on one side ; where I have by implication taken a side in any one of them, it is because I conceive that side to have the better arguments in its favour ; and further, that I do not think that a different judgment upon these matters, while it might well have altered my view of the importance of the whole question, would have affected the special point at issue. That point is merely this : that the recognition of Personality in God harmonizes better than any other conception of the Supreme Reality with the experience for which the problem of Evil reveals itself in its acutest form, namely with the experience which may be described as that of ' conviction of Sin.'

We may now turn to the other way in which the same question we have just been examining may be expressed from an opposite point of view by those who, holding to Divine Personality, think that in the existence of Evil,

[8] See above, Lecture V. p. 125.

and in particular of moral evil, they have the strongest possible argument for distinguishing God, the object of Religion, from the Absolute, the all-comprehending Reality. Only thus, they think, can God be relieved of responsibility for the evil in the world ; and only if he be relieved of that responsibility can he be a possible object of our unqualified reverence. This, however, he may be, if he be not the all-comprehending Being, but a Being comprehended in one universe along with other beings of whose existence either he is not the cause at all, or, if he is the cause of it, is so only under conditions due to a necessity to which he himself is subject, and to the limitations imposed by which he must perforce submit. He is, on this showing, not a Being of boundless power ; but he may be a Being of boundless benevolence. Only the effects of his benevolence are determined within certain bounds by the eternal nature of things, himself included.

To this way of thinking, however, there appears to me to be one fatal objection. It relieves God of the responsibility for the evil in the world only at the cost of depriving him of Godhead. I do not say that such a Being as the champions of this view describe under the name of God would not be a Being whom we could venerate, with the veneration which we pay to the saints and heroes of our race, though, if you will, indefinitely increased. But what he would not be, is what, when once we have come to mean no less than this by God, we cannot, I feel sure, cease to demand in whatever is offered to us under that name. He would not be, in a word, the ' Supreme Being.' He would not be, so to put it, at the back of everything. There would be for him as for us a mysterious background. It seems to me a point in which the theology of Mr. Wells's ' new religion ' has an advantage over that of some who agree with him in affirming their God to be finite, while demurring to his distinction of God from what he calls the ' Veiled Being,' that it recognizes this consequence of the view in which he and they are at one.

The dogmas of no religion are to be taken by us here as authoritative. But religious dogmas may prove suggestive to us, just as do other speculations which have appeared in the course of the history of thought upon these subjects. And so it may be worth pointing out that, in affirming the bond of unity between all who share mediately or immediately in the Divine Life to be a Spirit not independent of, but ' proceeding from ' both Father and Son, a Spirit whose concrete reality is neither greater nor less than that of those from whom it proceeds (so that it is called a *person* just as they are), the Christian Church has decidedly taken up a position adverse to the view which sets God against the background of a necessity which limits from without, as it were, the eternal process of love wherein the Divine Life is conceived by the Christian religion to consist.

What I have attempted to show in these last observations is that the existence of Evil, though it must always present itself as a problem for the Philosophy of Religion, does not, as is urged from two opposite quarters, so especially affect the acknowledgment of Personality in God as to put us to a choice between denying to God either personality or that ' infinity ' (if we are so to call it) without which, unless I am completely mistaken, he cannot really be at all what a philosophically cultivated theology can mean by God. But we have still to ask ourselves whether the consciousness of Sin in ourselves must modify that conception of the relation between

13

our spirits and the divine Spirit which we saw reason in the last Lecture for adopting, and, if it must, then in what way.

A young English theologian, Mr. Oliver Quick, has lately dwelt in an interesting manner upon the important fact that the problem of Sin cannot satisfactorily be treated by sinners as a merely speculative problem.[9] In so far as we are not concerned to fight against Sin and overcome it we are not really conscious of it *as sin*. We are only conscious of a certain kind of action, which, under certain circumstances, done thus, here, now, and so forth, is sinful, but under other circumstances would be nothing of the kind. This is a fact well worth bearing in mind, when we approach the question how our spirits, conscious as they are of sin, can be taken up into the divine life, and share in that intercourse of love the presence of which therein we hold to be presupposed in the personal relation to God whereof we have experience in religion. We are all familiar with a solution of this problem expressed in the form of a myth (if we are to call that notion of a Mediator, the value of which we saw in the last Lecture, by this name of ' myth,' remembering, as we use that word, the dignity of its Platonic associations rather than the common custom of contrasting it with the ' truth '). The mediator may be viewed not merely as the Perfecter but also as the Redeemer ; and the religious spirit may be led to a satisfaction in the whole process which can find utterance in those bold words of the famous hymn for Easter Eve :—

O felix culpa, quæ tantum et talem meruit habere Redemptorem.

It is not altogether surprising that to some there has

[9] *Essays in Orthodoxy,* p. 78 ff.

seemed to be an utter incompatibility between a genuine
sense of the evil of Sin and the contemplation, suggested
by those words, of such a transcendence of sin as to
permit of satisfaction in its mediation of an ultimate
good higher than without it could (for what we know)
have been attained. On this subject, however, I will
not dwell further, except to point out that (as I have
elsewhere tried to show [10]) the thought implied in the
hymn which I have just quoted should not really lead,
as its critics would doubtless insist that it is logically
bound to lead, to regarding sin as no sin. For since sin
can only be done away by atonement, and the indispensable
condition of an effective atonement is repentance, there is
no room for the antinomian attitude, as we may call it,
in which one could say ' Let us do evil that good may
come ; ' [11] an attitude which might attempt to justify
itself by an appeal to the sentiment of the apostrophe
O felix culpa ! Only through repentance can a sinful
will pass into a good will : and " the repentance which a
man could intend while sinning would be no real repentance at all. Real repentance could only supervene
through a complete change of will upon the state in which
a man should set out to sin with the intention of repenting
and then obtaining something better than innocence." [12]

Yet I do not think that Religion can finally acquiesce
in the view that, as it has been put in Christian language
by a modern mystic (the originality of whose genius
deserves more recognition than it has received) : " If
God had really known all from the beginning, he would
not have allowed such circumstances to arise as would
make the Passion necessary." Rather it must assure

[10] *Problems in the Relations of God and Man*, p. 274 ff.
[11] See Rom. iii. 8.   [12] *Problems*, loc. supra cit.

itself that, in the words of the same writer, " God does not merely get out of evil by a wonderful device, leaving the evil as a thing that had better not have been." [13]

In my last Lecture I ventured to suggest that Signor Benedetto Croce had by his observations upon Religion shown himself but indifferently well qualified for forming an adequate estimate of the contribution made by religious experience toward our knowledge of Reality. But it has perhaps for this very reason been easier for him than for one better equipped in this respect to elaborate what in the phraseology of modern theology may be called a doctrine of mere *immanence* ; for we have seen reason to think that Religion can never dispense with *transcendence*, although it can dispense with the representation of its transcendent object as *personal*. The importance assigned to History in Signor Croce's philosophy gives to it an advantage over that of Spinoza, who, as we saw in an earlier Lecture, also put forward an extreme doctrine of immanence. But I think that a comparison of the two systems will suggest that our contemporary's philosophy is, after all, even a more extreme doctrine of immanence than his predecessor's ; and that this is not unconnected with the fact that, while the great Jewish thinker found a religion in his philosophy, Signor Croce (however he may sometimes claim to have done the like) has only found his philosophy enable him to dispense with a religion.

Nevertheless we shall find it instructive to consider briefly in relation to our topic of Divine Personality the principle involved in Signor Croce's theology of immanence. It is, I think, the same principle which is expressed in Hegel's doctrine that the Absolute cannot be understood

[13] R. M. Benson, *Spiritual Readings for Advent*, p. 286.

except as a ' result,' [14] to the knowledge of which there
can be no shorter way than that of patiently tracing out all
the stages of the evolution in which its very life and being
consist. The principle is also perhaps related not very
distantly to James's repudiation of a ' block-universe.' [15]
It is the principle that there is not to be sought beyond
the Reality which lives and moves and develops around
us and within us, whereof we ourselves are a product
and a part, some other yet more real Being complete in
itself apart from that living process which is the history
of the world, a process that is going on still and is never
finished. In accordance with this principle Signor Croce
will not hear of a God " before the world was " or of a
Last Judgment to be passed, superfluously enough, upon
a world which has already come to an end and is no more.[16]
The divine transcendence which he is concerned to deny
is a transcendence of the historic process of which our
lives are an integral part and which is for him the one
and only Reality.

Now I think we need have no hesitation in admitting
that, whatever obligation members of particular religious
communities may sometimes have considered themselves
to be under to the letter of their sacred books, Religion
has no real interest in maintaining (in accordance with
the theology of the Wandering Jew in Shelley's *Queen Mab*)
that God awoke " from an eternity of idleness " [17] to
create the world, nor yet that he is to relapse into
inactivity after the destruction of the world which he

[14] See *Phänom. des Geistes*, Vorrede (*Werke*, ii. p. 15).
[15] The phrase is used by James in *A Pluralistic Universe*, pp. 310,
328.
[16] See *Saggio sullo Hegel* (ed. 1913), p. 137 (Eng. tr. p. 201) ;
Filosofia della Pratica, pt. I, s. I, c. 6, p. 65 (Eng. tr. p. 93).
[17] *Queen Mab*, § 7.

then created. The religious experience of communion
with God is an experience of communion not with a
prehistoric or post-historic Being, but with a *living* God.

Again, all philosophy to which the supreme Reality is
Spirit—and Signor Croce's is such a philosophy—even if,
like Signor Croce's, it repudiates any suggestion of a
Reality transcending the unbeginning and unending
series of acts which constitute the history or evolution
of the world, makes affirmations concerning the nature
and character which is manifested in this perpetual
process. According to Signor Croce [18] himself, we may
even describe this process as directed by a Providence,
but by a Providence which only " becomes actual in
individuals and acts not on them but in them." " This
affirmation of Providence," he goes on to declare, " is
not conjecture or faith but evidence of reason." But
what is this evidence ? He goes on to tell us. " Who
would feel in him the strength of life without such an
intimate persuasion ? Whence could he draw resignation
in sorrow, encouragement to endure ? Surely what the
religious man says with the words ' Let us leave it in God's
hands ' is said also by the man of reason with those other
words ' Courage and forward.' " There seems to me,
indeed, to be so great a difference between the temper of
these two exclamations that I cannot but consider one
who, with Signor Croce, sees no more in the former than
in the latter as thereby showing himself a stranger to
genuine religious experience. But it is not upon this
point that I would dwell here. I would rather ask whether
such a persuasion as the Italian philosopher here speaks
of, while I should be the last to deny it to be the voice
of Reason within us, is not just what has usually been

[18] *Filos. della Pratica*, pt. I, s. 2, c. 5, pp. 178 f. (Eng. tr. p. 257).

meant by ' faith ' ; for example, in the famous definition by the author of the *Epistle to the Hebrews* : " The assurance of things hoped for, the evidence of things not seen " [19] things not seen because, if Signor Croce be right, they are not yet *made*. It is a *reasonable* faith indeed, though not what the rationalistic philosophy which is dominant in popular thought would recognize at once as Reason ; but Signor Croce is ready to admit that there is sometimes more philosophy in Religion, " troubled by phantoms " [20] though it be, than in crude Rationalism.

It is a cardinal point in Signor Croce's philosophy that *mystery* is to be found only in History, the future course of which cannot be foreseen and the detail of which must be first *enacted* before it can be *known* ; in Philosophy, which is exclusively concerned with universals, there is no place for mystery. But it is precisely the presence of the same eternal and universal Spirit at every point of the historical process which enables Signor Croce to affirm the infinite progress of man,[21] though for him neither man nor God can know the concrete forms that progress will assume. And it is this presence that I should describe as a mystery, and a mystery in Philosophy ; and this is made not more but rather less obscure in the light of the religious experience of a personal relation of our individual spirits to the Spirit " which worketh in us both to will and to do." [22] The confidence which Signor Croce has in the nature and character of this Spirit is of a kind which we can hardly describe except in terms which are most properly applied to the kind of confidence which we have in a *person* ; and it

[19] Heb. xi. 1.
[20] *Filos. della Pratica*, pt. ii. s. 2, c. 2, p. 314 (Eng. tr. p 450).
[21] Ibid. Eng. tr. p. 260.   [22] Philipp. ii. 13.

cannot be justified except by such a view of the relation of this Spirit to our individual spirits as is expressed in religious language and realized by our individual spirits in their religious experience. I do not deny, I rather desire strongly to emphasize, that religious experience differs from the experience of acquaintance with finite persons in that it is freed from what is merely casual and empirical in the latter [23]; just as, on the other hand, it differs from the knowledge of universals, principles, or laws by the presence therein of that peculiar *rapport* (I know no English word so fitting to express my meaning) which elsewhere exists only between two persons in intimate mutual intercourse. The condescending, not to say arrogant, language held by Signor Croce towards those who, though not without pretension to philosophy, are yet not ready to leave Religion behind them as " a creed outworn " [24] which for the philosopher has already accomplished its work and is now ready to vanish away, ought not to divert our attention from a mystery which he has after all failed to banish from his own philosophy, and our only reasonable attitude to which is what we call Religion.

I said just now, perhaps somewhat too hastily, that Signor Croce had rather considered himself as dispensed by philosophy from the need of a religion than had, like Spinoza, found a religion in his philosophy. For after all there is religion in Signor Croce's philosophy, which, indeed, he admits will, when it has absorbed Religion, " have the value of true and complete Religion " [25] and if it does not utter itself in religious language and religious

[23] Cp. *The Notion of Revelation* (Pan-Anglican Paper), p. 4.
[24] Wordsworth's sonnet, " The world is too much with us."
[25] See *The Task of Logic* in Windelband and Ruge's *Encyclopædia of the Philosophical Sciences*, Eng. ed. p. 210.

practice, that is only on account of a prejudice against the associations of such language and practice which is very evident in Signor Croce's writings, but which one need not share in order to profit by what is of permanent value in his speculations.

What can better deserve the name of a mystery than that contradiction in its own nature which perpetually distracts and baffles the human soul when it realizes that it is " haunted for ever by the eternal Mind " [26] and unable to set limits to the range of its thought or the scope of its concern, and yet notwithstanding is at the very same time hurried along without pause by the ever-rolling stream of Time, " never continuing in one stay," [27] but each moment leaving something of its past self behind and always beset with intimations of mortality ?

No doubt the name of a mystery is misapplied when no more is meant than that some fundamental feature of our experience cannot be explained in terms of something else. The relation of the Particular to the Universal is not a mystery because it is not a case of the relation borne by a copy to its archetype or by the part of a body to the body of which it is a part. We understand quite well what it is ; and, if we did not, the simplest conversation would soon become unintelligible to us. In like manner the conception of Time involves at once the evanescence of its successive moments and the persistence of its continuous course ; and the relation of the former to the latter factor in so familiar and indispensable a notion is not the less understood because any attempted comparison of it to something else will prove to be in some respects inadequate. To the contemplating mind Universal

[26] Wordsworth, *Ode on Intimations of Immortality*, § 8.
[27] *Burial Service* : " Man that is born of a woman," etc.

and Particular, or again the permanence and the lapse
of Time, are mutually correlative, each understood in
its relation to the other, and neither otherwise intelligible
or real. We may justly say that there is no ' mystery '
here, properly so called.

But the case is otherwise when the Soul turns back
upon itself and reflects upon its own nature, as a particular
aware of itself as a particular, as transient but conscious
of its transiency ; and as, in that awareness, that consciousness of its transiency, apprehending its universal and
eternal nature as its own, yet not its own ; as its unrealized
and perhaps unrealizable ideal, its unattained and
perhaps unattainable perfection. I cannot persuade
myself that the word ' mystery ' is not applicable here,
just as Signor Croce admits it to be applicable to the
anticipation of a future the detail of which, because it
does not yet exist, cannot from the very nature of the
case be foreseen by the anticipating mind.

Professor Alexander, in his Gifford Lectures at Glasgow,
has just been contending that the religious consciousness
witnesses to the reality of such an ideal, yet not to its
actuality. The world is (he tells us) pregnant with deity,
and in Religion we are aware that it is so, but God is not
yet born. We may, indeed, learn from the sacred stories
of Buddhism and of Christianity [28] that the thought of
worship paid to a divine Lord while yet in his mother's
womb has nothing in it uncongenial to the temper of
religion ; but the context, legendary and doctrinal, of
these same stories testifies not less unequivocally to the
impossibility of resting in the thought of the object of
worship as not yet actual. The future Buddha as soon
as born miraculously proclaims his own greatness and is

[28] See Luke i. 43 ff.

adored by a venerable sage and by his own father ; and
he is further described as descending into his mother's
womb from an assembly of glorified beings, the presidency
among whom he is said in some later forms of the story
to have left to the being who is to be the Buddha of the
next age, and who even now receives prospectively the
veneration of Buddhists in that capacity.[29] So too the
belief of the Christian Church in the pre-existence of her
Founder is already manifest in the New Testament in
the writings of St. Paul and of the author of the Fourth
Gospel.[30] I find it therefore difficult to believe that, as
Professor Alexander thinks, the embryonic deity of which
he tells us will satisfy all the demands of theism.

I will, then, venture to assert, in opposition to Professor
Alexander, that the religious consciousness demands not
merely a prospective but an actual God, already possessing all to which we can aspire. And yet at the same
time it is no less true that it is not content to regard
the worshipper's own religious life—which is certainly
not yet complete—as without significance for God.

Hence it comes about that the religious imagination
tends to represent God to itself as being already beforehand " all " (to use an expression of Green's [31]) " which
the human spirit is capable of becoming " : and then
making us with the intention that we shall become what
he already is. This representation may be criticized as
reducing our religious activity to a process of *copying*.
We seem to have presented to us here a theological
analogue of that ' copying theory of truth ' with protests

[29] Warren's *Buddhism in Translations*, pp. 42, 49 ; Rhys Davids'
Buddhist Birth Stories, pp. 64, 69; Bigandet, *Legend of Gaudama*,
Eng. tr. ; pp. 27, 41.

[30] E.g. 2 Cor. viii. 9 ; Philipp. ii. 6 ; John i. 1 ff, xvii. 5.

[31] *Prolegomena to Ethics*, iii. 2 § 187, p. 198.

against which we have in late years become so familiar in
discussions of the nature of Knowledge. We can understand why a philosophy deeply interested in maintaining
the creative activity of the mind that thinks in us must
be inevitably hostile to a scholasticism which, by reducing
that activity to a mere reproduction of a reality to the
constitution of which it makes no difference, " denies "
according to an epigram I quoted before,[32] " the divinity
of the human spirit " ; and why such a philosophy is
even suspicious of Religion, since it seems as though
Religion cannot be satisfied with any other system than
one which condemns the human spirit to walk for ever
in a vain show, and disquiet itself [33] in order to do over
again less well what has already been done perfectly.

How are we to solve the antinomy with which we are
thus confronted ?

I spoke just now of the ' copying theory of truth.' This
phrase means, as I understand it, an attempt to explain
what knowing is by describing it as a kind of *copying*.
We may recall how Bacon says that *templum sanctum ad
exemplar mundi in intellectu humano fundamus*,[34] a model
of the universe in the human understanding. There can,
of course, be no objection taken to the occasional employment of such a metaphor, but there is a grave objection
to treating it as a serious *explanation* of that to which
such words as ' copy ' or ' model ' are transferred from
their original significance. It is just because it is so
treated in a ' copying theory of truth ' that such a theory
is rightly to be condemned. Knowing is not copying ; it
is quite as familiar an experience as copying ; some degree
of it must indeed precede any copying, as in its turn

[32] See above, Lecture VII, p. 156.
[33] Psa. xxxix. 6.   [34] *Nov. Org.* i. 120.

copying a thing may become a help towards knowing it better.

Those who have in recent times been most severe upon the ' copying theory of truth ' have been, I think, specially inclined to insist upon the point that it reduced the real world to something finished and done with, beyond our mending—a ' block universe '—and condemned our intellectual activity to a mere barren repetition, in the course of which nothing substantial is added to the universal stock. And of the defenders of any form of what is often called Realism, which asserts the independence of the object of knowledge upon the mind's activity in knowing, even though it may not vainly attempt to elucidate the meaning of knowledge by a reference to *copying*, it may very well be asked : What *difference*, on your view, does being *known* make to a thing ?

Now it seems to me clear that in regard of the lifeless, so far forth as it is lifeless, it makes *no* difference. This is why the doctrine of a Naturalist like Huxley that consciousness is a mere ' epiphenomenon ' and that of an Idealist like Green that it is not a part of nature— doctrines which, though advanced in opposite interests, make the same point—are irrefutable, so long as in speaking of *nature* or *phenomenon* we are thinking, as both Huxley and Green were thinking, of a mechanical and not a spiritual system ; and if in speaking of knowledge or science we are thinking of the kind of knowledge which we have in the sciences of physics and chemistry.[35] But when we come on the one hand to spiritual being and specially to that grade of spiritual being which we designate as Personality, and on the other to that sort

35 See above, Lecture I, pp. 26 f.

of knowledge which we have in personal intercourse with
our fellow-men, here it is no less evident that to be known
makes a very great difference to the person known. The
knowledge which we call 'acquaintance' cannot be onesided. What has more to do with making us what we
are than the knowledge others have of us, their attraction
towards us or repulsion from us, their agreement or dissent,
their approval or disapproval, their hatred or their love ?
Holding, as I do, with the Realists that it is to contradict
the very notion of Knowledge to suppose its object
created by the subject in the act of knowing it, I would
at the same time insist that the mutual independence
of subject and object is at its maximum in the lowest,
at its minimum in the highest kinds of Knowledge. It is
where the knowledge makes least difference to the thing
known that the knower is least interested in the existence
of the thing known outside of his possible experience of
it. In what may be called (if we ignore for the moment
the knowledge of God in Religion) the highest kind of
Knowledge, the knowledge which we have of our fellow-
men in social intercourse with them, we find that such
intercourse makes all the difference to those who are
parties to it, and also that we are profoundly interested
in the independent existence of our friends ; indeed in
proportion to our devotion to them the greater will be our
concern for them, even apart from the maintenance of
their relations to ourselves.[36]

If we accept the testimony of religious experience to
the possibility of a knowledge of God which can be in
any way likened to our personal knowledge of the fellow-
men with whom we are acquainted, we shall find here
also this insistent interest (all the more insistent for the

[36] Cp. *Problems in the Relations of God and Man*, p. 37.

absence of that sensible verification which can be
had in the case of our human friends) upon the existence of its object. It is in vain that certain schools
of thought have attempted to evade the difficulties
raised by this insistence by laying stress on the value
which may be ascribed to religious emotion or religious imagination whether or no God exists independently thereof. I do not deny that such schools
of thought have supplied a much-needed correction of
the mistake committed by those who have sought for
' proofs of God's existence ' apart from religious experience. For this is as great a mistake as it would be to
hope to demonstrate the existence of Beauty apart from
an æsthetic experience. Nevertheless the common demand for certainty that *God exists*, that *there is a God*,
however it may often express itself in forms which betray
a misconception of the kind of proof which could avail
to satisfy it, proceeds from a sound instinct. Religion
has a genuine interest in the assurance of the existence
of God as no mere " vision of fulfilled desire " [37] or creature
of the imagination.

But can we say here, as we ought to say if our analogy
is to hold, that we believe our devotion to God to make
a difference to him even greater than our friendship makes
to our friends ? We feel a natural hesitation in answering
in the affirmative. It is characteristic of Religion to
shrink from such an assertion, and to make God so far
the predominant partner in our intercourse with him,
that even our knowledge of him is ascribed to his own
activity in us. He reveals himself to us and in us ; only
so far as he does so can we be said to find him either
in the world or in our hearts. The initiation, the

[37] Fitzgerald, *Rubáiyát of Omar Khayyám*, § 67 (3rd ed.).

action, and the success are all to be referred to him. He " worketh in us both to will and to do." [38]

Nevertheless, if we are to do justice to all sides of our religious experience, it is certain that there is present in it also an element which seems to meet the expectations which our analogy with other levels of experience had led us to form.

There is the consciousness of an insistent demand upon us for our *worship*. It is easy to see in this no more than a survival from a primitive theology which envisaged its God as a despotic chieftain, greedy of his subjects' abject submission. And of course such a conception of God may have left traces in our religious phraseology ; though even this conception was not, when it was alive, the base thing that it seems when opposed in rivalry to the nobler thought inspired by a later teaching. But probably only those with little religious experience of their own will be content to dismiss it thus. We shall do more wisely to recognize the splendid flower sprung from that apparently unlovely seed in the passionate experience which has found immortal utterance in the greatest religious poem of our own age and country— the poem in which Francis Thompson has told us of his soul's unavailing flight from her " tremendous Lover," the Hound of Heaven.

In such an experience the consciousness of an imperious summons of the worshipper to a complete surrender of himself is fused with the consciousness of an " unchanging love " which can say, " Can a woman forget her sucking child that she should not have compassion upon the son of her womb ? Yea, these may forget, yet will I not forget thee." [39] It cannot be denied, then, that there

[38] Philipp. ii. 13.   [39] Isa. xlix. 15 ; Cowper's 18th Olney Hymn.

is a phase of religious experience in which the devotee
is conscious of his devotion as 'making a difference' to
God.

But how, then, can God be regarded as perfect from all
eternity if he can also be represented as needing and
desiring our worship and our love ? Are we not here in
the presence of an inevitable contradiction, such as must
compel us, with Mr. Bradley, to regard God, the object
of religious worship, as *appearance* only, and not as the
ultimate Reality, wherein all contradictions must of
necessity be harmonized ?

Now, as I have already said, there may be a sense in
which Religion need have no fear of this view. As Mr.
Bradley is himself fully aware, we have not to learn for
the first time from the philosophical critics of to-day
that God's ways are not as our ways nor his thoughts
as our thoughts,[40] or even that the distance between
them is so great that God's cannot properly be called
' ways ' or ' thoughts.' [41] Nor is there any novelty in the
doctrine that the Word, or (as we may in this context
quite legitimately translate, using Mr. Bradley's expression)
the Appearance, was in the beginning with God, and was
God.[42] The only thing, as I venture to think, that Religion
is here interested in repudiating, is an attempt to
undo the work of those Christian theologians of the age
of creed-making who fixed their own community in the
faith that the Appearance and that of which it is the
Appearance are one undivided God, the only lawful
Object of worship, because the only one which will not
fail the worshipper when he endeavours to give a reason·
able account of the faith that is in him. It is only in

---

[40] Isa. lv. 8.   [41] *Essays on Truth and Reality*, p. 436*n*.
[42] John i. 1.

so far as Mr. Bradley's distinction of God from the Absolute may be thought to " divide the Substance " [43] of which these theologians affirmed the indivisible unity that it endangers Religion. And I should not speak thus if I considered that the danger was a danger merely to the religion of one particular religious community—although that community were the one of which I myself am a member—if I did not hold that the community whose explicit formula of faith is here directly threatened were in this respect the defender of a fundamental interest of Religion, the nature of which has been less fully realized by other communities than by the Christian Church.

The difficulty which we find in reconciling the divine perfection with the divine demand upon us (both of which are in my judgment what Mr. Bradley would call ' ideas necessary to the religious consciousness,' and therefore, in his view true, although not ultimately true)—a difficulty which we, as finite spirits, cannot, I think, so completely overcome as to possess its answer in an experienced fact—is an indication that we are here in the presence of a problem beyond our powers to solve, and therefore of one not less legitimately entitled to be described as a ' mystery ' than that of the detail of the future, to which, as we saw, Signor Croce would allow the name.

But it is, I think, relevant to the main purpose of these Lectures to point out that it is precisely in the instance of personal character that we come nearest to understanding how perfection might not exclude the desire of self-communication ; since in this instance the notion of a self-sufficient perfection strikes us as displeasing, and as really contradictory of our notion of what would be perfect in that kind. And, as Plato says,[44] speaking of

[43] See the *Quicumque vult*.   [44] *Tim.* 28 c, 29 E.

" the Father and Maker of the universe," in words which were adopted by Athanasius [45] as an axiom of his theology : " He was good, and therefore he grudged existence to nothing." What I have called (using the word ' myth ' in its high Platonic sense) the myth of a Mediator has been turned to account to express the problem before us. For here the necessity of self-communication to a perfect being is expressed in the representation of the eternal Sonship as an intrinsic factor in the Godhead ; and the part of finite and imperfect beings in this self-communication is expressed in the thought of their archetypes or patterns as included within the eternal nature of the divine Son or Word.   And here again we must note that in the instance of personal character we seem to find no incompatibility between the thought of a perfection on which we can place entire dependence and that of a living activity, whose course could by no means be settled beforehand, but would afford to the spectator the joy of anticipating ever new and unexpected manifestations of power and wisdom and goodness.   We may here find confirmation for the view that the religious consciousness to which intercourse with the supreme Reality has the intimacy and passion of personal converse is that which takes us farthest into the heart of that Reality and gives most assurance of the solution of problems which yet to us remain mysteries indeed, but ' joyful mysteries,' mysteries of love, which may be said not so much to baffle Reason as to enlarge its scope and opportunity.

In the two remaining Lectures of this course I must essay, however tentatively and modestly, the difficult task of gathering together the suggestions which may

[45] *de Incarnatione Verbi*, iii. § 3.

be obtained from the historical and critical discussions which have in the main occupied us so far, into something which may pass for a constructive account of the place to be assigned to Personality in our conception of the Supreme Being, whom we apprehend in Religion as God ; bearing in mind that, in the memorable words of Lord Gifford's will, " the true and felt knowledge—not mere nominal knowledge—of the relations of man and of the universe to him is the means of man's highest well-being and the security of his upward progress."

LECTURE IX

RELIGION AND PHILOSOPHY

THE preceding Lectures will have, I think, brought out the fact that the problem of Personality in God is the same as that which is expressed in asking " Is God the Absolute ? " or again : " What is the relation of Philosophy to Religion ? " It may at first sight seem as though the undeniable existence of religions and even of great religious systems which do not ascribe Personality to God were a sufficient argument against this identification. It may be remembered that in the historical portion of this course I was so far from disputing the existence of Religion apart from a doctrine of Divine Personality that I dwelt upon the evidence that such a doctrine it was not easy to find explicitly held outside of Christianity, and that the expression " Personality *of* God " as distinguished from " personality *in* God " will be sought in vain in the authorized formularies (or at least in those of not quite recent origin) accepted by any of that large majority of Christian Churches and sects which has adhered to the main Christian tradition by retaining the doctrine of a Trinity of Persons in the Unity of the Godhead.[1] Nevertheless I think it will be found that it is just in proportion as we interpret our relation to God as a *personal* relation

[1] See Lecture III.

213

—and only in such an interpretation can I find a sound basis for a doctrine of Divine Personality—that our religious experience will prevent us from being overborne by what we may call the dialectical difficulties, drawn from considerations which abstract from the specifically religious consciousness, that beset the attribution of personality to the supreme Reality. It is the fact that Religion is, in the words of Lord Gifford's will, a *felt* knowledge of God, calling into play emotions unmistakably akin to those excited towards our fellow-men in intercourse with them—emotions of reverence and of love—which differentiates it from Philosophy, and gives meaning to the remark which comes naturally to our lips in reading certain passages in the *Metaphysics* of Aristotle and in the *Ethics* of Spinoza, that those great men, who seem beyond most others of the famous teachers of our race to move in a region of thought remote from ordinary religious practices, have after all found in their philosophy itself what is unquestionably a religion.

Perhaps I may be allowed to state what I take to be the truth as to the relation of Religion to Philosophy in words which I have already used elsewhere when dealing with the same subject.

" When men have begun to put to themselves questions of the kind in attempting to answer which Philosophy consists, and to ask what is the true nature of this mysterious world in which they find themselves, how it comes to be there and what is at the back of it all, they have never approached these inquiries with a mind completely free from prepossessions. In a far-distant past their fathers had begun dimly to feel the presence of the mystery which encompassed them on every side. With a fearful sense of its strangeness to them, its weirdness and uncanniness, there was mingled an anticipation of the possibility of establishing a familiarity or of proving a kinship with it, which might be the hope of a securer, freer, more powerful existence for themselves than was possible under other conditions. During a long course of ages such fear of the mystery and desire of coming to terms with it, in combination with the more disinterested emotions of awe and curiosity, had everywhere given rise to some complicated system of forbearances and actions, of ceremonies and stories, expressive of the habitual attitude of a people towards the powers that surround them and whose ways are not as theirs —in a word, to a religion.   Thus the philosopher, when he begins to philosophize, is already accustomed to a certain way of approaching the riddle which he desires to solve, by which he cannot fail to be affected, whether or no he be himself inclined to take it for a clue in his own investigations. But it belongs to the very essence of Philosophy that it should not so take anything for granted as to refuse to test and examine it before admitting it as true.   And so neither the initiators of a new philosophical movement nor an individual who is beginning philosophical studies for himself can avoid in the first instance taking up an attitude of independence towards religious tradition, which, if the representatives of that tradition do not tolerate it, may easily pass into hostility. The opposition between Philosophy and Religion, which we so frequently observe, is thus both natural and inevitable. It arises from the fact that they are both concerned with the same object.

" It does not, however, follow that Philosophy must eventually take the place of Religion as a better way of doing what Religion has tried to do in an inferior manner This might be so if the theories of

the origin and course of nature which often form part of
a religious tradition constituted the whole or the most
important part of Religion.[2] But this is not so. Rather
it would seem that men do not cease to find in the universe
that which evokes and " in divers portions and divers
manners " satisfies their instinct of reverence, their
impulse to worship. This experience can only find expression in some sort of Religion. But, just because
Religion is a response to what is felt to be the innermost
heart of Reality as a whole, the whole nature of man
necessarily claims to take part in it. Hence a religion,
when once the level of spiritual development is reached
at which Philosophy can come into existence, can no more
ignore or evade the criticism of Philosophy, without
abdicating its claim to express the response of the whole
man to the Divine, than Philosophy can in its turn
without self-mutilation ignore the testimony of religious
experience to the nature of that ultimate Reality which
it seeks to apprehend as it truly is." [3]

Philosophy is from the first and throughout a search
for the one in the many, which, if successful, must issue
in the knowledge of a single ground of all things, or of
an all-inclusive unity—in other words, of ' the Absolute '
of modern philosophers. Now the aspiration after such
a knowledge has its original and constant stimulus in
that hope and promise of its fulfilment which the religious
experience supplies,[4] so that I think it would not be too
much to say, not only that Philosophy could not have

[2] Thus Croce, who thinks that Religion is doomed to vanish in
Philosophy, states expressly that " Religion is nothing but knowledge" (*Estetica I*, c. 8, Eng. tr. p. 102).

[3] *History of Philosophy* in Home University Library, pp.
78–80.

[4] *Group Theories of Religion*, p. 189.

arisen, but that it can never long flourish, except in the soil of Religion.[5]

An industrious school of thinkers in France who lay especial claim for themselves to the title of sociologists—I regret that we have had within the last year to lament the death of their distinguished leader, M. Emile Durkheim—have contended that such elementary and, to science, indispensable notions or ' categories ' as those of Time, Space, Number, Causality, have their origin in the arrangements of primitive society, arrangements which excite in the members of the groups to which they belong emotions of the kind which we call religious. I have elsewhere attempted to deal somewhat fully with this theory, which has been presented by the writers of whom I have just spoken in a form which appears to me to be highly misleading, and in connexion with a general view which I take to be philosophically unsound. Nevertheless in my judgment it contains, although mixed with some error, a genuine truth of high importance.

This truth may be stated as follows. It is characteristic of the human mind to concern itself with the All ; it is, indeed, in virtue of this characteristic that it can properly be called rational. But in thus concerning itself with the All it always starts with its immediate social environment. The measures of Time and Space used by primitive man, the interest taken by them in certain numbers, the ways in which they account for striking events in their experience, although, since they presuppose the notions of Time and Space, Number and Causality, they cannot without a fallacy be described as the source of these notions, yet are certainly determined by this immediate social environment. Only gradually have men come to

[5] *Group Theories of Religion*, p. 188,

realize that their immediate social environment is not
the dominant fact in the universe. Only gradually has
their consciousness of the world, which at first was, as
we may put it, mediated to them through the consciousness
of their group, become the consciousness of a Reality
which cannot be identified with even the most comprehensive of human communities. But, as ever wider and
wider horizons have opened to their view, the religious
emotion which was from the first excited in the performance of those actions whereby men shared in the
common life of their tribe has continued to attend the
consciousness of the all-embracing Unity wherein they
" live and move and have their being." [6] The French
sociologists whom I mentioned above are apt to speak of
the object of their religious consciousness as though it
were a merely subjective fact, the product of man's social
nature. But it would in my judgment be better to
acknowledge that the very social consciousness wherein
consciousness of the supreme Unity has from the first
been implicit is rooted in the spiritual nature of that
supreme Unity itself, which in the movement of man's
spiritual and social life has been carrying on that perpetual revelation and communication of itself which
belongs to its own innermost being.

Although it would no doubt be idle to contend that
whatever has at any time " been called God and worshipped " [7] has been explicitly conceived as a single
Ground of all existence or as an all-inclusive Unity, the
' Absolute ' of modern philosophers, yet I am persuaded
that no God that is explicitly distinguished from the
Absolute can prove a satisfying object to the religious
consciousness in any one who has attained to the level

[6] Acts xvii, 28.   [7] 2 Thess. ii. 4.

of intellectual development at which he can ask himself
the question what is behind and beyond the God whom he
worships. Anthropologists have been puzzled by the
' high gods ' of primitive peoples, who are but little
worshipped themselves but are thought of as older and
more venerable than deities more frequently in the thoughts
of their adorers. I suspect that these ' high gods,' whatever the original application of the names given to them
(which may differ widely in different instances), reflect
an early and embryonic form of speculation upon that
one ultimate Ground of all existence which philosophers
call the Absolute, and which, as soon as it is distinguished
from " whatever gods there be," [8] at once appropriates
to itself the attributes of genuine and primary Godhead,
reducing all other objects of worship to a comparatively
lower grade. These lower gods may be more familiar,
more intimately known, more practically worth pro-
pitiating ; but they are as Gods inferior to the Beings
who stand for the ultimate Reality at the back of everything in these rudimentary attempts at a metaphysical
system for the Absolute. Thus something less than
the Absolute, or what stands for the Absolute in any
particular system, may be and often is " called God and
worshipped " and may even be far more considered and
worshipped, and that, very likely, because more feared,
than that which *does* stand for the Absolute. But it is
to that which stands for the Absolute that in the end
the greatest reverence must be paid ; nor can the religious
consciousness forbear the demand that the supreme God
should be the supreme Reality, the Abso'ute and nothing
less. Over against this statement, however, must be set
another, namely, that apart from the religious conscicus-

[8] Swinburne, *The Garden of Proserpine.*

ness the Absolute cannot be known as God. The former statement indicates the intimate connexion, the latter the distinction, never to be neglected, between Religion and Philosophy.

When modern philosophers speak of the Absolute and ask what is or stands for the Absolute in any particular system of thought, what they have in view is the principle of Unity which is reached at last by that search for a ' One in the Many ' upon which every philosophy is engaged. But of course a search for a ' One in the Many ' may not go further than the attainment of some subordinate principle which claims to unify not the whole multitude of appearances which make up the world of our experience but only some restricted group of them. And we may, I think, learn something to our purpose from a study of some subordinate principles of unity, and of the light which may be thrown by such a study upon the nature of that more comprehensive principle with the discovery of which we could be satisfied and find rest from our labours.

A principle of unity in multiplicity which ~~easily~~ early attracted the notice of philosophers is the Universal. We may perhaps profitably ask how far the manner in which the Universal unifies its particulars can be supposed to throw light on the nature of the supreme principle of unity— the Absolute.

A Universal, taken in its widest sense, is an identical nature manifested in many instances each of which is, as an instance of it, entitled to the common name. For example, the common name ' horse ' is used with an equal right of every animal which exhibits a certain nature which we may call ' horse-ness.'

Now it is clear that we cannot regard the Absolute

as a ' universal ' in the sense that it is an identical nature
exhibited by many instances, each of which may bear
the common name and be called an Absolute. To speak
of many Absolutes would be self-contradictory. When
Mr. Bosanquet 9 insists that the Absolute is individual—
is, indeed, according to him the only genuine individual
—he is calling attention to that feature in any notion that
we can form of the Supreme Unity which differentiates
it from a logical ' universal.' On the other hand, the
expression ' universal ' is sometimes used (often, as I
venture to think, without sufficient care being taken to
indicate that we have here passed beyond the limits of
the meaning given to it above) for a ' systematic whole.'
It is not difficult to understand how this use is connected
with the former. The identical nature may appear
in each of its instances with a definite modification ; a
genus is a ' universal ' of this kind, and the species are
its ' particulars.' Where these species can be arranged
in a serial order and exhaust between them all the possible
alternatives of which the identical nature common to
them all is capable, there we may be said to have a systematic whole which determines the mutual distinctions
and relations of all its parts. It is among the abstract
objects of mathematical science that one can most readily
find illustrations of an exhaustive series of alternative
species whose differences are determined by nothing but
the generic nature itself. It is thus that numbers must
be either odd or even, lines either straight or curved,
triangles equilateral, isosceles, or scalene, and so forth.
But cf course for the construction of an ideal of a systematic whole we should be far from finding an adequate
pattern in this region of mere abstractions. We should

9 See above, Lecture I, pp. 18 f.

gain more from reflection on the nature of a complex work of art, or of a rich and many-sided character. Such wholes as these are (what ' number ' and the like are not) eminently individual ; and the supreme Unity must certainly be conceived as possessing in the highest degree the attribute of individuality.

We may now turn to another principle of unity, that of *Substance* : and in this case the attempt to construe the Absolute in térms of it has been made, as is well known, by one of the world's greatest thinkers. But the few observations which I shall submit to you will make no sort of pretension to be a general criticism cf the philosophy of Spinoza. It would be rash to take for granted that by pointing out the inadequacy of the common account of Substance as a description of the nature of the Absolute one must be disposing of any system in the terminology of which the word ' Substance ' happens to play an important part. Words are, indeed, less amenable to dictation in respect of their meanings than Lewis Carroll's ' Humpty-Dumpty ' [10] supposed : but as " customs," according to Shakespeare,[11] " curtsey to great kings," so do the usages of language to great philosophers.

. The ancient contrast of Substance and *Accident* will not, I think, help us in the present inquiry. It belongs to the Aristotelian philosophy, in which substances coexist with other substances as real as themselves. But the Absolute cannot thus coexist with other Absolutes. Hence we find the Schoolmen maintaining that in God there are no Accidents ; and when Spinoza confines the term ' Substance ' to the Absolute, we find that its correlate in his system is not *Accident* but *Attribute*. It is possible

[10] *Alice Through the Looking Glass*, c. 6.
[11] *Henry V*, Act V, Sc. 2.

to speculate on the possibility of a Substance existing
without Accidents ; but a Substance is nothing apart
from its Attributes, nor Attributes apart from the Substance to which they belong ; thus only bodies can
gravitate, and gravity can only belong to bodies. It may
seem that an ultimate principle of unity, such as we seek
under the name of the Absolute, would not be what we
are looking for, if it were not a unity of this type—if the
detail of the Universe were not in the last resort such as
could only belong to this Universe or (to express the same
thing in other words) if the Universe might have equally
well been differently constituted. But here serious difficulties seem to threaten us. Can we, and especially can
our religious consciousness, acquiesce in what would
appear to be a system of rigid determination throughout,
wherein nothing can be otherwise than it is and whatever
is is at once the best and the worst because the only thing
possible ? It is just because of these difficulties that so
many have found themselves unable to subscribe to that
famous doctrine of the Absolute Substance to which I
have already referred, and that the religious world in
particular, both in Spinoza's own day and long after,
could see in him, though he wrote as one to whom God
was all in all, the very prince of atheists.

The inadequacy of the notion of Substance as a guide
to the nature of the Absolute is seen most obviously in
this, that it is no less applicable to the inanimate or
material than to Life and Spirit. Since, however, the
Absolute manifests itself in Life and Spirit as well as in
lifeless Matter, a notion which abstracts from the difference between these two spheres of being cannot be the
adequate ground and principle of both and also of the
distinction between them. And that universal deter-

minism which strikes so terrible a chill to the heart does so because what it at once suggests to the mind is not a spiritual activity, such as we know in our own thought and will, but rather some kind of blind mechanical process, the discovery of the universality of which would make our thought and will themselves a mockery and an illusion.

Can we, then, find in Life the clue we desire ? Life too is a principle of unity with an infinite variety of manifestations. In our own day the imaginative genius and persuasive eloquence of M. Bergson have been lavished on a brilliant presentation of Life in the character of the Absolute.

In this philosophy of ' creative evolution ' we are offered, in place of the determinism associated with the doctrine of the Absolute as Substance, a theory which, denying that the road yet to be traversed by Life is determined beforehand either after the manner of the regular working of a machine or after that of a plan directed to a predestined end, leaves, in M. Bergson's striking phrase, " the gates of the future open " [12] ; a theory which has seemed to many to be an inspiring call to adventure and a message of hope. Yet after all perhaps it is only to cheerful and sanguine temperaments that we can fairly expect it to be a message of hope ; for to persons of a timid and apprehensive disposition the thought of those open gates might become rather a source of fear and trembling in the presence of a boundless uncertainty.

I am convinced that we should do better to follow M. Bergson in representing to ourselves the Absolute as a universal Life than to think of it as a lifeless Mechanism

[12] *Devant l'évolution de la vie . . . les portes de l'avenir restent grandes ouvertes* (*L'Évolution creatrice*, p. 114). Cp. Bosanquet, *Value and Destiny of the Individual*, Lecture X.

And, before indicating what notwithstanding seems to me wanting even in this representation of it as Life, I will dwell briefly on some especial advantages which it may be held to possess, not only over any attempt to conceive the Absolute after the analogy of a lifeless mechanism, but even over views which seek for a clue to its nature rather in Thought or Will than in mere Life.

These advantages consist mainly in this, that animated nature, when studied apart from any metaphysical or theological presuppositions, appears to present the spectacle of a constant effort after adaptation to environment, not such as to indicate some determinate end in view to which we could give a name and could fancy it as established beforehand by some external designer, but rather such as to suggest in the case of each species of organism an instinctive desire to preserve and perpetuate itself, without any regard to the interest of other species ; and also what we can hardly describe otherwise than as a wonderful ingenuity displayed in the gratification of this desire, although at the same time an ingenuity divorced from any appearance of those processes of discursive reasoning and calculation which we associate with ingenuity in the case of human beings.

Now it has always been the grand obstacle to the adoption either of a theistic theory of the universe, or even of a pantheistic theory which would emphasize the unity and goodness of the immanent Spirit, the Soul of the ' one stupendous whole ' (to quote the poet Pope's classical expression of this kind of view),[13] that the world of living beings is revealed to our most careful inspection as the theatre of a vast conflict, ' a struggle for existence,' wherein pain and self-seeking (the typical

[13] *Essay on Man*, Ep. i. 9.

instances of physical and moral evil respectively) are indispensable conditions of the result achieved, and in which there occur not only success and victory, but also failure and defeat. Can we not, it may plausibly be asked, avoid these difficulties by frankly admitting that in contemplating Life, the impulse manifested in this great movement with its general upward tendency attested by the actual evolution of reason and civilization, science and morality, but also with its patent indifference to the standards by which we judge of individual human conduct we are face to face with the general character of the ultimate Reality ? And we must not overlook, in estimating the attraction of such an admission, the appeal which it is found to make to the poetical or artistic temperament. The possessor of such a temperament is quick to see interest and beauty in situations from which the moralist turns away with disgust and condemnation, and is accustomed to rely rather upon intuition than upon reasoning. It is here interesting to note, though I do not propose to examine the application by M. Bergson of artistic intuition to the ' instinct ' which is most strikingly exhibited in bees and ants rather than to the ' intellect ' characteristic of human beings alone among the living inhabitants of this planet.

To one more point in favour of this representation of the Absolute after the fashion of an all-pervading Life I must call your attention. It undoubtedly is capable of meeting, to a certain extent at least, the demands of the religious consciousness.

' Half a beast is the great god Pan ' [14] ; yet he is a great god too. The felt presence of that mysterious Power has at all times availed to call forth from the hearts of

[14] Elizabeth Barrett Browning, *A Musical Instrument*.

men the sentiment of solemn awe, in intimate fusion, however, with the sensuous excitement proper to the mood of abandonment to impulses which are the very vehicles and instruments of Nature's divine fecundity.[15] Nay, to tell the truth, religious *emotion* is perhaps more easily to be found in such worship as this than in one paid to a God conceived mainly as a Supreme Reason and Goodness ; although no doubt at what we are accustomed to call higher levels of religious experience there is found in exceptional cases a mysticism like that of the " undaunted daughter of desire," [16] which, although disassociated from the satisfaction of animal instincts, is for all its " large draughts of intellectual day " at least no less passionate than any that the most orgiastic rites of nature-worship could show.

In passing from the description of this mode of conceiving the Absolute to the criticism of it, I would emphasize the point that it is not the positive side of it, the importance attached to Life as a manifestation of the ultimate Reality, but the negative side of it, the depreciation in comparison of Reason and Goodness, which seems to me open to objection. The Reason and Goodness for which a claim can be made with any hope of success to be regarded as characteristic of the Supreme Being will certainly be a *living* Reason and an *active* Goodness, no mere stereotyped formula or rule for thought or action such as is (it would appear) suggested to some minds by the mention of these words.

I will do no more than mention in passing that those

[15] I borrow the expression from the title of an essay by the late George Tyrrell, read to the Philosophical Society at Oxford very shortly before his lamented death; see *Essays on Faith and Immortality*, pt. 2, c. 14.

[16] Crashaw, *The Flaming Heart* (of St. Teresa).

who conceive the Absolute on the analogy of Life, no
less than those who conceive it as Mind or Spirit, may be
challenged to give an account consistent with their view
of what we call the material world, which is *not* alive,
and yet is commonly regarded as indisputably real.
Attempts to explain material things as no more than
'ideas,' in the sense of modifications of the spirit or soul
that 'perceives' or 'conceives' them, will be uncongenial to thinkers to whom part of the attraction of the
notion of Life as that which will bring us nearest to the
nature of the ultimate Reality is certainly its comprehension of subconscious and unconscious processes along
with such as rise, in the phrase now so familiar, 'above
the threshold of consciousness.'

M. Bergson, whom I have already taken as the chief
representative at present of the mode of thought which
I am now considering, sees in inert matter only the living
movement around us observed from the point of view of
one particular living and moving individual, or perhaps
it would be more strictly in accordance with the spirit
of M. Bergson's philosophy to say, an individual life and
movement ; for there is for this philosophy no individual
substance of which movement and life are states alternative to rest and death. Just as from a train in motion
another train moving alongside at an equal speed appears
to be standing still, so to us as individuals the movement
of life around us presents the appearance of motionlessness
and gives rise to the notion of an inert matter existing,
where in fact there is a life going on no less real than that
of which we are aware in ourselves.[17] I will candidly
confess that this account of Matter has never struck me

[17] See *L'évol. créatr.* p. 273. I follow the interpretation of
Dr. Wildon Carr, *Henri Bergson,* p. 30.

as illuminating ; but rather as an example of a certain tendency, characteristic of M. Bergson, to disappoint his readers by offering a vivid picture of a familiar object as the explanation of something else of a quite different nature which we find it difficult to understand. I think that this objection to M. Bergson's account of Matter would hold even if one were able to admit more fully than I could admit the principle of his philosophy to which it is accommodated, namely that there are in very truth no moving *things* but only movement itself, not, strictly speaking, even many distinct movements; but only one continuous indivisible movement, which needs no substance in which to inhere and is itself the only Reality, itself at once the World and Life and Time.

It is not, indeed, necessary that all partisans of the claim of Life to be our sufficient clue to the nature of the Absolute should adopt this particular theory of Matter which we find in M. Bergson. But it is, as I have said, worth noting that they will in any case be in no better position in this respect than the defenders of other views which are not naturalistic. The fact that Life may seem to be, so to speak, more deeply immersed in matter than Spirit does not enable us any the more to explain Matter out of that which we contrast with it, whether that be Spirit or whether it be Life. In either case Matter is, within our experience, the medium of its manifestation, the instrument of its communication, the treasury of its past gains. We may not unreasonably suppose that it exists for its sake and in order to its service. But this is no less reasonably to be supposed in the case of Spirit than of Life, no more capable of demonstration in the case of Life than of Spirit. The assertion must in both cases rest upon a judgment of value which declares the subordination in some such fashion as has been suggested of Matter to Spirit or Life, as the case may be, to be preferable to that of Spirit cr Life to Matter as a mere by-product of the latter. For, as the history of the Cartesian philosophy proved long ago, a theory which makes them quite independent of each other will never be found tenable in view of their intimate mutual relations, especially in the case nearest and most interesting to ourselves, that of the union of body and soul in human beings. I am in no way inclined to dispute the judgment of value in question ; but it is quite as necessary to the position of the thinker who envisages the Absolute as Life as it is to him who envisages it as Spirit.

Nor can I feel satisfied that there is not in the tendency to emphasize Life rather than Spirit or Reason or Goodness as the highest category under which we can consider Reality a risk of taking refuge from certain difficulties which beset the adoption of these rival claimants in what is after all an evasion rather than a solution of the problems raised. That Spirit is more than Life and that in Spirit we have made explicit what in Life was only implicit it would be hard for any one to deny who was influenced in his preference for Life as the most important characteristic of Reality by such notions as have been described above. But if so, must it not be in Spirit rather than in Life that we shall find the secret even of the latter ? Again, while it has seemed sometimes as though Life would afford a satisfactory mean between mere Mechanism, which seems plainly inadequate to our purpose, and Reason or Intelligence, to which the facts of experience seem to be inadequate, are we sure that this is not only because we have not made up our minds as to whether Life is in truth Mechanism or Intelligence and willingly leave it to be taken for either or both and so avoid the responsibility of decision ?   For my part I suspect that the words used in a remarkable article on *Mechanism, Intelligence, and Life* contributed some time ago to the *Hibbert Journal* [18] may contain the truth on this subject.   " It will, I think, appear," says Mr. Joseph in this article, " that the real antithesis to Mechanism is Intelligence, and that Vitalism assumes in living things activity such as nothing known to us except Intelligence can show."

Lastly, if we study the language used of Life by its devotees, we shall, unless I am much mistaken, discover a singular oscillation in this view of it as respects its relation to Goodness.   On the one hand they seem to regard it as a point in its favour that it is, so to say, indifferent to our values, whether ethical or economic (to use a distinction brought into use by Signor Croce).   On the other hand, they sometimes appear to find in this very indifference something of greater worth, and more apt to stir us to awe and reverence—something, in fact, in the widest sense *better*, at the heart of things, than would be a puritanically rigorous Moral Law or a Providence solicitous of our private comfort.   We are thus led to wonder whether we can really get away, under cover of accepting Life for the Supreme Reality, from that search for Reason and Goodness as the ultimate moving principle of the Universe in which the classical tradition of philosophy from Plato and Aristotle downwards has found the true business of the would-be ' spectator of all time and all existence.' [19]

Yet perhaps the attempt to set up Life as the true type of Absolute Reality may serve a useful purpose in counteracting a tendency to interpret too narrowly the words

[18] Of April 1914.   [19] See Plato, *Rep.* vi. 486 A.

'Reason' and 'Goodness' as designations of the object of
our search. We have seen that this attempt makes a
special appeal to the artistic temperament ; and it may
be that theists have too often, especially in their arguments for the existence of God, shown a disposition to
represent the Divine Intelligence too exclusively after
the pattern of a philosopher rejoicing in the faultless
concatenation of his inferences ; of a judge dispensing
rewards and punishments according to exact desert ; or
of a skilled mechanic adapting means ingeniously to ends ;
forgetting that not only in such as these, but also in the
creative passion of the artist (of whom we are more
reminded by the study of Nature), we have an image of
the eternal Love " che move il sole e l'altre stelle." [20]
" The world," it has been said, in scornful rejection of
what seemed to the author of the epigram an ignoble
optimism—" the world is a tragedy, and not a pudding."
The saying expresses in a striking way a sentiment
which is probably widely spread among cultivated men
to-day. But does not it point to the fact that a view
of the world which ignored the tragedy in it or was
content to suppose it merely abolished as if it had not
been, would not be a veritable optimism ?

The great religious poet of Italy had such happy thoughts
of the ultimate issues of universal experience that he could
call the pilgrimage in the course whereof he imagined
himself as entering into all its phases not a tragedy but
a comedy. Nevertheless, it was certainly for him a comedy
which enclosed a tragedy within itself, yet a tragedy
of which he could ascribe the authorship to no less than

la somma sapienza e il primo amore.[21]

---

[20] Dante, *Paradiso*, xxxiii. 145.　　　[21] *Inferno*, iii. 6.

I am far from saying that there may not be in the details of Dante's exposition of his tremendous theme much which as it stands one could not accept ; that we may not miss in his mood some strains of feeling which we might think of too high worth to be thus missing without grave loss. But at least he bears impressive witness to the power of the religious consciousness to recognize the supremacy of Reason and Goodness in the world, while in no way failing to appreciate the place of tragedy therein.

It is, I think, from Plato that we shall best learn the possibilities of a view which finds in Reason and Goodness that supreme principle of unity in the search for which Philosophy may be said to consist. I speak here of Reason and Goodness together, for the intimate connexion of the two is fundamental in his teaching. He has told us [22] of the disappointment which his master Socrates expressed with the work of Anaxagoras wherein after the promise, which had seemed to Socrates so full of hope that he would account for the order of the world by Reason, he fell back in every particular case on merely mechanical explanations and did not give the kind of answer which his announcement of Reason as the grand principle of explanation had led his readers to expect. For when we ask the reason of a man's, of a reasonable being's actions, we look for a statement of his motives—that is, for an answer to the question : ' What is the good of doing that ? ' If we ask why Socrates does not escape from his prison, as his friends urge him to do, we do not give a reasonable reply if we simply describe the mechanism of his limbs which make it impossible for him to move while he is sitting still ; but we do give a reasonable reply if we allege his conscientious objection to disobeying his

[22] *Phædo*, 97 B ff.

country's laws. The famous doctrine of the Idea or
Form of Good in the *Republic* of Plato is but the
expansion of this Socratic thought.

In that dialogue [23] we are shown how the soul comes
to distinguish among the objects of perception by the
senses a solid body from what *seems* at first to be a solid
body, but proves, on the application of the rational principle that what is real cannot be self-contradictory, to
be only the reflection or shadow of a solid body. Then
we watch the same principle applied even to these real
objects of sense, as we may call them, and find that they
too are found to be full of contradictions, if we essay to
treat them as objects of Knowledge or Science properly
so called.

The line A is long compared with the line B, but short
compared with the line C ; this act is just done here and
now, but unjust done there and then ; we may be mistaken about the straightness of a visible track, or the
courage of a particular man ; but what straightness is,
and what courage is, we *know* ; and, if we did not, the
question whether this road is straight or this man brave
would be as idle as the celebrated riddle propounded at
the mad tea party about the raven and the writing desk.[24]
It is with the ' Ideas ' or ' Forms,' the eternal natures
which are single and permanent in all the shifting multitude of instances, that Knowledge in its various depart-
ments is concerned. But the impulse to seek the one
in the many must drive us farther yet. We must ask the
reason why the different orders of reality stand, as it were,
side by side, the science of each resting upon its own
peculiar principles, yet in the world wherein we find ourselves intricately intermingled. We may think—I do

[23] vi. 509 c ff.   [24] *Alice's Adventures in Wonderland*, c. 7.

not here pretend to be closely following my Platonic text—
of the indifference of the mechanism of Nature to considerations of Beauty or of Duty, while yet the worlds
which it is the business of the artist or the moralist to
explore rest upon the foundation of the physical order
and presuppose it at every point. We may note that,
as Lotze [25] has well pointed out, except in a world of
necessary connexion, wherein the issues of actions may be
depended upon, the freedom of the will could have no
scope for exercise. Yet to seek to subordinate the laws
of one kind of science to the principles of another—for
instance, to deduce mathematical truths from moral
premises or *vice versa*—can only lead to sophistry and
confusion. Everything, in Butler's often-quoted phrase, [26]
is what it is, and not another thing. The only hope of
reaching an ultimate satisfaction of that aspiration after
unity which is the very mainspring of Reason and to
which the sciences which we already possess themselves
owe their origin, must lie, I am persuaded, in the direction
which Plato has indicated to us, when he speaks of the
vision of an Idea or Form of the Good, in the light whereof
all the orders of Reality should be exhibited as good,
because filling a place in one supreme system, which would
not satisfy us were any of them missing from it. Should
we not readily allow that with the absence of any of them
the world would be *worse* off ? And if we could, like the
Creator in the Book of Genesis, [27] see the whole world to
be ' very good,' would not that give satisfaction to our
reason, so that we should not feel constrained to ask
any further ' Why is this, or wherefore is that ? '

It will be evident from what I have just said that, in

25 *Philosophy of Religion*, c. 7 § 61, tr. Ladd, p. 102.
26 Preface to the *Sermons*.   27 Gen. i. 31.

speaking of the Reason and Goodness in which our search for an ultimate principle of unity in the world of our experience could come to rest, we must not suppose ourselves to have to do with some restricted type of the one or of the other. It would be wholly in vain to ask, for example, that a reason should be given for everything, if by reason we mean a syllogistic premise or a mathematical axiom. We see quite clearly that neither syllogism nor mathematics can from their own resources account for, say, poetry or patriotism or self-sacrifice. Nor, when I speak of Goodness as the supreme principle, have I in view merely the right conduct of men in society. Great art has no moral nor has exact science. Yet these things are most certainly *good*. On the other hand, we have not to do with a mere verbal equivocation, for, in speaking of Reason and Goodness as the goal of our inquiries, we do not lay aside what we have learned of their nature in the narrower field of mathematics or of morals. In thus meaning by Reason and Goodness, when regarded as one supreme principle, at once far more than the reason used in mathematics, or than the goodness of human conduct, and yet as that for the contemplation of which the soul is educated by the mathematical sciences and by the discipline of social life, I am, as all who recollect his *Republic* will perceive, merely repeating what we find in Plato's account of the methods and aims of the philosophical life, an account which on the whole has, I think, not been bettered by any of his successors.

But, while we acknowledge the profundity of Plato's insight into the intimate connexion of Reason with Goodness, and the significance of the assertion that Goodness, as the satisfaction of Reason, is the supreme principle of unity in the world, we have to observe that he does not give so clear an answer as we might desire to the question which we may naturally raise as to the relation of this supreme principle of Goodness or the Good to God. This may seem surprising if, as Professor Burnet says,[28] it was no other than Plato that first made Theism a philosophic issue. But, when we turn to the treatment of this theme in the tenth book of the *Laws*, we find that what Plato is there concerned to maintain is that the movements of the heavenly bodies attest the existence of a Soul or Souls, having every sort of excellence, by which these movements are directed. Yet the " visible gods," the stars with the sun as their chief and centre, or rather the intelligences or souls which guide these in their courses, are not for Plato the supreme and ultimate Reality. This is to be found in the eternal Ideas or Forms, forming a single system under their unifying principle, the Form or Idea of Good, which is the Sun of the intelligible universe.[29] It is no doubt of this highest reality of all that he is speaking in a figure when he says in the *Timæus* [30] that the Maker and Father of the world is hard to discover, and to speak of his nature to all men impossible. But it is only in a figure that he is here speaking. Where he speaks of God plainly, it is of a Soul most excellent that he speaks, not of the Good which is no Soul but a Form or Idea. Professor Burnet has well pointed out (as I have already observed [31]) that the controversies determined at the Council of Nicæa have as their philosophical background the problems to which this Platonic distinction of God from the Good neces-

---

[28] See *Greek Philosophy, Thales to Plato*, § 254, p. 336.
[29] Cp. *Studies in the History of Natural Theology*, p. 94.
[30] *Tim*. 28 c.
[31] Lecture VII, p. 174. See Burnet, *Greek Philosophy, Thales to Plato*, § 255, p. 337.

sarily gave rise. We may put it thus, that the religious consciousness of the Christian Church (whose thinkers were at that time trained for the most part in Platonic traditions) could not find satisfaction in an object of worship which, however exalted, was less than the Highest ; and hence was driven to affirm an absolute equality between the Logos, the Word or Manifestation of God, and the Supreme Father, whose manifestation and utterance he was acknowledged to be. Apart from this affirmation we may say that an impersonal Goodness is left beyond and above the personal God—the divine Being with whom personal relations are possible. According to this affirmation, on the other hand, the Highest is *personal*. He is not, indeed, *a* person, because the highest personal activities, those of knowledge and love, demand an intercourse of person with person ; and yet the Highest (it was thought) could not be dependent for what is intrinsically necessary to its nature upon beings less exalted. But there is nothing impersonal above and beyond the Persons to whom the supreme Good belongs, or rather who in their eternal mutual intercourse are that supreme Good.

The view thus outlined is one which it is quite possible to criticize. Especially perhaps is this the case with respect to the insistence implied in it upon the transcendent self-sufficiency of the Divine Being. But it is not to this that I now wish particularly to call attention. It is rather to the following two points. In the first place, though we certainly do not conceive that Goodness is no more than an affection of this or that good person ; for we may recognize the imperfection by which every good person falls short of the ideal in virtue of his approximation to which he is called 'good' at all ; yet on the other hand an impersonal Goodness seems something incomplete and abstract. " There is none good but one, that is God," [32] because none other is Goodness, the Good. But if not even God is that, then there is no exception to the statement that none is in the fuller sense good ; and where in that case is this Goodness really after all ? In the second place, we see the peculiar contribution of the religious experience to the metaphysical problem of the ultimate principle of unity in its consciousness of a personal intercourse therewith, which will not be content to regard itself as consciousness of a personal intercourse with anything less than ultimate Reality ; though it welcomes the conviction that this personal intercourse is not something accidental, as it were, to the essence of that ultimate Reality, but is an admission to participation in what is from all eternity its inner activity.

It is a familiar reflection that in the activity of right thinking or knowing we take our thought to be just what must be in any mind that is occupied with the same objects, so far as it is thinking aright, or genuinely knowing. We have no such sense of a private property in knowledge as we may have in opinions in respect of which we may agree to differ. It belongs, we may say, to the nature of Mind as such so to think. If we care to introduce the mention of a Divine Mind, we may put it that we are rethinking the thoughts of God ; or we may prefer the expression that God is thinking thus in us. In Aristotle's theology the Divine Life is conceived as nothing else than an activity of knowledge ; and our highest intellectual activity is represented as not distinguishable from God's except by being temporary and intermittent, while his is eternal.[33] Just in the same way does the religious

[32] Mark x. 18.   [33] *Eth. Nic.* x. 8. 1178 B 25 ff.

experience which has expressed itself in the dogmatic system of Christianity recognize its consciousness of personal intercourse as nothing less than the consciousness of an eternal process within the Godhead.

We have now reached what appears to be a definite contribution made by the religious experience to our conception of the supreme principle of unity. As the æsthetic experience reveals in Nature a spirituality which apart from that experience cannot be shown to be there, so does the religious experience reveal in the ultimate Reality something which apart from religious experience is not there discoverable. This may be properly called Personality, for it is revealed in and through an experience of personal intercourse. It will be my task in the concluding Lecture of the present course to dwell more in detail upon the implications of the revelation in such experience of this aspect of the Divine Nature.

LECTURE X

DIVINE PERSONALITY

THE claim that Theology should be based upon Religious Experience has in our times become very familiar to those interested in such matters. But it is a thought of which little use can be made, unless we possess a fairly clear conception of the nature and scope of that which we describe by the name of Religious Experience. To the important part played in drawing attention to the subject in this country by the well-known Gifford Lectures of the late Professor William James on the *Varieties of Religious Experience* is perhaps to a considerable extent due the fact that this expression is apt to suggest too exclusively either the emotions and excitements associated with what is called ' sudden conversion ' or the extra-ordinary states of consciousness so often described in the biography of those to whom the name of ' mystics ' is commonly applied.

The prominence of these types of religious experience in James's treatment of his theme is easily explicable. In the first place the facts collected and classified by Professor Starbuck [1] which formed the basis of James's induction were drawn almost exclusively from accounts

[1] In his *Psychology of Religion* (2nd ed. London 1901), to which James contributed a Preface.

16

given by members of American Protestant communities
accustomed to require proof of a definite individual
change of mind in their younger adherents as a condition
of admission to full religious privileges. In the second
place the individualism characteristic of American religion
and encouraged by this traditional tendency in certain
churches to lay so great a stress on the importance for
spiritual life of individual feelings was thoroughly congenial to the bent of James's own mind ; while his interest
in abnormal psychology naturally directed his attention
to those phenomena which pass by the name of mystical,
and which may also be said to belong rather to the private
than to the corporate aspect of religious life. This latter
aspect seems to have appealed to him but little, and his
comparative neglect of it was the proximate occasion of
his friend and colleague Josiah Royce's striking reassertion
of its significance in the last book that he wrote, *The
Problem of Christianity*.[2]

But, though the records of conversions and of mystical
raptures are by no means to be neglected by the student
of religious experience or ignored in the construction of
a theology claiming to interpret such experience, it is, I
am convinced, a great mistake to forget here, or indeed
in the investigation of any form of human experience,
the lesson taught us in Plato's *Republic*,[3] that we shall
find it easier to read what in the individual soul is written
in letters hard to discern, if we turn first to their reproduction on a larger scale in the institutions of society.

In the public theologies and ecclesiastical polities of
mankind we have the best expression of the normal
religious experience of the peoples among whom they have
arisen. This is by no means to say that they merely

[2] New York, 1913. [3] ii. 368 D.

represent the feelings and desires of average and common-place individuals. The founders of religions and of churches, without whom they would not have come into being, have, for the most part, been prophets—that is to say, men of original religious genius ; and the same is true to a considerable extent of the organizers and reformers through whom these religions and churches have assumed their present form ; but these prophets have themselves sprung from and have exhibited in its most highly developed form the general religious type of their nation or community ; and in the creeds and institutions which have taken their rise from their teaching we have a mirror of their activity, so far as it has proved effective in stimulating and raising the level of spiritual life around them, and in maintaining it at the height to which it has thus been lifted. Without wishing to deny that the ' questionnaire ' may sometimes extract information of value even in this region of inquiry, one may not unreasonably suspect that the characteristically religious sentiments of reverence and awe may make it an instrument of investigation peculiarly unfit for wholesale employment in the field of Religion. No doubt there is a risk, to which we do well to be alive, of forgetting that the language or behaviour which has become traditional in religion may often reflect rather the thoughts and feelings of those who first introduced them than of those who at present use them. Nevertheless we are more likely to discover what men's thoughts and feelings are from the language and behaviour in which they are at any rate content to acquiesce, and under whose influence their religious life has unfolded itself, than from answers given or refused in a cross-examination to which they are not accustomed, and which may, by its apparent lack of delicacy in touching on the most sacred intimacies, reduce them at once to an indignant or obstinate silence.

I have already, in the first Lecture of this course [3] expressed my general view of the relation of the religious experience embodied in historical religions to the Natural Theology which Lord Gifford chose to be the theme of the Lectures appointed under his will. I said there that, in my judgment, while every actual system of Natural Theology presupposes a definite type of religious experience expressed in a historical religion, the ultimate goal in all speculations must be a system which shall presuppose the whole religious experience of mankind. Of course the speculations which I am offering in these Lectures make no pretence to be at any but a very remote distance from that goal. Nevertheless no one can claim in dealing with this subject to be in touch with the general movement of the civilized thought of to-day who does not extend his view beyond the boundaries of a particular system of organized religion and does not keep before his mind the ideal of a universal religion and a universal theology whose shrine and school shall be " neither in this mountain nor yet in Jerusalem " but " in spirit and in truth." [5]

So long, however, as the personal experience of any one engaging in the pursuit of this ideal is inevitably of a character far from comprehensive, he will do well to guide himself by two considerations.

In the first place he will recognize it as his special task to discover, so far as he may, the universal significance of that particular tradition whereof he is by his training and convictions an inheritor, the contribution which it has to make toward any final synthesis. In the second place,

4 P. 31 ff.   5 John iv. 21, 23.

he will frankly acknowledge that in classifying religious traditions or experiences among themselves as ' higher ' or ' lower,' although he may very possibly be often mistaken as to the particular rank to be assigned to a particular tradition or experience, he is in no wise disloyal to the ideal mentioned above, which does not and cannot require that all religions be placed upon one level, or that the student of these should hold himself debarred from preferences resting not upon mere prejudice, but upon a deliberate application of a suitable criterion.

But what is a suitable criterion ? I think that there is one, but that it is easier to apply than to formulate it. Two statements, however, about it I would venture to make, which may at first sight appear to contradict one another. One of these statements will be that we may rightly test a religion by its success in encouraging, and being itself encouraged by, moral and intellectual progress among its votaries. The other statement will be that the only true test of the rank of one religion as compared with another is to be sought in the greater or less extent to which it exhibits the specific nature of Religion, and not that of Science or of Morality as distinguished from Religion. How these two apparently inconsistent positions can be reconciled may be perhaps most conveniently suggested by an illustration from a different region of experience. We should most of us readily admit that in ranking *Venus and Adonis* and *Love's Labour's Lost* below *Hamlet* and *King Lear* we were taking into account the greater moral and intellectual interest of the latter as compared with the former. Yet we should not consider ourselves bound upon that account so to judge of poetry by the excellence of its ' moral,' or by the correctness of the scientific or historical information imparted in it, as to run into danger of placing Mrs. Turner's *Cautionary Stories* above *Romeo and Juliet* or the well-known doggerel verses which give the dates of the Norman Conquest or the Fire of London above the *Æneid* or the *Divine Comedy*. What we should ask about a poem would be, not ' What conduct does this advise ? ' or (as the legendary mathematician is reported to have asked about *Paradise Lost*) ' What does this prove ? ' but rather ' Does this express emotions consistent with moral and intellectual self-respect in the mind of him who entertains them ? '

Yet it may be objected that this question too is surely one which only a prig would put to himself, at any rate in this explicit form ; and in dealing with this objection (which has my full sympathy), we shall, I think, discover by the way an important difference between the sphere from which I took my illustration, the sphere of Art, and that which is at present our chief concern, the sphere of Religion.

When we are enjoying the nonsense of the *Walrus and the Carpenter*, the exciting incidents in the *New* (or for that matter in the old) *Arabian Nights*, or even the delightful society of the ladies and gentlemen whose doings Jane Austen has chronicled for us, we should without hesitation reply in the negative to any one who should ask us the question whether we should be content if literature never penetrated further and deeper into the mysteries of life, never took a more comprehensive view of the world than we find in these charming works of fancy and imagination. But we are content to refresh ourselves with these, to spend a holiday with them without impairing our moral and intellectual self-respect—even feeling, indeed, that to keep an eye all the time on the fact

that we are not impairing it is somehow to fail in the true
holiday spirit of enjoyment and to write ourselves down
as prigs.

But in Religion we are directly concerned with the whole
of life and experience ; hence while we may no more
estimate the rank of a religion by the application of a
non-religious standard,—as though Religion were (as it
has sometimes, indeed, been held to be) merely a means
to morality or to intellectual culture,—than we may apply
non-æsthetic standards in the criticism of works of art ;
yet we may here speak not merely of a negative consistency with the spiritual atmosphere of a high morality
and of a disinterested search for truth, but of a positive
harmony with such an atmosphere as a consideration
which may determine us in calling one form of faith
higher or lower than another.

I now come to the use which I would make for my
present purpose of these general considerations. It
falls under two heads. In the first place, if we compare
the religions of the world on some such principle as I
have just indicated, we shall, I think, have no difficulty
in acknowledging that there is none which has shown
more capacity for maintaining and even developing itself
in the atmosphere of what would be generally admitted
to be the highest moral and intellectual culture to be found
at present in the world than the religion which, as we have
had occasion to see,[6] has more than any other laid stress
on the presence of Personality in God. This will justify
us in attaching especial importance to the witness of
Christian experience ; and this is also, as it happens,
the only form of religious experience of which I myself
can claim that intimate knowledge which training and

[6] See above, Lecture III,

conviction alone can impart. And, in the second place, so far as a greater stress on Personality in God than is elsewhere to be observed is characteristic of Christianity among the religions of the world, it can, I think, be shown that this is no merely extrinsic nor accidental feature of that religion, but the fuller development therein of a factor in some degree present in all religion.

This factor is, as those who have followed the course of our discussions will have divined, no other than what passes under the name of ' divine transcendence.' Religion can never, as we have seen, [7] be content with a *merely immanent* object, though it is also no doubt true that it can never be satisfied with one *merely transcendent*. It is indeed in its discontent with either of these alternatives that it reveals itself as essentially concerned with nothing but the whole, the ' Absolute ' of modern philosophy. But while nothing seems to possess beyond question the character which, under the name of Transcendence, Religion has been shown to require in its object, the character of a reality fully equal to that of the subject, except what can claim to be, like the subject itself, *personal*, it would also be difficult to deny that even where there is no explicit assertion of Personality in the object of Religon, the religious relation is on the whole thought of as exhibiting an emotional quality of the sort especially associated with personal intercourse, whether hostile or friendly. We shall moreover, I think find that the more definite ascription of personality to the object of Religion will generally correspond to a fuller realization of his own personality by the worshipper. I shall not dwell upon this correspondence at present; for it will fall to be more fully considered

[7] See Lecture VII, p. 159.

in my second course. But it goes along with the other circumstances which I have mentioned immediately above to justify my assertion that the express affirmation of Personality in God, though made, strictly speaking, by one alone of the great historical religions of the world, is the natural culmination of a tendency traceable in all Religion, and therefore deserving of especial attention from any one desiring to construct a theology upon a broad basis of religious experience.

It will, I think, be not unprofitable to point out how, in the case of some of the principal religious conceptions —I will take for consideration those of Sin, Forgiveness, Justice, Sacrifice, Union—the acknowledgment of Personality in God does actually add both to their intelligibility and to their moral power.

It must not be supposed that the conception of Sin cannot or does not exist except in connection with the thought of an offended personality. The history of Religion shows that this is very far from being the case. Among primitive peoples it is probably more often imagined as a kind of uncleanness or infection which can by some act such as expectoration, imposition of hands, or what not, be transferred to some other person or thing and so got rid of. The terrible consequences which it is thought to entail are represented as ensuing upon it rather after the manner of direct physical effects than after that of punishments inflicted by a person whose displeasure it has incurred. On the higher levels of religious development it may still be regarded as working out its baleful issues after an impersonal fashion, as we find it regarded, for example, in ancient Greek tragedy or in the Indian doctrine of Karma, rather than as bringing them about only through the intervention of a divine Judge. It may even be contended that this view of the matter is a higher one, because assimilating the moral order of the universe to the august likeness of inexorable natural law instead of using language which may appear to aim at introducing into it the arbitrary element of personal feeling.

In opposition to this suggestion, I can but declare my conviction that to regard Sin as an offence against a personal authority, and still more to regard it as an affront to a loving Father, is a more intelligible and a more ethically significant way of thinking about it than it is to conceive it after the analogy of a physical defilement or an automatic mechanism. It is no doubt true that in our experience of the personal action of human rulers or parents there is present not only an element which, in Kant's famous phrase, is fit to be law for all rational beings, and is recognized as such by our common reason, but also an element which depends on the idiosyncrasies of the individual's peculiar temperament. But, even allowing for the moment that the latter element is un-questionably something of inferior worth, and that nothing corresponding to it is to be sought in a divine personality, should we be doing any more violence to our imagination in representing the divine character to ourselves as a *personal* character wherein desire and will are completely coincident with the requirements of Reason than in supposing an *impersonal* order which should yet be capable of inspiring in a supreme degree the veneration and the confidence which we render in varying measure to wise and good persons ? It seems to me clear that the former presentation does but take for real a perfection our comprehension of which is implied in the very contrast with it of the imperfection of human personality, whereas the latter unites by a merely verbal device characteristics which cannot really be thought together, while secretly cancelling the inconsistency by indulgence in an emotional attitude which presupposes a quite different, indeed a personal, object.

We may, however, before leaving this subject, consider a little more closely what may for the m ment be called the impersonal view of Sin, with a view of bringing it into a more detailed comparison with that which interprets it as essentially a personal offence. It may be thought, indeed, that to speak of any view of sin as ' impersonal ' must be misleading, since Sin must be regarded as at any rate committed *by* if not *against* a determinate person. But we may here recall the significant fact that Buddhism, while adopting the doctrine of Karma, which is characteristic of Indian religion in general, eliminated Personality by its denial of the existence of any substantial soul, and thereby gave an interesting illustration of the close connexion which always exists between a religious doctrine of Personality in God and a genuine concern for Personality in man.

The experience of mankind has not confirmed the belief in a detailed dependence of the course of nature upon the social conduct of men which is often found in the earlier stages of religious development. The prevalence of sexual irregularity among a people does not lead, as primitive men sometimes suppose, to the blighting of its crops ; and however true as a general rule it may be that a virtuous life conduces to the maintenance of physical health and a vicious life to its decay, yet moral goodness and bodily vigour are far too often divorced from one another to make possible an identification of the rules of hygiene with the law of holiness. Thus that ancient view of Sin which assimilates its connexion with its penalty to a natural sequence of cause and effect, and does not greatly, if at all, interest itself with the question against *whom* it is committed, seems destined to disappear with the advance of knowledge and the consequent subversion of the sanctions by which the avoidance of it was formerly secured. The doctrine of Karma, indeed, is not necessarily involved in the ruin of this view, for it cannot be subjected to the same empirical tests, since it is only from the observed fates of individuals in one life that we can ascertain the moral quality of those deeds done in other lives which, according to this doctrine, have entailed those fates. But those who share the conviction expressed above, that the recognition of a personal relation in the sinner to God makes the whole conception of Sin more intelligible and more ethically significant than it can be without such a recognition, cannot but hold that the lack of it is a serious drawback to the doctrine of Karma, as well as to cruder views of Sin which resemble it in dispensing with a God against whom Sin is committed and by whom it is judged.

It would, however, be unfair to pass over altogether without comment an argument which is not infrequently met with and which challenges the morality of introducing the notion of personal displeasure into our view of Sin, by pointing to its consequence in the doctrine of a *forgiveness of sins*, a doctrine which is (it may be alleged) of a distinctly *immoral* tendency. This is a challenge to be taken up, especially as this doctrine is one which, while it is intimately associated with the conception of Sin as a personal offence, very specially distinguishes the *religious* from the *merely ethical* view of the world. On the general question of the mutual relations of Morality and Religion

I do not here propose to dwell, because we shall encounter
it again in the course of the discussions which I have
reserved to my second series of Lectures. But on this
particular matter of the morality of the Forgiveness of
Sins it will be in place to say something at this point of
our investigations.

Insistence upon the importance of the Forgiveness of
Sins is obviously connected with the peculiar horror of
Sin which is a mark of Religion rather than of Morality
when considered apart from Religion. Yet this religious
horror of Sin need not be combined with a faith in a provision for its forgiveness. The doctrine of Karma is a
religious doctrine resting upon and expressing a profound
sense of the seriousness of Sin, but it leaves no room for
the *forgiveness* as distinct from the *expiation* of Sin. While
therefore the objection which is sometimes raised from
the side of ' mere Morality ' to the religious view of Sin
as diverting the mind from positive activity in well-doing
to gloomy meditation upon the ill-spent past may be
brought (I do not say that it would be justly brought)
against the doctrine of Karma as against doctrines embody-
ing a similar view of Sin under other religious systems,
the disciple of that doctrine may be tempted to join with
the exponent of a Morality divorced from Religion in
charging the believer in the Forgiveness of Sins with
weakening the sense of the gravity of those inevitable
consequences of ill-doing which no change of mind on the
part of the doer or of any one else can undo.

Nevertheless I think it may be shown that only if a
doctrine of the Forgiveness of Sins falls short of being
what it *professes* to be does it deserve this reproach ; and
that, when it is what it pretends to be, it possesses an
ethical depth and value beyond that of rival doctrines

which may at first sight present an aspect more awe-inspiring in their uncompromising disregard of human weakness, their vigorous enforcement of the melancholy lesson of the ' vanity of human wishes.'

Here, however, I can only attempt a very summary indication of the way in which this claim on the part of the doctrine of the Forgiveness of Sins may be maintained. In my second course of Lectures I hope to deal at greater length with the problems upon which at present I can do no more than touch.

A genuine forgiveness of sins must imply a thorough recognition, both by the sinner forgiven and by him who forgives, of the nature of the sin committed. It must thus be quite inconsistent alike with impenitence on the sinner's part or with indifference to the gravity of the offence on his who forgives. No doubt it is possible to speak of a forgiveness of those " who know not what they do," [8] but in such a case those who are said to be forgiven must miss the full experience of forgiveness, except in so far as by such a subsequent understanding of their action as necessarily involves repentance they appropriate the pardon which has been by anticipation already pronounced. And on the other hand, a sinner who does not find in what is offered him under the name of forgiveness a comprehension of the heinousness of his offence correspondent to the depth of his own penitence cannot but feel that he has failed to attain that for which he seeks. Here at once we see how, if personal relations exist only between human beings, the penitent sinner must be often thus defrauded ; while if, on the other hand, he can always pass beyond the neighbour he has offended to God and say with the Psalmist of the *Miserere*, " Against *thee*

[8] Luke xxiii. 34.

have I sinned " 9 he can attain in the experience of divine forgiveness what otherwise he must for ever go without.

But the supposed immorality of the Forgiveness of Sins disappears if we regard it in this way ; and no kind of Forgiveness which falls short of this has any claim to rank as an idea which, in Mr. Bradley's phrase,[10] " is really required in practice by the highest religion." And as to the superior dignity which may be attributed to an eternal Order conceived impersonally, whether after the manner of Karma in Indian religion or otherwise, I can but repeat what I have in substance already said, that we can only reverence it in so far as we impart into our attitude towards it an element which is at home only in personal intercourse ; for a system definitely realized as impersonal, of which we can say that it " as impotently rolls as you or I " [11] we are far more likely, when we find ourselves helplessly in its grip, to loathe and curse than to venerate. And yet, even in loathing and cursing it, we shall not cease to illustrate the unconquerable tendency of the human soul to envisage its relation to the ultimate Reality in terms of personality ; we shall but be treating it as a devil instead of as a God.

I am not forgetting in what I have just said the austere and lofty piety of the Stoics and Spinoza which would find freedom and peace in the world by willing that what we cannot help happening should happen. But I feel sure that here again the use of the name of God is really in contradiction with the conception of his nature explicitly held. " Our wills are ours to make them " [12]

9 Psa. li. 4.
10 See *Essays on Truth and Reality*, p. 433. Cp. p. 439.
11 Fitzgerald, *Rubáiyát of Omar Khayyám* (3rd and 4th eds.), § 72.
12 Tennyson, *In Memoriam*, introductory verses.

God's, but this saying has no meaning if God's will is a *mere* figure of speech, if it is not at least as really what we mean by will as ours is. But here, as in all similar cases we must remember, if we are to be true to our purpose of basing our theology upon religious experience, that our starting-point must be our experience of submission to the divine Will and not an attempt to imagine the divine self-consciousness in abstraction from that experience.

Having dealt so fully with the conceptions of Sin and of Forgiveness as religious ideas which seem to possess a greater value in the context of a personal relation to God than otherwise, it will not be necessary to dwell in the same detail on the others which I mentioned as agreeing with these in that respect—that is, on Justice, Sacrifice, and Union. But some few observations may, perhaps, be profitably made upon each in turn.

In the case of Justice it might plausibly be argued that ideal or absolute Justice may be best conceived on the analogy rather of the working of a law than on that of an award by a personal judge. It might be pointed out that we regard the establishment of a legal system, whereof persons are but the ministerial agents, as an advance upon the stage of social development in which one is left to the chances of finding on the judgment-seat a Solomon or an unjust judge who " fears not God nor regards man " [13] as the case may happen to be. This seems to point to the progressive diminution or elimination of the personal factor as indicating the direction we should follow in our attempts to work out the thought of a supreme Justice.

On the other hand, we must note that there is much reason for doubting whether the notion of a personal

[13] Luke xviii. 4.

source of Justice, whether in a sovereign or in God, is
not on the whole younger than that of a custom or law
valid on its own account and only declared by the
individual judge.

But I shall do no more than call attention to this fact,
and shall not now pursue the consideration of it ; it will
come before us again when in my second course of Lectures
I attempt to trace the bearing of the conclusions reached
in this course upon our view of the various activities in
which human Personality expresses itself. I only mention
it at present to show that the elimination of the personal
element is far from constituting the whole story of the
development of our notion of Justice. What I would
rather insist upon here is that our preference for an impersonal law over the personal discretion of the judge is
due chiefly to the security afforded by it against the
uncertainty which must prevail where the discretion
must be now one man's and now another's. There are
persons to whose discretion one would commit oneself
with far more confidence than to the generalities of a
legal rule ; and hence our care to leave as little scope as
possible in human tribunals for the vagaries of personal
caprice does not at all carry with it an ultimate preference
for the impersonal over the personal, which we must
needs carry over even into our notion of divine justice.

Again, impersonal Justice is contrasted with *Mercy*.
So opposite to one another may the two conceptions
seem to be that men have sometimes imagined them to
be the respective attributes of different divine persons.
But we should in fact scarcely call an unmerciful person
just ; and, in speaking of a person as unjust, we should
think rather of his hard treatment of those who do not
deserve it than of his comparative over-leniency to others ;

17

we should certainly think it strange to describe him on account of such over-leniency as a merciful man. The truest Justice would seem to include Mercy, and Mercy in the highest sense would vindicate for itself the name of Justice ; and it is, I am convinced, easier to represent to ourselves such a union as realized in a personality than after any other fashion. It is not unworthy of remark in this connection that in political communities the prerogative of *mercy* is habitually left to be *personally* exercised by the head of the State or by those who rule in his name, after everything possible has been done to exclude his or their interference in the administration of *justice*.

In turning to another important religious conception, that of Sacrifice, we find that investigation of its history by no means goes to show that a sacrifice is always thought to be offered to a determinate person any more than Sin is always thought to be committed against a determinate person or Justice to be that which is in accordance with the decree of a determinate person. Thus it is not a merely trifling proposition to say that we see the notion of Sacrifice in its most intelligible and ethically significant form where Sacrifice is regarded as an act of personal intercourse between a worshipper and his God. It belongs to Sacrifice in the fullest and highest sense that what is sacrificed should be, in the very surrender of it, recognized by the sacrificer as good. Hence there may seem to be at the heart of the notion a contradiction ; there is certainly a paradox, in so far as something is treated at once as good (since, if it is not good, there is no sacrifice in the surrender of it) and as not good (since it is not pursued, but, on the contrary, declined). This paradox becomes intelligible only where the thing in question being surrendered to God is regarded as safe in him ; in whom, although not directly in itself, its goodness is enjoyed, even when surrendered. To this an analogy may be easily found in the mutual relations of persons but hardly elsewhere ; and it cannot be disputed that to such mutual relations of persons as those of which one is here thinking we attribute a value superior to any which could be assigned to Sacrifice as a religious act on any theory but that of an intercourse with the God capable of expression in terms of personal relations.

The religious idea of Union with the Supreme Reality, the ruling idea of Mysticism as we may call it, is the last of those which I propose to take in illustration of my thesis that the recognition of Personality in God imparts to religious ideas generally an increase of intelligibility and of ethical significance. A particular interest belongs to this idea in connexion with our present inquiry. For some thinkers who lay especial stress on Divine Personality are inclined to be suspicious of all mystical language, just because to them a union of two personalities in any such intimate sense as that which mystical language suggests appears to them impossible 14 ; while, on the other hand, thinkers of a different turn of mind are disposed to appeal to this same mystical language, which is so recurrent in the history of Religion, in proof of the inadequacy of the notion of Divine Personality to the requirements of the religious consciousness. I cannot, however, here enter upon anything like a full examination of this controversy, my general view of which may be easily inferred from the discussion of kindred issues in preceding Lectures. There is a celebrated phrase which might seem to suggest a loss of Personality in the climax

14 I am thinking especially of Dr. Rashdall.

of Union—I am thinking of the figure under which entrance upon Nirvana, the goal of the Buddhist's spiritual ambition, is described in the words : " The dewdrop slips into the shining sea." [15] In this phrase there is, in fact, nothing to mark the existence of Personality on *either* side. The dewdrop is no more personal than the ocean into which it is absorbed. In itself this might indicate no more than that the contrast of the personal existence of the saint in this life with the impersonal nature of the Eternal Being from which at death he ceased to be distinct was absent from the mind of the framer of the phrase. But it is doubtful if even finite Personality has any place in the original philosophy of Buddhism. On the other hand, the great mass of mystical literature in which the union with God is described under the imagery of a marriage between lovers bears impressive testimony to the truth that the human soul is for the most part best satisfied when in the culmination of its religious experience it recognizes the antitype of the most intimately personal form which human fellowship can assume.

Now it is doubtless possible to admit (as Mr. Bradley would, he tells us,[16] be willing to admit) that our relation to God may be rightly represented as a personal relation, while insisting that this will not entitle us to attribute Personality to the Absolute, the supreme and ultimate Reality. For to do this would (according to this way of thinking) be to transfer the imaginative language of Religion without modification to Metaphysics which, as it is sometimes hinted, is in a very special sense the sphere of ' bitter earnest.'

It is certainly not my intention to deny that the language

---

[15] See Edwin Arnold's *Light of Asia*, bk. viii. *ad fin.*
[16] See *Essays on Truth and Reality*, pp. 432, 451.

of Religion is always imaginative and in a sense mythological, and that to take it to be literally and prosaically true as it stands will be apt to lead us into error. Nor would I have the metaphysician abate a jot of his determination to pursue the intellectually satisfying at all costs. But (and here Mr. Bradley would assuredly agree) it is not the test of the intellectually satisfying that it should be expressible in prosaic language. Nor can Religion be content that her language should be treated as ' merely figurative ' [17] in the sense in which the term might be used of an eighteenth-century poet's conventional invocation of the Muse. The language of Religion we must no more dismiss without discrimination as figurative than accept it without discrimination as scientifically exact. I will go back to an illustration of which I made use earlier in these Lectures.[18] A child's picture of his elders' lives is no doubt very unlike indeed to those elders' lives as known to themselves from within. Or again, we may think of the distance which may separate a savage's notion of what the ruler or generalissimo of a great civilized State has to do from such an one's actual conduct of government or warfare. Yet as the child grows up or the savage is educated, there need be no shock in their gradual discovery of the unlikeness in many respects of their earlier picture to the reality. But what if it should dawn upon the child that those he called his parents

[17] I have seen an eighteenth-century translation of the New Testament intended to satisfy readers to whom the Authorized Version seemed written in a style which, tried by the standard of Hume and Robertson, was rude and unpolished. John vi. 63 was (if my memory does not deceive me) thus translated : " The discourse which I have been addressing to you is entirely figurative ; and to take it in any other sense would be to be guilty of the highest absurdity."

[18] See Lecture V, p. 131.

were not real persons at all ? Were he only to learn
that they were no more than foster parents, or that they
did not love him as they seemed to do, the discovery
might be baffling, disheartening, discouraging enough.
But what would it be in comparison to the discovery that
they had no more independent existence than the cor-
respondents of Mr. Toots ? [19] Would not this be a complete subversion of the world in which he had grown up
and a grave threat to his sanity ?

The application of this to our present subject will, I
think, be obvious. We shall readily believe that in personal
intercourse with God we behold so small a part of his ways [20]
that nothing we could report of them but would probably
or even certainly require drastic revision from the point
of view of a fuller knowledge. We shall indeed all the
more readily believe it, the more deeply penetrated we
are with the sense of being truly in communion with the
Highest. But that this intercourse is not a genuinely
personal intercourse at all ; that personality in " him
with whom we have to do " [21] is no less figurative than
the image of the father's table or the mother's breast or
the bridegroom's embrace, which we may use, turn and
turn about, despite their mutual inconsistency, as suits
our mood ; that there is no reciprocal knowledge and love
coming to meet us at all ; or that, if there is, it is not on
the part of the true God, who is, as we may say, at the
back of everything ; to discover this—and really to believe
in our discovery—would it not mean the overthrow of
our religion, the revelation of such an incoherence in the
world as must confound the reason and shake knowledge
from its very foundations ?

[19] In Dickens's *Dombey and Son*, see c. 12.
[20] See Job xxvi. 14.   [21] See Heb. iv. 13.

I think that it would ; and yet, before we conclude that religious experience favours the affirmation of personality in God, we must turn aside to consider a possible assertion by the opponents of this position of a religious interest which may be enlisted upon their side. Is it not a principal interest of Religion, it may be asked, to be kept from falling into Idolatry ? And is there not in the view which has been maintained in this Lecture, and in the reasons by which it has been supported, an encouragement of a tendency in that direction, full of danger to the very cause we have been endeavouring to serve ?

From the point of view of a philosophical theology we must understand by Idolatry the worship as God of that which, at the moral and intellectual level occupied by the worshipper, is less than the Highest. The acquiescence by thinkers like Mr. Bradley and Mr. Bosanquet in the distinction of God from the Absolute must, it would seem, imply the condemnation of any one who stands at their high level of philosophical culture to a choice between Idolatry and no Religion at all. I suspect that Signor Croce would agree with me in drawing this inference from their premises, and for himself would frankly embrace the second of the alternatives allowed. Of Mr. Bosanquet I will speak later on ; but Mr. Bradley would, I think, prefer the former, while disclaiming the insinuation of disparagement conveyed by the word Idolatry, for which he would probably prefer to substitute ' worship of an Appearance.' I must confess to an unwillingness to accept either alternative, and am ready to justify this unwillingness on the ground that, as I have elsewhere said in another connexion, " I do not think it possible to remain content with the reduction of an experience so manifestly substantial, rational, and harmonious as a genuine religious experience can be to the rank of mere mirage or sheer illusion." [22] And, while no doubt this is by no means what Mr. Bradley and Mr. Bosanquet intend to effect, I am convinced that denial of the claim of Religion to take as its object nothing less than the supreme and ultimate Reality can have no other issue.

In the history of Religion the idolatry of to-day is often the true religion of yesterday, and the true religion of to-day the idolatry of to-morrow, but only if we look for the identity of a religion merely in the identity of the symbolism which it employs. But that religion which has its face set ever towards the Supreme Reality and which does not lower its thought thereof to accord with its symbols, but rather adapts its symbols, or replaces them by others better adapted to the highest and best that it can conceive, this is true Religion, whatsoever symbols it may use.

On the other hand, such a new religion as Mr. Bradley [23] seems to desire, which metaphysics, although its full requirements would still not be met, might be able, " in some sense " (as he says), " to justify and support," would, I fear, like the worship of the Golden Calf in Horeb, wear from the first the air of a ' substitute ' provided to satisfy those whose impatience will not allow them to wait for, or to do without, the genuine article, and could hardly in the long run be able, any more than that worship, to escape condemnation as an idolatrous service.

In personal intercourse with our friends, if we rest content with our first impressions or even with the impressions gained at any stage of our friendship and cease from further exploration of their characters we are so

[22] *Group Theories of Religion*, p. 181.
[23] See *Essays on Truth and Reality*, p. 446.

far falling short of the ideal of such intercourse. It may be that our own limitations or those of our friend really make this check to our activity inevitable. Still it is a failure. The most successful marriage is that where romance does not culminate with the wedding bells, but where each partner can to the end address the other in those brave words of Browning's :—

> Grow old along with me!
> The best is yet to be.[24]

But if we can go so far as this in speaking of the converse of human lovers and friends, it is surely the very essence of that other converse which we call Religion, where we have to do with no finite being, but with the Supreme and Eternal, that the possibilities of discovery therein are inexhaustible. To suppose that, on the attainment of any level of insight, we have seen all there is to see, this is surely to commit the sin of Idolatry, no matter how free we may be from any temptation to "bow down to wood and stone."[25] But it is not necessary, because we must not suppose God to be no more than that of which we have experience in the personal intercourse of our religion, to deny that this is personal intercourse at all We know that it is, and, so far as to speak of Personality in God expresses this knowledge, it is more than a mere symbolical phrase ; although any imaginative repre-sentation of this Personality, such as we cannot but form, may fairly be called symbolical, and be acknowledged to be such without any derogation from the reality of the experience in the service of which it is formed.

That when once the stage of religious development

---

[24] *Rabbi ben Ezra*, § 1.
[25] Heber, *Hymn before a Collection made for the S.P.G.*

is reached at which religious experience takes the form of
an experience of personal intercourse, the denial that
there is truly Personality in God must in the end lead
to the denial that religious experience is an independent
and autonomous form of experience at all, I feel for my
own part no doubt whatever.

I think that the Philosophy of Religion owes a considerable debt to Signor Croce for bringing this clearly
out. I am of course very far from disputing the sincerity
and deep conviction of Mr. Bosanquet in adopting as he
does a different view. But it seems to me that his thought
about the Absolute is constantly coloured by the religious
associations of the language which he employs—the
language of the religion which has above all others insisted
on Personality in God. The difference between his
intellectual temperament and that of Signor Croce corresponds to a conspicuous difference between the national
characters of the peoples of which they are such eminent
representatives ; a difference which shows itself in politics
in the fact that the ' anticlericalism ' of the Latin countries
of Europe has no precise analogue in Great Britain. I
sympathize, I will admit, far more with Mr. Bosanquet
than with Signor Croce in regard to their respective
attitudes toward Religion ; but I think that Signor Croce
is in this matter the more logical of the two.

In an earlier Lecture [26] I discussed the antithesis
between Personality and Reason. We saw that while
Reason was an essential feature of our conception of Personality, it was nevertheless a difficulty felt in ascribing
Personality to God that there seemed to be involved in
Personality something which, unlike Reason, was not
common to all persons, in so far as they reasoned aright.

[26] Lecture V.

Yet should we not, in ascribing to the thought of a Divine Mind any variation from this common Reason, anything capricious or arbitrary or susceptible of an explanation only from some peculiar circumstances of the thinker, be ascribing to it something incompatible with the perfect Wisdom and Truth which are at any rate an important part of what we mean by God ?

On the other hand, the characteristic religious emotion of Reverence was one which it appeared hard to refer to an *impersonal* object. The dilemma in which we find ourselves thus placed has more than once come into view in the course of our discussions, without having been ever finally disposed of. I would now at last invite your attention to some few considerations which are all that I have to contribute to the solution of a very real difficulty.

In what has been said above of a common Reason, it will be clear that we have had in mind the kind of Reason which is exemplified in what are often called the exact Sciences. These Sciences, as was pointed out in the first Lecture of this course, may be said to take as little account as possible of personal differences. Though of course not all men are equally endowed with the capacity or the opportunity for carrying on the investigations proper to these branches of knowledge, so that personal differences affect in this way the history even of the exact Sciences ; yet we regard the trains of thought employed therein as throughout capable of statement in generally intelligible terms and communicable not only in respect of the results but also in respect of the processes which have led up to those results. We suppose that from the same premises any person competent to understand them must draw the same conclusions as any other. Moreover, as we saw in the fifth Lecture, when examining the ethical doctrines of Kant and Fichte, we seemed to find in the field of Practical Reason also the same neglect as characterized the exact sciences of a factor no less indispensable to Personality than the rationality which distinguishes it from other forms of individual existence. But, if we turn from the exact sciences to the field of Art, we perceive at once an interesting difference. We should never say that any competent musician or man of letters could see how a symphony of Beethoven or a play of Shakespeare should be completed, if only he had the earlier movements or acts before him. On the other hand, we do not regard this fact as meaning no more than that the composer or poet may do as he likes, and that he might have finished off his work in half a dozen ways as well as in that upon which he actually hit. On the contrary, we are disposed when we see how it is done to say ' That is the only possible way in which it could satisfactorily have been done.' [27] Reason, the common Reason, could not anticipate but can endorse it, and can say, as Albert Dürer is reported to have said of a picture of his own, " Sir, it could not have been better done." In the creative activity of the artist we seem to see Personality and Reason no longer contrasted but reconciled and at one. God, it was said of old, plays the geometer ; [28] but does he not play the artist too ? Or rather, is not the artist made in his image as well as the geometer and the moralist ? And was not the writer of Genesis happily inspired when he imagined the Creator,

[27] I am especially conscious here of a debt to the conversation of my friend Mr. C. J. Shebbeare, though he is in no way responsible for my use of thoughts suggested to me by him. Cp. his *Challenge of the Universe*, p. 183, and Mr. Temple's *Mens Creatrix*, p. 154.

[28] Plutarch, *Quæst. Conv.* viii. 2, p. 718 c. ff.

like a greater Dürer, beholding " all that he had made, and behold it was very good " ? [29]

These reflections upon the possibility of conceiving a factor in the Divine Mind distinguishable from that which seemed, when supposed to exist in absolute perfection, to exclude something necessary to Personality, and yet by no means describable as an irrational factor, may, I think, be supplemented by some observations intended to suggest that a Reason of what may conveniently be called the mathematical type is not adequate to interpret even the world with which the investigations of the natural sciences themselves are concerned.

In the first place, it is to be borne in mind that even according to that view of the physical world which we may call pre-evolutionary, but which has not always been abandoned by thinkers who have won fame as exponents of a philosophy of Evolution—I mean the view which looks to the laws of matter in motion and of the compounding of simple elements for a complete explanation of all phenomena—there must, as John Stuart Mill pointed out,[30] be supposed an initial collocation of material elements, inexplicable by those laws themselves, but necessary before they could begin to operate. Such an original collocation would in theistic language be referable only to the Divine Will ; and thus even an account of the world in terms of a pre-evolutionary natural science would seem to involve in its cause not merely a Reason whose workings could be traced out by a calculating intelligence from certain premises, but a Reason which could establish those premises—in other words, a Reason which, working, in the phrase of Leibnitz [31] in accordance with the principle

[29] Gen. i. 31.   [30] *Logic*, iii. 5 §§ 8, 9.
[31] See *Théodicée* i. 8.

of the *best*, is more easily conceived—is perhaps only conceivable—after the analogy of a personal intelligence.

If, however, the conception of development be taken seriously, we must refuse to accept the pronouncement of the Hebrew Preacher that there is no new thing under the sun,[32] and must acknowledge, with M. Bergson, that evolution is creative ; and in that case it is clear that the Intelligence which is manifested in the world-process must be thought of rather after the analogy of the dramatist than after that of the geometer ; so that there will not seem to be the same incongruity in the attribution of Personality to it which there certainly is when, in representing to ourselves the Supreme Mind, we employ the analogy rather of the mathematician or moralist than that of the artist.

Shall I be thought too fanciful if I add to these two considerations a third, drawn from the implication of such judgments as we constantly make when we speak of certain events imagined or even actual as grotesque or fantastic, or as like bad dreams or nightmares ? We seem to appeal herein to a certain mood or style as we may put it, which, though we could no doubt not describe it in detail, we feel to be that of Reality, and with which the imaginations or experiences in question are, as it were, out of tune. Although no doubt we often speak of this as especially manifested in what we call Nature, that is to say in the world as unaffected by the deliberate operations of man—the thought which inspires such language is of course the ruling idea in the poetry of Wordsworth— yet it is possible sometimes to find Nature itself strike a jarring note. We may recall the familiar lines of Tennyson :—

[32] Eccles. i. 9.

Are God and Nature then at strife,
That Nature lends such evil dreams ? [33]

And the very outcries of pessimistic spirits to whom the
world seems a ' city of dreadful night ' remind us of those
dream experiences in which we comfort ourselves in
the midst of horrors by an assurance that we shall awake
out of what must be after all a dream because it has not
the familiar sanity of the real world.   It is not of the mood
of Nature as contrasted with Man or with Spirit so much
as of the mood of Ultimate Reality that I am here thinking.   Coleridge said [34] that the World was no goddess
in petticoats but the Devil in a strait waistcoat.   And
certainly, since the evil wills of men undoubtedly produce
their evil effects in the real world, I cannot affirm *a priori*
that there are no evil wills other than human to which
what we cannot but hold to be evil in the world beyond
humanity may be traceable. [35]   I should rather hold
it to be likely that there are such.   But that does not
affect our capacity of apprehending what we may call
the standard mood or style—as we may speak of the
mood or style of a particular poet or artist—whether
what we call Nature fully express it or no.   Such a capacity
seems, indeed, to be implied in our æsthetic judgments
generally.   We appreciate and take pleasure in all kinds
of eccentric moods and feel that it is well to have them
isolated and expressed by individual artists, yet we fall
back for more enduring satisfaction on the great masters—

Who saw life steadily and saw it whole. [36]

But even these are only relatively universal, only relatively

33 *In Memoriam*, § 55.   34 *Table Talk*, April 30, 1830.
35 See *Problems in the Relations of God and Man*, p. 270.
36 Matthew Arnold, *To a Friend.*

satisfying. They are not always in accord with one another, and we reach forward after a supreme mood which will harmonize them without loss in no merely eclectic or artificial fashion.[37] What are we here speaking of but of that in the Supreme Spirit whereof what we call the 'personally characteristic' in a finite spirit is the image, just as in that which in knowledge and morality is common to all rational beings philosophers have been ever ready to recognize the thoughts or ideas of the Eternal Mind ? I do not know that I have made intelligible the drift of a speculation which it would take too long to attempt further to develop here. But I hope I may have done so sufficiently for my present purpose, and will now pass on to the last topic to which I shall call your attention in my present course.

It will perhaps have occurred to my readers that the arguments of this Lecture have pointed rather to a single personality *of* God than to that distinction of persons *in* God which, as we saw before, was taught by the theology which, among the great theologies of the world, had been most in earnest with the task of working out the implications of Divine Personality.

It has been my contention throughout that, although the existence of Personality must in any case give rise to problems which cannot but embarrass every philosophy unable to allow to it any but the subordinate significance assigned to it by all systems except those which may be classed as theistic, yet a satisfactory defence of Divine Personality can only be founded upon the facts of religious experience. Nor, in my judgment, can a theological account of such religious experience as takes the form

[37] Here too I am conscious of a special obligation to the conversation of Mr. Shebbeare.

of the consciousness of personal intercourse with the Supreme stop short of conceiving this personal intercourse as itself falling within the divine life, and thereby translating the personal distinction which it involves into a fundamental factor in the Supreme or Absolute Experience itself. But this personal distinction cannot be interpreted as involving a difference in personal character without abolishing that unity behind and through all differences which is what we primarily have in view in speaking of the Absolute at all. It could only involve such a difference for those who could accept a genuine pluralism, which would appear in a religious form as a true and thorough-going polytheism.

Such a thorough-going polytheism, we must observe, we shall not find in doctrines of a hierarchy of many gods under a single chief, but rather in such as leave us at the end with an eternal opposition of a good and an evil Principle.[38] If, however, the personal distinction within the Supreme Experience to which our religious experience testifies is not to be regarded as involving a corresponding personal difference of character, then the analogue, or rather archetype, in God of the personally characteristic element in human souls will not be diversified by the existence of the personal distinction which, in the language of Christian theology, is called the distinction of the Son from the Father ; and the language used about it will not vary from what would be used by theists who recognize no such personal distinction within the Divine life.

This is not, of course, to say that the rich variety of personal character wherein lies the great interest of personal intercourse is lost in the Supreme Experience. In its relation to the personal distinction which we may call

[38] See St. Thomas Aquinas, *Summa contra Gentiles*, i. 42 ad. fin.

18

that of the Son or Word from the Father, it is probably best represented as constituting the content of the Word, and the corresponding variety of moods as " broken lights " [39] of what I have called the supreme mood, of which may be given the name which the poet gives it from whom that phrase is taken—the name of " immortal Love."

On the other hand, care must be taken to avoid the suggestion that this richness of content is absent from the other term of the personal distinction, which Christian theology calls the Father. For it would destroy the very meaning of that religious faith in following the implications of which we have been induced to borrow the terminology of the Christian schools, if the wealth possessed in the religious life is more or less or other than that supreme Good which is the nature of the Father, and therefore that of whosoever can call himself his Son.

It is for this very reason that this bond of union, this common nature itself, can come to be described in theological phraseology as *Person* also. It might seem that the analogy of human intercourse would suggest another word. Two human persons' love of one another may be the best thing about each of them ; yet we describe it as an affection or sentiment on the part of each rather than as something no less real than they themselves who feel it. They may come to lose it and yet remain real. On the other hand, if we think of the bond which binds human beings together as a community or society to which they belong, and of this as something no less real than its members, or rather as something more lasting, more sacred, more august than any of its members, something for which they may even sacrifice their lives, yet

[39] Tennyson, *In Memoriam*, introductory verses.

we know how even here it does not seem to possess, despite
its greater permanence and dignity, that special assurance
of reality which comes to the individual members in their
consciousness of self. The intention of the theological
phraseology to which I have referred I take to be no other
than this—to claim for the life of mutual knowledge and
love which, in the intercourse of Religion, the worshipper,
so far as he realizes his sonship, enjoys with the Supreme,
and in enjoying it recognizes to be no other than the
very life itself of the Supreme—to claim for that life a
complete concrete reality, in no respect less than that
of those who share in it and have their being in it.

Here I must leave the subject of Divine Personality :
in the sequel I hope to consider what is the bearing upon
our conception of human Personality and of its manifestation in the various phases of human life, of that
conception of Personality in God which I have attempted
to outline in the present course of Lectures.

INDEX

Straightness, 21
Stuckenberg, J. H. W., 119
Subject, 57
Subjective, 56 f.
Substance, *Substantia*, 37 ff., 44, 222 ff.
Suetonius, 35 n.
Swinburne, 219

Temple, Dr. W., 268 n.
Tennyson, 30, 95, 255, 270 f., 274
Teresa, St., 227
Tertullian, 27, 44 f., 66 f., 137
Theodorus of Gadara, 38 n.
Thomas Aquinas, 64, 75, 90, 273 n.
Thompson, Francis, 208
Thompson, James, 271
Time, 22, 201 f., 217
Transcendence, 33, 70, 73, 75, 140, 148 ff., 196, 248
Trinity, 20, 42 ff., 51, 57, 61 ff., 82, 102, 130, 145 n., 161, 213, 272 ff.
Turner, Elizabeth, 246

Turretinus, 56 n., 69 n.
Tyrrell, George, 227 n.

Union, 249, 256, 259 f.
Unitarianism, 62 ff., 84 f., 160 f., 163
Unity, 218, 220 ff.
Universal, 175, 201, 220 ff.
Usener, Hermann, 47 n.

Valentinus Gentilis, 62 n.
Virgil, 246

Wallace, W., 59 n.
Warren, H. C., 203
Watson, Sir W., 29
Wells, Mr. H. G., 103 ff., 135 ff., 147, 192 f.
Will, 55, 59
Wilson, J. Cook, 119 n.
Wisdom of Solomon, 39
Wolff, 58, 62 n.
Wordsworth, 28, 122, 171, 178, 200, 270

Zeller, 37 n.

Printed in Great Britain by
UNWIN BROTHERS, LIMITED, THE GRESHAM PRESS, WOKING AND LONDON

Social Purpose
A Contribution to a Philosophy of Civic Society

By H. J. W. HETHERINGTON, M.A.

Professor of Logic and Philosophy in the University College of
South Wales and Monmouthshire, Cardiff

AND J. H. MUIRHEAD, LL.D.

Professor of Philosophy in the University of Birmingham

Demy 8vo.   10s. 6d. net.

"The authors keenly analyse the problems . . . and show how the
ideals of democracy bear upon them."—*Athenæum.*

Elements of Constructive Philosophy

By J. S. MACKENZIE, LITT.D.
(Camb.); HON. LL.D. (Glasg.)

Emeritus Professor of Logic and Philosophy in University College, Cardiff;
formerly Fellow of Trinity College, Cambridge

Demy 8vo.   12s. 6d. net.

"The book is sufficient. In its pages is all that the educated man
needs to know or is likely to care to know. The arrangement is
methodical; the style is crisp and conclusive."—*Expository Times.*

Scientific Synthesis

By EUGENIO RIGNANO

TRANSLATED BY W. J. GREENSTREET, M.A.

Demy 8vo.   7s. 6d. net, postage 6d.

"Exceedingly valuable and suggestive."—*Glasgow Herald.*
"Takes the reader through many a fascinating field of research and
speculation."—*Scotsman.*
"Especially fruitful in ideas leading to further research."—*Athenæum.*

The Metaphysical Theory of the State

By PROFESSOR
L. T. HOBHOUSE, D.LITT.

Demy 8vo.   7s. 6d. net.

"No modern writer has so clearly worked out the main theoretical
relations of the State to the individual citizen and to other social forces
and institutions. The reasoning is close and cogent. Prof. Hobhouse is
an admirable guide."—*Manchester Guardian,*

Outlines of Social Philosophy

By J. S. MACKENZIE, Litt.D., LL.D.

Demy 8vo.   10s. 6d. net.

"Dr. Mackenzie's able and interesting work is of special value at the present time. It is written with much literary grace."—*Scotsman.*

The Rival Philosophies of Jesus and of Paul   By I. SINGER

Demy 8vo.   10s. 6d. net.

The author's contention is that there are two distinct and mutually destructive philosophies in the Gospels, one by Jesus and one by Paul. He vindicates the philosophy of Jesus on scientific grounds, but rejects the Christology of Paul as unhistorical and irrational.

The Nature of Being
An Essay in Ontology

By HENRY H. SLESSER
Barrister-at-Law

Demy 8vo.   10s. 6d. net.   Postage 6d.

The author, in pleading for a closer consideration of the Problem of Ultimate Being beyond the confines of Knowledge, justifies a mystic attitude in Metaphysic on logical grounds. In his essay on Ontology, Mr. Slesser explores a field of philosophy much neglected since the time of the early Greeks.

The Relationship between the Mystical & the Sensible Worlds

By HERBERT N. G. NEWLYN

Crown 8vo.   4s. 6d. net.

"As publishers of scientific and sociological treatises, Messrs. George Allen & Unwin Ltd. have justly earned a reputation. This has been added to by the publication of 'The Relationship between the Mystical and the Sensible Worlds,'"—*Edinburgh Evening News.*

The Six-Hour Day

And Other Industrial Questions

By LORD LEVERHULME

With an Introduction by
THE RT. HON. VISCOUNT HALDANE OF CLOAN

Demy 8vo. Edited by Stanley Unwin. Second Ed. 12s. 6d. net.

"Deserves the attentive study of all who are now thinking of reconstruction—that is to say, of all the electors of the country."—*Westminster Gazette.*

"Here is the one clear voice from the side of enlightened capitalism heard above the babel of reconstructive chatter. Lord Leverhulme's scheme has been deftly woven into a volume which demands earnest attention from social and economic thinkers."—*Christian World.*

"In the consideration of the knotty problems of capital and labour the views of Lord Leverhulme must carry weight."—*Truth.*

The Idea of Public Right

Being the first four Prize Essays in each of the three divisions of *The Nation* Essay Competition

With an Introduction by the Rt. Hon. H. H. ASQUITH.

Demy 8vo. 8s. 6d. net.

Our Democracy: Its Origin and its Tasks

By JAMES H. TUFTS
Professor in the University of Chicago

Large Crown 8vo. 7s. 6d. net.

"Is popular in its treatment. It attacks large problems in a bold and clear-sighted fashion, remarkable for the clearness and directness of its exposition."—*Scotsman.*

After-War Problems

By the late EARL OF CROMER and Others

Edited by William Harbutt Dawson

Demy 8vo. Fourth Impression. 8s. 6d. net. Postage 6d.

"Valuable, clear, sober, and judicial."—*The Times.*
"A book of real national importance, and of which the value may very well prove to be incalculable."—*Daily Telegraph.*

Problems of the Peace

By WILLIAM HARBUTT DAWSON
Author of "The Evolution of Modern Germany"

Demy 8vo. REVISED EDITION. *8s. 6d. net. Postage 6d.*

"A notable book."—*New Statesman.* "Stands out conspicuously." —*Times.* "A careful and consistent theory."—*Westminster Gazette.* "His knowledge entitles . . . a respectful hearing."—*St. James's Gazette.* "Written with cool judgment and knowledge."—*Yorkshire Post.* "An excellent book."—*Glasgow Herald.*

Problems of the International Settlement
WITH AN INTRODUCTION BY G. LOWES DICKINSON

Demy 8vo. *6s. net.*

This volume is a series of papers by eminent European and American jurists and publicists on the more important of the problems that must be faced in arriving at any lasting international settlement.

The Choice Before Us
By G. LOWES DICKINSON

Demy 8vo. THIRD IMPRESSION. *7s. 6d. net. Postage 6d.*

"There are many pages in this volume which express admirably the opinions of calm, clear-thinking men."—*The Times.* "A noble book which every one should read."—*Daily News.*

The International Solution
By H. E. HYDE

Crown 8vo. Cloth. *3s. 6d. net.*

"Sketches in confident detail the machinery for an international Parliament to rule and police the world."—*Athenæum.*

A Century of British Foreign Policy
By G. P. GOOCH, M.A., AND THE REV. CANON J. H. B. MASTERMAN, M.A.

Crown 8vo. Cloth. FOURTH IMPRESSION. *2s. 6d. net.*

"Both authors have the historic instinct, and have won reputations as historians."—*Sheffield Telegraph.* "An admirable little book—concise, well arranged, well combined."—*Nation.*

Keeling Letters and Recollections EDITED BY E. T.

WITH AN INTRODUCTION BY H. G. WELLS

Demy 8vo.   12*s.* 6*d. net.*

"Though every age is in its way an age of transition, this age, this red dawn of world-unity, in particular is to be marked as a period of transition and conflict between two widely differing phases of human thought upon political and social questions. And Keeling was as lively and sensitive as a compass needle to every shade of conflict and transition. . . .

"His letters and articles upon the opening of the war and the events of his service are a valuable picture of the state of mind of the English *intelligentsia* of his time. I wish some of this most characteristic matter could be put before German readers to make the quality of our spirit plainer to them."—H. G. WELLS.

Reminiscences & Reflexions of a Mid and Late Victorian

BY ERNEST BELFORT BAX

Demy 8vo.   7*s.* 6*d. net.*   *Postage* 6*d.*

"A fascinating volume."—*Sunday Telegram.*
"Reasoned, systematic, and judicial survey."—*Observer.*

The Life of Francis Place

BY GRAHAM WALLAS

Demy 8vo.   NEW EDITION.   8*s.* 6*d. net.*

"We have here not only a record of history, but, what is much more important, the interpretation thereof, the whole carried through with a lucidity and mastery of detail which is as charming as it is rare."—KEIR HARDIE in the *Labour Leader*, February 19, 1898.

"A very fine piece of work in which an immense amount of material hitherto unused is drawn upon without in the least overweighting a fascinating narrative."—*Manchester Guardian*, March 1, 1898.

"Not only a vivid picture of a most interesting man, but a new light upon a period of English domestic history."—*Saturday Review*, Feb. 26, 1898.

"Mr. Graham Wallas has restored to life a figure of unique interest, and he has opened up a new mine of English history."—*Daily Chronicle*, January 24, 1898.

An Autobiography

BY ROBERT F. HORTON, M.A., D.D.

Demy 8vo.   THIRD EDITION.   7*s.* 6*d. net.*   *Postage* 6*d.*

"It is a fine, a noble, a most moving book."—*Church Times.*
"It is, above everything, the frank record of a man whose life continues to glow with passion for the salvation of men."—*The Christian.*

Library of Philosophy

General Editor : Professor J. H. MUIRHEAD, LL.D.

ANALYTIC PSYCHOLOGY. By G. F. Stout. Two Vols. 21s. net.

APPEARANCE AND REALITY. By F. H. Bradley. 12s. net.

ATTENTION. By Prof. W. B. Pillsbury. 10s. 6d. net.

CONTEMPORARY PSYCHOLOGY. By Prof. G. Villa. 10s. 6d. net.

HISTORY OF ÆSTHETIC. By Dr. B. Bosanquet. 10s. 6d. net.

HISTORY OF ENGLISH UTILITARIANISM. By Prof. E. Albee. 10s. 6d. net.

HISTORY OF PHILOSOPHY. By Dr. J. E. Erdmann.
    Vol. I. Ancient and Mediæval. 15s.
    Vol. II. Modern. 15s.
    Vol. III. Since Hegel. 12s.

HISTORY OF PSYCHOLOGY: Ancient and Patristic. By G. S. Brett, M.A. 10s. 6d. net.

MATTER AND MEMORY. By Henri Bergson. Translated by N. M. Paul and W. S. Palmer. 10s. 6d. net.

NATURAL RIGHTS. By Prof. D. G. Ritchie. 10s. 6d. net.

PHILOSOPHY AND POLITICAL ECONOMY. By Dr. J. Bonar. 10s. 6d. net.

RATIONAL THEOLOGY SINCE KANT. By Prof. O. Pfleiderer. 10s. 6d. net.

THE PHENOMENOLOGY OF MIND. By G. W. F. Hegel. Translated by J. B. Baillie. Two Vols. 21s. net.

THOUGHT AND THINGS; or, Genetic Logic. By Prof. M. Baldwin.
    Vol. I. Functional Logic.
    Vol. II. Experimental Logic.   } 10s. 6d. net per vol.
    Vol. III. Real Logic (I., Genetic Epistemology).

TIME AND FREE WILL. By Henri Bergson. Translated by F. L. Pogson. 10s. 6d. net.

VALUATION: THE THEORY OF VALUE. By Prof. W. M. Urban. 10s. 6d. net.

THE PSYCHOLOGY OF THE RELIGIOUS LIFE. By G. M. Stratton. 10s. 6d. net.

THE GREAT PROBLEMS. By Prof. Bernardino Varisco. Translated by Prof. R. C. Lodge. 10s. 6d. net.

KNOW THYSELF. By Prof. Bernardino Varisco. Translated by Dr. Guglielmo Salvadori. 10s. 6d. net.

ELEMENTS OF CONSTRUCTIVE PHILOSOPHY. By Prof. J. S. Mackenzie. 12s. 6d ne

LONDON : GEORGE ALLEN & UNWIN LIMITED